ESCHATOLOGY IN THE OLD TESTAMENT

ESCHATOLOGY IN THE OLD TESTAMENT

DONALD E. GOWAN

T&T CLARK
EDINBURGH

T&T CLARK LTD
59 GEORGE STREET
EDINBURGH EH2 2LQ
SCOTLAND

www.tandtclark.co.uk

First edition 1987
Second edition 2000

ISBN 0 567 08665 0

British Library Cataloguing-in-Publication Data
A catalogue record for this book is available from the British Library

Printed and bound in Great Britain by MPG Books Ltd, Bodmin

CONTENTS

PREFACE TO THE NEW EDITION

The reissue of this book makes it possible for me to write a new Preface, adding some material that will supplement the rather brief Introduction to the original text, and to add in the form of an Appendix some reflections on a broad subject associated with eschatological material: language about time and the Old Testament's choices of ways to talk about the future.

Apocalyptic thought continues to attract a great deal of attention from scholars, and at another level it has an ongoing fascination for many in the general populace, as well. Given the extravagant eschatological schemes that appear in most apocalyptic works, one might have expected an increased interest in the eschatological materials in the Old Testament to have appeared in recent years, but since this book was published in 1986 there has not been a flurry of activity in that field corresponding to the work on apocalyptic, so it seems appropriate to reissue it with a few additions.

During much of the twentieth century, English-speaking readers have depended on the works of R. H. Charles, *Eschatology: The Doctrine of a Future Life in Israel, Judaism and Christianity* (1899) and Joseph Klausner, *The Messianic Idea in Israel from Its Beginning to the Completion of the Mishnah* (Hebrew, 1949; English, 1955) for thoroughgoing surveys of the available material. Those scholars used the source-critical approach that prevailed in their time, dealing with the prophetic books in chronological order, with the portions of those books considered to be later than their reputed authors removed to the appropriate places. Three German monographs have approached the material differently, but they have not become available in English translation. Siegfried Herrman located the origins of Israel's hope in three major traditions: the promise of land, the covenant, and the promise to David.[1] H. D. Preuss dealt briefly with almost every aspect of Old Testament theology, since his premise was that eschatology is of the very essence of the Yahwistic faith.[2] H. P. Müller considered God's acts in history, blessing and curse, and the covenant to be the sources of eschatology, and showed how the tension between these beliefs and real life led to projections into the future.[3] My approach is partly similar in its use of the history of tradition, but focuses on different traditions. The recent Old Testament theologies need not be surveyed here, since they devote very little space to eschatology.

If a better word than "eschatology" could have been chosen for the title of this book, it surely would have been preferred. The word is not commonly used outside of theological scholarship and those who use it disagree over its meaning. As yet, however, no better technical term to denote the special hope for the future which appears in the Old Testament prophets has been proposed.

The etymology of the word suggests it ought to mean the "doctrine of the end," leaving us free to decide "end of what?" But etymology has not governed everyone's usage. In Christian theology, the term is often used to refer to the destiny of the individual after death, so that its contents deal primarily with judgment, immortality and resurrection, heaven and hell. Since the Old Testament shows almost no interest in those subjects, that is not a significant use of the term for this study, except for the very few passages where the resurrection of individuals is considered.

The chief interest of the Old Testament is the destiny of peoples and of the world in which they live, and all of the uses of "eschatology" by Old Testament scholars focus on those concerns. Unfortunately, the word is not always used to denote the same body of material, as the following survey will show.

The term is sometimes virtually equivalent to "hope," and as such it can then include much of the message of scripture. Since the Old Testament is filled with divine promises and looks toward the future almost throughout, some scholars call this futuristic element "eschatology."[4] The promise to Abraham (Gen. 12:1–3), the general promise of the land to Israel, the Sinai covenant (Exod. 19:3–6), and the covenant with David (2 Samuel 7) have all been so designated.[5] But this usage creates two problems. First, it makes the word unnecessary, since we already have the clear words "promise" and "hope" to describe these futuristic elements of the Old Testament. Second, it leaves us without a term by which we can identify a peculiar form of hope which is significantly different from the normal expectations of a better future which many peoples share with the ancient Israelites. Such a distinctive form of hope does appear in the Old Testament and it needs a term to denote it.

A persuasive approach to the identification of that peculiar form of hope has taken the expectation of the inbreaking of a *new age* to be its definitive feature. Whenever two eons are in mind, there we have the kind of expectation that should be called "eschatological," it is argued.[6] The new era must be one which is completely different from the present, but it need not necessarily involve the end of history of the world. A definition of this type which focuses on the negating of the old era is offered by Gerhard von Rad: "The prophetic teaching is only eschatological when the prophets expelled Israel from the safety of the old saving actions and suddenly shifted the basis of salvation to a future action of God."[7] This definition has proved to be useful in identifying a distinctive aspect of the prophetic message, and some form of it will be encountered frequently.[8] Other scholars insist, however, that this is an inaccurate and inappropriate use of the term.

The descriptions of the future that are characteristic of apocalyptic literature speak of a complete change in the nature of reality: the end of the world, the end of history, the move from time to eternity. Sigmund Mowinckel and others have insisted that this more extreme form of the two-age concept is the only one which is appropriately called eschatology. But there is almost no trace in the Old Testament of such thinking, of what Mowinckel calls "the severance of the future hope from historical reality, from the contingent, from any causal connection with circumstances, so that it assumes an absolute character."[9] This definition restricts the word to the futurism of apocalyptic literature, leaving us without a technical term to denote that distinctive hope which appears in the prophetic books. For that reason, most Old Testament scholars have been unwilling to restrict the definition to this extent. Von Rad says of this narrow definition: "The most outstanding element in the prophetic message is left without a proper explanation and without a name."[10]

If one insists on the temporal sense of "doctrine of the end," as J. M. van der Ploeg does, then the only appropriate use of the word eschatology is to denote material which speaks of the "end of this period, this time, and of the rather short space of time which precedes the end."[11] This definition has the same effect as Mowinckel's, since language about "the end" appears only in the latest book of the Old Testament, Daniel.

The opposite extreme, "realized eschatology," defining it without any reference to time at all, as in the works of C. H. Dodd and Rudolf Bultmann, does not seem to have been found useful by Old Testament scholars.

Since "eschatology" is a modern word created by scholars for their own convenience, its definition can be an arbitrary matter; the debate does not concern "what the word really means," as it would if we were discussing a biblical term. This is a label, and the differences just outlined concern the contents which are most usefully to be identified by that label. A fresh look at these contents suggests a perspective different from that taken in the past.

I have not included the prophets' messages of judgment as a part of their eschatological message, as some other scholars have done, so some explanation of that should be offered. "Last Judgment" is a traditional part of Christian eschatology, and this may have influenced those scholars, but the judgment of Israel functions in a quite different way from Christian teachings about the

Last Judgment. The latter represents the vindication of God's people; the wicked are condemned while the elect are confirmed in their righteousness and receive the victory. But for the prophets there was no righteousness to be vindicated (cf. Jer. 5:1; Ezek. 2:3–7; 20:1–31). Form critical studies have identified two distinct prophetic genres, the oracle of judgment and the oracle of deliverance, and they do not appear in combination. Within an individual unit of speech, a prophet who addresses the present sinful condition of Israel moves no further into the future than the announcement of impending judgment. When a prophet announces deliverance, it is from the perspective of those who have *already* come under judgment; it is part of the present, not the future. It has seemed appropriate, then to use "eschatology" only of the promissory texts in the prophetic books, as other scholars have also done.

There is general agreement that the prophets offered promises different from passages such as Gen. 12:1–3 and also different from the grandiose and comprehensive depictions of the future which appear in later apocalyptic books. A series of examples will begin to clarify what is distinctive about these promises:

> In that day the branch of the LORD shall be beautiful and glorious, and the fruit of the land shall be the pride and glory of the survivors of Israel. And he who is left in Zion and remains in Jerusalem will be called holy, every one who has been recorded for life in Jerusalem, when the LORD shall have washed away the filth of the daughters of Zion and cleansed the bloodstains of Jerusalem from its midst by a spirit of judgment and by a spirit of burning. (Isa. 4:2–4)

This picture of the glorious future calls for the washing away of filth and the cleansing of bloodstains.

> He shall judge between many peoples, and shall decide for strong nations afar off; and they shall beat their swords into plowshares, and their spears into pruning hooks; nation shall not lift up sword against nation, neither shall they learn war any more. (Mic. 4:3)

This one calls for an end to war.

> Then the eyes of the blind shall be opened, and the ears of the deaf unstopped; then shall the lame man leap like a hart, and the tongue of the dumb sing for joy. (Isa. 35:5–6a)

Human infirmity will be no more.

> I will make the fruit of the tree and the increase of the field abundant, that you may never again suffer the disgrace of famine among the nations. (Ezek. 36:30)

No more hunger.

> I will cleanse them from all the guilt of their sin against me, and I will forgive all the guilt of their sin and rebellion against me. (Jer. 33:8)

Sin and guilt will be erased.

> They shall not hurt or destroy in all my holy mountain. (Isa. 11:9a)

No more killing or harming of any living thing.

The ethical aspect of these futuristic passage has not been emphasized enough, I believe. These are examples drawn from a lengthy series of prophetic promises which have as their central concern what is presently *wrong* with the world and with humanity. And it is a sense of radical wrongness that they convey. They confront the evil in this world without the optimism of law or wisdom, traditions which seek to make humanity and the world better by educating and by regulating behavior. They differ from cultic texts, which provide "religious" ways of dealing with sin: means of cleansing and assurances of forgiveness. They struggle with evil in a way that does not appear in the promises of the Abrahamic or Sinai or Davidic covenants—promises which do not confront an insoluble problem, but which assume that God can work with what presently exists to make it better. They differ also from descriptions of the traditional work of institutional prophecy, which dealt with sin by exhorting and warning and calling to repentance (e.g. 2 Kings 17:13; Jer. 26:4–6).

These are texts which spring from the conviction that something is radically wrong in this world, so that only radical change can make it right. To this extent they have something in common with later apocalyptic thought, but they do not yet personalize evil, give to evil a cosmic dimension, or systematize and periodize their picture of the triumph over evil. Their vision of the future still deals with this world, with a nation of Israel, the city Jerusalem, other nations, farmers and children and old people. The radical victory over evil which is hoped for does not call for "going to heaven" or the complete abolishment of the world we know. The prophets share Israel's basic, world-affirming spirit. All was made by God, so nothing is bad in itself—but sin has by now left it hopelessly corrupted. These texts promise *transformation* as the radical victory over evil. If, then, we consider again the literal meaning of eschatology, "the doctrine of the end," as "end of what?" I believe we shall find it helpful to consider the major theme of all the prophetic promises to be "The End of Evil."[12]

The writing of this book in the mid-1980s was stimulated in the early stages by conversations with my colleagues at Pittsburgh Theological Seminary, Marjorie Suchocki, George Kehm, Walter Wiest, and James Walther, and their contributions to my thinking should be acknowledged again. The willingness of T&T Clark to keep the book in circulation by this reprint is much appreciated.

1 November 1999

Notes

1. S. Herrman, *Die prophetische Heilserwartungen im Alten Testament*, BWANT 85 (Stuttgart: Kohlhammer, 1965).

2. H. D. Preuss, *Jahwehglaube und Zukunftserwartung*, BWANT 87 (Stuttgart: Kohlhammer, 1968).

3. H. P. Müller, *Ursprünge und Stukturen alttestamentlicher Eschatologie*, BZAW 109 (Berlin: Walter de Gruyter, 1969).

4. E.g. A. A. Hoekema, *The Bible and the Future* (Grand Rapids: Wm. B. Eerdmans, 1979), ix.

5. E. Jacob, *Theology of the Old Testament* (New York: Harper & Row, 1958), 317–18, 327; E. Jenni, "Eschatology," *IDB* 2:126–33; O. Procksch, "Eschatology in the Old Testament and in Judaism," in *Twentieth Century Theology in the Making*, ed. J. Pelikan (New York: Harper & Row, 1969), 1:231–2; Preuss, *Jahwehglaube und Zukunftserwartung*, 205–14.

6. J. Lindblom, *Prophecy in Ancient Israel* (Philadelphia: Fortress Press, 1962), 360; G. Fohrer, "Die Struktur der alttestamentliche Eschatologie," *TLZ* 85 (1960): 401–20; cf. R. E. Clements, *Prophecy and Covenant*, SBT 43 (London: SCM Press, 1965), 105.

7. G. von Rad, *Old Testament Theology* (New York: Harper & Row, 1965), 2:118.

8. J. Bright, *Covenant and Promise* (Philadelphia: Westminster Press, 1976), 19; T. M. Raitt, *A Theology of Exile, Judgment/Deliverance in Jeremiah and Ezekiel* (Philadelphia: Fortress Press, 1977), 212–22.

9. S. Mowinckel, *He That Cometh* (Nashville: Abingdon Press, 1954), 153–4; cf. p. 149.

10. G. von Rad, *Old Testament Theology*, 2:114–15.

11. J. M. van der Ploeg, "Eschatology in the Old Testament," *OTS* 17 (1972), 93.

12. The preceding paragraphs are intended to provide additional support for the brief statement concerning "end of evil" in the Introduction to the 1986 edition. After that book was published, my former colleague, Marjorie Suchocki, advocated a similar definition, taking a very different approach, that of process theology: *The End of Evil: Process Eschatology in Historical Context* (Albany: State University of New York Press, 1988).

ABBREVIATIONS

Ancient Documents

Pseudepigrapha

Adam and Eve	*Books of Adam and Eve*
2 Apoc. Bar.	*Syriac Apocalypse of Baruch*
As. Mos.	*Assumption (Testament) of Moses*
Jub.	*Jubilees*
Pss. Sol.	*Psalms of Solomon*
T. Ash.; T. Benj.; T. Dan; T. Jos.; T. Jud; T. Levi; T. Naph.; T. Sim.; T. Zeb.	chapters of *Testaments of the Twelve Patriarchs*

Qumran Documents

CD	Damascus Document (Cairo Geniza text)
4QpIsa[a]	Pesher on Isaiah from Qumran Cave 4

Rabbinic Literature

b. Ta'an	Babylonian Talmud, Tractate *Ta'anit*
Exod. Rab.	*Midrash Rabbah on Exodus*
Hag.	Babylonian Talmud, Tractate *Ḥagiga*
Midr.	*Midrash*
Midr. Qoh.	*Midrash on Ecclesiastes*
Midr. Rab.	*Midrash Rabbah*
Pesiq. R.	*Pesiqta Rabbati*
Pesiq. Rab Kah.	*Pesiqta de Rab Kahana*
Tg. Cant.	*Targum of the Song of Songs*
Tg. Isa.	*Targum of Isaiah*

Tg. Ket.	*Targum of the Writings*
Tg. Neb.	*Targum of the Prophets*
Tg. Ps.-J.	*Targum Pseudo-Jonathan*
Yalq.	*Yalqut*

Other Abbreviations

AARSR	American Academy of Religion: Studies in Religion
AASF	Annales Academiae Scientiarum Fennicae
AnBib	Analecta biblica
ATANT	Abhandlungen zur Theologie des Alten und Neuen Testaments
BA	*Biblical Archaeologist*
BBB	Bonner biblische Beiträge
BibOr	Biblica et orientalia
BKAT	Biblischer Kommentar: Altes Testament
BZAW	Beihefte zur *ZAW*
BZNW	Beihefte zur *ZNW*
CBQ	*Catholic Biblical Quarterly*
ConBNT	Coniectanea biblica, New Testament
EstBib	*Estudios Biblicos*
ExpTim	*Expository Times*
GThA	Göttinger Theologische Arbeiten
HeyJ	*Heythrop Journal*
HR	*History of Religions*
HSM	Harvard Semitic Monographs
HTR	*Harvard Theological Review*
HTS	Harvard Theological Studies
IB	*Interpreter's Bible* (Nashville: Abingdon Press, 1953).
ICC	International Critical Commentary
IDB	G. A. Buttrick (ed.), *Interpreter's Dictionary of the Bible*
IDBSup	Supplementary volume to IDB
IDOC	*IDOC International: North American Edition*
Int	*Interpretation*
JBL	*Journal of Biblical Literature*
JSOT	*Journal for the Study of the Old Testament*
JSOTSup	*Journal for the Study of the Old Testament*—Supplement Series
LD	Lectio divina
MT	Masoretic Text (of the Hebrew Scriptures)
NCBC	New Century Bible Commentary
NEB	*New English Bible*
NT	New Testament

NOVT	*Novum Testamentum*
OT	Old Testament
OTL	Old Testament Library
OTS	*Oudtestamentische Studiën*
PTMS	Pittsburgh Theological Monograph Series
RHPR	*Revue d'histoire et de philosophie religieuses*
RSR	*Recherches de science religieuse*
RSV	*Revised Standard Version*
SBLDS	Society of Biblical Literature Dissertation Series
SBT	Studies in Biblical Theology
SHR	Studies in the History of Religions
SIDIC	*SIDIC: Journal of the Service Internationale de Documentation Judeo-Chrétienne*
SJLA	Studies in Judaism in Late Antiquity
SJT	*Scottish Journal of Theology*
TDNT	G. Kittel and G. Friedrich (eds.), *Theological Dictionary of the New Testament*
TDOT	G. J. Botterweck and H. Ringgren (eds.), *Theological Dictionary of the Old Testament*
TEH	*Theologische Existenz heute*
TEV	*Today's English Version*
TToday	*Theology Today*
TZ	*Theologische Zeitschrift*
USQR	*Union Seminary Quarterly Review*
VT	*Vetus Testamentum*
VTSup	Vetus Testamentum, Supplements
WMANT	Wissenschaftliche Monographien zum Alten und Neuen Testament
WTJ	*Westminster Theological Journal*
ZAW	*Zeitschrift für die alttestamentliche Wissenschaft*

INTRODUCTION
A New Approach to Eschatology in The Old Testament

This is a study of the theology of the eschatological traditions of Israel. By "theology" I mean both an effort to describe the faith of Israel and the application to contemporary issues of insights drawn from that faith. I emphasize traditions in conscious distinction from previous works that have tended to focus on the eschatological teachings of individual biblical authors.[1] Earlier approaches, which became deeply involved in the usual historical-critical questions of unity, date and authorship, have produced few widely accepted results. There is no agreement whatever, for example, on what legitimately can be said about "eschatology" with reference to the eighth-century prophet Isaiah. I take a different approach partly because of the unsatisfying results of earlier studies, but also for more positive reasons. Form-critical and traditio-historical studies have already shown us that the teachings of individuals such as Isaiah, even if they can be determined with certainty, are actually of less significance than what *Israel* believed. Since it was the book ascribed to Isaiah which became canonical, then what Israel believed included his teachings plus whatever else may have been added, and they are all important. This concurs with recent emphases on taking the final, canonical form of the tradition as the basic unit to be interpreted. This is not a synchronic presentation of the type that has sometimes appeared in biblical theologies, putting everything on the same level and ignoring historical change. That would be a reversion to the past which would deprive us of many of the valuable contributions that historical-critical scholarship has made to exegesis. This is a history of eschatological tradition.

The OT contains many promises concerning a better future, but this book does not deal with all aspects of hope. Rather, it is confined to those promises that speak of a future with significant discontinuities from the present. They speak of circumstances that scarcely could be expected to arrive as the result of normal, or even extraordinary, human progress, and so most scholars agree in distinguishing them from ordinary hopes for a better future by calling them "eschatology."[2] Although the word literally means "doctrine of the end," the OT does not speak of the end of the world, of time, or of history.[3] It promises the end of sin (Jer. 33:8), of war (Mic. 4:3), of human infirmity (Isa. 35:5–6a), of hunger (Ezek. 36:30), of killing or harming of any living thing (Isa. 11:9a). One of the distinctive features of these hopes is their sense of the radical wrongness of the present world and the conviction that radical changes, to make things right, will indeed occur "in that day," that is, at some time known only to God.[4] The OT vision of the future deals throughout with the world in which we now live. All was made by God, so nothing is bad in itself, but sin has by now left it hopelessly corrupted. These texts promise transformation as the radical victory over evil. To the challenge that has been raised concerning the appropriateness of calling the OT hope "eschatology," asking "end of what?" it will be shown that a clear answer can be given. The answer is: "the end of evil."

My approach is thematic, like some earlier theologies and monographs, but it is more comprehensive and organized in a different way. Since the history of the various traditions will be traced, decisions about the probable dates of certain passages still have to be made. The principal concern will be thematic development, however, rather than attempting to connect passages with particular historical events. Authorship seldom will be a concern, since the value of each text is to be found in its adoption by Israel as to some extent a legitimate expression of its hopes.

Two discoveries led me to organize this study as I have. First came the observation that the comprehensive picture of the ideal future in Ezek. 36:22–38 acknowledges that for God to make things right, a threefold transformation of the world as it now is will be required. God must transform the human person; give a new heart and new spirit (Ezek. 36:25–27). God must transform human society; restore Israel to the promised land, rebuild cities, and make Israel's new status a witness to the nations (36:24, 28, 33–36). And God must transform nature itself, to make the produce of the land abundant and to banish hunger forever (36:30, 35). The same pattern occurs elsewhere, and it includes everything the OT needs to say about the ideal future—except possibly providing a place for the resurrection of the dead. That subject doesn't fit the pattern very well, but it also is a rare topic for the OT, so perhaps that is appropriate.

The transformation of the human person comes about through eschatological forgiveness, the kind that truly erases the past and never has to be repeated; through an act of re-creation, giving a new heart and spirit, to produce a truly new person whose most obvious improvement is the ability to obey God.

The transformation of human society must first bring Israel back to the promised land and glorify Jerusalem, the center of all hope for the future. A righteous king will provide for good government in the new society and ways will be found for all nations to live together in peace.

The transformation of nature calls for two essentials, the elimination of hunger and the creation of a new order in which the rule will be "they shall not hurt or destroy."

The second discovery that has influenced my study is that Jerusalem appears with a prominence unparalleled by any other theme. It was surprising to find a "center" of OT eschatology, but the evidence strongly suggests Jerusalem does play such a role. Hence the hope that focuses on Zion will be the first theme undertaken. Its study will shed considerable light on the distinctive nature of the hope of Israel, and it also will provide an introduction to the other major themes, since each of them appears in a significant relationship to Zion in more than a few texts.

Each of the themes will be approached in the following way: Since the OT has selected the best from Israel's past and present in order to express its hope for the future, it will be necessary to begin with the history of the non-eschatological forms of each tradition. Next the new use of the tradition in an eschatological form will be taken up and explained with reference to selected passages that shed the most light on it. The history of the eschatological theme will then be traced briefly, through the OT, into intertestamental Jewish literature and the NT, with indications of its continuing use in rabbinic literature and the early church. This book can do no more than provide a sort of index of where others may go to trace these themes in the later literature. The ethical overtones of eschatology will be considered at every step, and the conclusion of each section will try to alert the reader to the potential or actual contemporary relevance of each theme, in Judaism, in the churches, and in the secular world as well, since those hopes first expressed in the OT have by now had a far-reaching influence.

CHAPTER 1

ZION

The Center of Old Testament Eschatology

Why begin this study with Jerusalem? Why should the hopes of Israel for an ideal future have been focused on one city—that small and not very prosperous place up in the hills of Judah—amid all the desirable places on earth (not to mention heaven)? How did that preoccupation with Jerusalem come about, and how does the hope for the ultimate glorification of Zion affect other aspects of OT eschatology? These questions plus their consequences for the later hopes of Judaism, Christianity, and indeed for the modern secular world will be taken up here.

Zechariah 8: The City of the Future

A post-exilic text that speaks of the past, present, and future of Jerusalem provides a good place to begin. The restoration promised by earlier prophets is underway; some exiles have returned from Babylonia to settle in Jerusalem, and regular worship has already been inaugurated on the holy mountain. As the rebuilding of the temple was in progress (518 B.C.; Zech. 7:1), some of the people came to Zechariah with a question about a custom that had been followed in Judaism since the destruction of Jerusalem in 587 (Zech. 7:2–3): Should we continue to fast in mourning of that tragic event, now that restoration has begun? Perhaps one reason for the question was their keen awareness that not all the glorious things promised for Zion by earlier prophets had by any means come true as yet.

Zechariah's answers dealt with two issues that the question raised for him. One was a familiar prophetic subject, the true nature and value of worship (7:4–14). That one need not concern us now. The other was a fairly detailed answer to the question of where they stood at that moment, with reference to what God had done and intended to do, and also with reference to what *they* had done and needed to do. He recalled the days of pre-exilic prophecy in order to remind them of the now generally accepted explanation of the exile as judgment for their sins, a judgment that the remnant of Israel had survived (7:7, 11–12), and he took up a summary of that message and made it his own (7:8–10). But now he and other Jews have come back from exile, and he understands that they are standing at the turning point between judgment and blessing. With 8:1 he begins his combination of "realized and futuristic eschatology."

> Thus says the Lord of hosts: I am jealous for Zion with great jealousy and I am jealous for her with great wrath. Thus says the Lord: I will return to Zion, and will dwell in the midst of Jerusalem, and Jerusalem shall be called the faithful city, and the mountain of the Lord of hosts, the holy mountain. (Zech. 8:2–3)

All that Zechariah needs to say about his people and their future he can say with reference to Zion. He uses that name twice (8:2–3), the word Jerusalem six times (8:3, 4, 8, 15, 22), and he also speaks of the faithful city, the holy mountain, and the house of the Lord. Zechariah 7 and 8 make three helpful contributions to our study of eschatology: They reveal how a post-exilic prophet saw the relationship between past, present, and the ideal future, show how he understood the relationship between divine initiative and human responsibility (cf. 8:14–17), and demonstrate the sufficiency of Zion as an eschatological symbol.

Zechariah's vision of the new Jerusalem compares remarkably well with my outline of the major themes of OT eschatology:

1. God's people will be restored to the promised land (8:7–8). Note that Jerusalem is the only part of the promised land that needs to be mentioned.

2. No king is mentioned, but that is not to be wondered at, given the infrequent appearances of the "messianic figure" in the OT.

3. The nations will no longer mock and scorn (8:13), but they will instead come voluntarily to Jerusalem to "entreat the favor of the Lord, and to seek the Lord of hosts" (8:20–23).

4. The people of Zion will make it possible to characterize Jerusalem as "the faithful city" (8:3). The possibility that as in the past they will be unable to obey the *torah* which he recites (8:16–17) is not considered an option for the people of the city of the future.

5. Peace and security will be enjoyed by all: old men and old women, boys and girls. No one will be left out (8:4–5). In that day, to return to the question that prompted Zechariah's comprehensive view of past and future, there will be no reason for fasting, and the fasts for Jerusalem will be turned into seasons of joy and cheerful feasts (8:19).

6. The curse on nature had resulted in fruitless work in the past (8:10a), but the day is coming when "the vine shall yield its fruit, . . . and I will cause the remnant of this people to possess all these things" (8:12).

The good life that Zechariah projects for the inhabitants of Jerusalem is a mixture of the material and the spiritual. Peace, prosperity, and security are dominant themes, but this is no secular city. What makes it all possible is God, who carries out his purpose (8:2, 6, 11, 13b–15), and the source of the good life in Zion is the presence of Yahweh in its midst. Zechariah 8 begins, "I will return to Zion and will dwell in the midst of Jerusalem," and it ends, "we have heard that God is with you."

This is one beautiful picture of the ideal future, tied very closely to events and issues of the immediate present, as effective eschatology always is; containing clear ethical implications, as responsible eschatology always should; with an outlook that includes Gentiles as well as Jews, but finding no need to describe any other part of the world except Jerusalem. Is this perhaps a peculiarity of early post-exilic Judaism, whose home territory included just Jerusalem and the tiny province of Judah surrounding it—hence to be labeled an inadequate outlook? In order to answer this question one must compare this passage with earlier expressions of hope to see whether there is strong evidence for the centrality of Zion throughout OT eschatology.

History of the Zion Tradition

The claim was once made that the entire OT is "the epos of the Fall of Jerusalem."[1] That may be a slight exaggeration, but the statement is worth quoting in order to remind us of the magnitude and importance of the Zion tradition. It can only be sketched here in order to provide the necessary background for our survey of the place of Zion in OT eschatology.[2]

Jerusalem is a relative latecomer as an Israelite sanctuary. It is not associated with the patriarchs in the significant way that Shechem, Bethel, Hebron, and Beersheba are. Only from David's time on was it the site of a Yahwistic cult. Eventually the Mt. Moriah of Genesis 22 was identified with Jerusalem (2 Chron. 3:1), but that identification is uncertain, and in any case did not result in the establishment of a Yahwistic sanctuary in the early period. When David brought the Ark of the Covenant to the vicinity (2 Samuel 6), Jerusalem became for the first time a place where Yahweh was worshiped, and no effort was made to assert its antiquity as a Yahwistic sanctuary. Instead, the royal ideology that developed concerning God's election of David and the covenant made with him (2 Samuel 7) included also the affirmation that God had chosen Zion to be his resting place at that time. Psalm 132 clearly demonstrates this pairing of royal ideology and Jerusalem ideology. When Solomon built a temple to house the Ark and established a royally sponsored cult of some magnificence (1 Kings 6—8), a whole series of novelties, in addition to kingship, was introduced into Yahwism. One prominent theory, based largely on the Psalms but also using prophetic texts, has suggested that a Zion theology (or mythology) of Canaanite origins was among the elements adopted by the Israelites at this time. In Psalms 46, 48, 76, and others, Zion is glorified as something more than a place to come and worship God; it has qualities distinguishing it from every other place on earth. The suggestion that these are cult songs which reapply the traditional Canaanite mythology of Zion to the city chosen by Yahweh has been widely debated,[3] but the evidence that has been used in those discussions will be useful to us.

The following themes appear both in cultic and in eschatological materials:[4]

1. Yahweh has chosen Jerusalem for his dwelling place (Pss. 78:68; 132:13).

2. Zion is identified with Mt. Zaphon (Ps. 48:2, "in the far north"), theologically understood to be the highest point on earth (cf. Pss. 2:6; 68:18; 87:1; 99:9).[5]

3. Zion is the source of life-giving springs of water, as is true of the mountain of the gods in Canaanite myth (Ps. 46:4).[6]

4. Zion is the place were Yahweh defeats the waters of chaos (Pss. 46:2–3; 74:13–17; 93:3–4).

5. Associated with this mythological conflict is the theme of God's defeat of the kings of the earth, when they attack Jerusalem, and his unfailing protection of his city (Pss. 96:6–9; 48:3–7; 76:1–12).

6. Those who dwell in Zion share in the blessings of God's presence (Pss. 48:12–14; 132:13–18; 133:1–3; 147:12–20).[7]

It is clear that after Solomon installed the Ark of the Covenant into the temple, and after the schism between the northern and southern tribes subsequent to his death left Judah as the principal adherent to the ideology of Davidic kingship, the city of Jerusalem became more and more closely identified with the presence of Yahweh, and it eventually replaced the Ark as the focus of attention (cf. Jer. 3:16–18).[8] The miraculous deliverance of Jerusalem from Sennacherib's army, which captured every other city in Judah in 701, no doubt added to the aura that was developing about this city and either reinforced or produced the belief in its invulnerability, depending on whose theory one accepts. The ambiguity of the books ascribed to the eighth-century prophets Micah and Isaiah, which contain both strongly positive and strongly negative words concerning Jerusalem, has led to an inconclusive debate over the attitude of those prophets toward the city.[9]

As the seventh century neared its end, Josiah carried out extensive reforms intended to make Jerusalem the only legitimate Yahwistic sanctuary (2 Kings 23), and there is general agreement that his activities were guided by an early form of the Book of Deuteronomy (2 Kings 22:8). This means that the unnamed, exclusive sanctuary of Deuteronomy, "the place which the Lord your God will choose out of all your tribes to put his name and make his habitation there" (Deut. 12:5), had been identified by the seventh century (in Judah) with Jerusalem. The entire history of the monarchy from Solomon to the end is recorded in 1 and 2 Kings from the perspective of one who is absolutely convinced that Jerusalem is the sole legitimate Yahwistic sanctuary (1 Kings 12:25–33; 2 Kings 17:21–22; 21). The psalms of Zion and the pilgrimage psalms (e.g., Psalms 84 and 122) show how great the enthusiasm for that place had become and how intimately related were the praise of Yahweh and the praise of Zion.

There is, however, an event that would appear to be a thoroughgoing repudiation of this glorification of Jerusalem and it intervenes between these optimistic, cultic celebrations of the place and the beautiful pictures of the ideal city of the future that were affirmed in Zechariah's time: in 587 B.C. Jerusalem was destroyed. As that time drew near, both Jeremiah and Ezekiel condemned the popular faith in God's everlasting presence in Jerusalem and the consequent belief in the invulnerability of the city. Jeremiah is reported to have attacked temple theology (Jeremiah 7, 26), to have counseled those already in exile not to expect to return home in their lifetimes (chap. 29), and to have identified those left in Jerusalem after 597 as without hope for the future (chap. 24). Ezekiel was even more emphatic about insisting that Jerusalem must fall, as he ministered to exiles who thought their only hope was God's continuing presence in and protection of that city. He spoke of the complete and terrible destruction of city and people (Ezekiel 5), lived out its effects in his own symbolic actions (chap. 12), and witnessed in a vision the departure of Yahweh from that place he had chosen (10:18–19; 11:22–23).

These prophets were right. No almighty divine power intervened to save Jerusalem from Nebuchadnezzar's armies. In 587 B.C. the city fell, its walls were ruined, the city and temple were destroyed, and those who were left of the upper classes were exiled to Babylonia. That should have been the end of Zion theology (cf. Lamentations 1 and 2). The events of history had thoroughly demonstrated the falseness of any belief in invulnerability, and the prophets had already explained the inadequacy of such a belief in terms of their understanding of Yahwism. If anything new was to come out of that devastating experience, presumably it ought to have been a theology and practice that de-emphasized Jerusalem, since it had been the site of their greatest failure, both of obedience and of understanding.

Yet the Books of Jeremiah and Ezekiel also contain passages that speak of a new Jerusalem, to be established by God after the time of judgment has passed, and there are reasons for thinking at least some of these texts may come from those prophets themselves, near the end of their ministries.[10] That is a debated subject, but no one can question the predominance of Zion in the promise oracles of 2 Isaiah, a generation later. Instead of repudiating Zion theology, exilic Judaism had corrected it, had eschatologized it, had found a way to take account of judgment and to express their hope for a divinely accomplished future that would take all they had once believed to be present-tense truth about Jerusalem and make that, and more, come true in the days that are coming.

The Zion theme is thus a remarkable example of the persistence of ideas, even when they have been shown beyond any doubt to be completely wrong in one manifestation. Despite the embarrassment of the fall of Jerusalem and with it the end of all that Judeans trusted in; despite their eventual acceptance of the tragedy as fully merited judgment for their own sins, they could not, it seems, abandon that symbol of the city of God built on his holy mountain in favor of something better. They evidently found it to be the best way to express hopes that could not be suppressed, even in the time of Zechariah, when restoration proved to be another embarrassment because of the modesty of its success, and subsequently in many another time of turmoil for the holy place. That continuing potency of the concept of the *city* of God as an eschatological symbol, throughout history to our own day, is another reason for emphasizing Zion as the center of Israel's hopes.

The Centrality of Zion in Old Testament Eschatology

Although the books of the northern prophets, Amos and Hosea, did acquire some redactorial promises concerning David (Hos. 3:5; Amos 9:11–12) and Judah (Hos. 1:7, 11), they remain true to their origin in containing nothing concerning an eschatological Zion. The books of the Judean prophets of the eighth century, however, have Zion of the future as a major theme. It is found in Micah 4 and occurs perhaps twenty times in Isaiah 1—39.[11] In the books of the late seventh- and early sixth-century prophets, it is found in Zeph. 3:14–20, five times in the poetry of Jeremiah,[12] eight times in the prose of that book,[13] and ten times in Ezekiel.[14] In exilic and post-exilic books, it appears twelve times in 2 Isaiah,[15] eleven times in 3 Isaiah,[16] and eight times in Zechariah.[17] Jerusalem as the ideal city also appears in Joel 3:17–21; Obadiah 15—21; Hag. 2:9; Mal. 3:4; and Dan. 9:2, 24–26.

The eschatological Zion is thus widely distributed in the prophetic literature, although the distribution is admittedly uneven, with a heavy concentration in Isaiah and Zechariah and a relatively small number of references in Jeremiah and Ezekiel. Jeremiah contains 106 occurrences of the word Jerusalem, but only three passages use it in a positive, futuristic sense. Zion is used seventeen times, four of them in eschatological passages. Ezekiel never uses Zion in any sense, and never uses the name Jerusalem in a positive context. But he uses other terminology to speak of future blessings—city, mountain, hill, and sanctuary—and Jeremiah also uses the term "this place" in a positive sense. Given the life situations of these two prophets, described earlier, in which the positive Zion theology was a problem to be struggled with, such reticence is not at all surprising. Although the number of occurrences of the theme in each book is not large, there are significant texts that are evidence for a Jeremiah tradition and an Ezekiel tradition concerning Jerusalem of the future, supporting the proposal that expressions of hope in the OT could scarcely be formulated without putting that city in a prominent place.

A more significant indication of the centrality of Zion is the way it is involved with all the other major eschatological themes. The best way of making that point, in my opinion, would be to repeat the outline of this book along with a list of the occurrences of each theme in connection with Zion.

Transformation of Human Society

Restoration to the Promised Land: Isa. 27:13; 35:10; 51:11; 60:4; 66:20; Jer. 3:14; 32:37; Ezek. 20:33–44; 37:26; Joel 3:20; Mic. 4:6–7, 10; Zeph. 3:20; Zech. 2:7; 8:7–8.

The Righteous King: Isa. 11:9; 44:28; Jer. 33:16; Zech. 4:5–10; 6:12–13; 9:9–10.

The Nations (victory over): Isa. 34:8; Joel 3:1–21; Obadiah 16; Mic. 4:11–13; Zech. 1:14–15; 12:2–9; 14:1–3, 12–19.

The Nations (peace with): Isa. 2:2–4 = Mic. 4:1–4.

The Nations (conversion of): Isa. 66:18–23; Jer. 3:17; Zech. 2:11; 8:20–23.

Transformation of the Human Person

Eschatological Forgiveness: Isa. 33:24; 40:2; Ezek. 20:40–44; 43:7–9; Zech. 13:1; cf. repentance in Isa. 59:20; Jer. 29:10–14; Ezek. 16:59–62.

The Means of Re-Creation: Isa. 30:20–21; 59:21; Jer. 32:39–40 (cf. v. 36—city).

The New Person: Isa. 33:24; 35:5–6 (cf. v. 10—Zion); 65:20; Jer. 33:6; 50:5; Ezek. 16:60; Joel 3:17.

Transformation of Nature

Abundant Fertility: Isa. 4:2; Joel 2:23; 3:17–18.

A New Natural Order: Isa. 11:6–9; 65:25.

A New Earth: Isa. 35:1–10; 65:17–18; Ezek. 47:1–12; Zech. 14:4–8, 10.

Frequently, Israel summed up everything that needed to be said about a specific hope in its words about Zion.[18] Return to the promised land, for example, is frequently described simply as return to Jerusalem. And even a promise of cosmic scope, "Behold, I create new heavens and a new earth," very quickly concentrates its attention on the place which contains the essence of that new world: "for behold I create Jerusalem a rejoicing and her people a joy" (Isa. 65:17, 18).

Two types of description of the ideal Zion will now be discussed in some detail. Both are based on the traditional cultic glorification of the city mentioned earlier, but while most visions of the future city presuppose a cataclysmic break between the present and that ideal time, alluding to its destruction and usually to the exile, there is a group of texts which seem to remain close to their cultic origins in that they do not refer to a time of judgment. These passages are characteristic of the Book of Isaiah.

That famous text which occurs in almost identical form in Isa. 2:2–4 and Mic. 4:1–4 speaks of no dramatic intervention by God in order to produce the new era, and no radical changes are described. The contrast between present and future that is so typical of eschatology is only alluded to, in "neither shall they learn war any more." What is said in these few verses has made them one of the most striking passages in the Bible, but what is left unsaid is just as surprising. Without the overcoming of great obstacles, without drama or conflict the new era is just placidly described. Somehow Jerusalem has become the center of a kind of United Nations—one that works. Presumably Israel is there, round about, but this text finds it unnecessary to comment on that. It reveals a universalism that also occurs in other texts dealing with the nations, which will be discussed more fully when the theme of the nations in the last days is taken up. Unlike certain later strands of eschatology, this text does not speak of Israel ruling the world: there is no messianic king who is expected to bring all peoples under his control; instead peoples and nations still exist as independent entities. The prophecy is realistic enough to acknowledge that wherever there are nations there will be disputes. What is different about the new age is that no longer does anyone settle a dispute by going to war. The establishment of peace among all peoples is the point of the text, and Jerusalem will provide the means for that to be done. The vision sees nations coming freely and without any coercion to learn how to live together peacefully, because somehow (and that is what makes this eschatology) they have become convinced that Yahweh is the sole source of that wisdom. For the Israelite who produced and the Israelites who reaffirmed this hope, it was assumed that knowledge of Yahweh was to be found in Jerusalem.

But something else has happened, according to Isa. 2:2 (= Mic. 4:1). That little hill, Mt. Zion, not even as high, at present, as the Mount of Olives next to it, is to become the highest mountain on earth! This is a theological, not a topographical, statement. In the mythology of the ancient Near East, the World Mountain was an important theme, and its meaning in myth reveals to us what the OT intended to say by speaking of the height of Zion.[19] The

World Mountain was the highest point on earth, located at the center of the earth, the point from which creation began, and thus the point par excellence where God could be encountered. The emphasis on its height simply expressed in physical terms the belief that this place was the point of contact between heaven and earth.[20] So the prophets are saying in a way readily understood by people of their time something we will find emphasized throughout the visions of the new Jerusalem: God will be there.

Although many scholars suggest an early date for Isa. 2:2–4, the oracle in Isa. 4:2–6 is regularly given a very late date. As we compare its contents with other pictures of the city of the future, however, we find that it seems to be more closely related to Isaiah 2 than to the typical Zion prophecies that appear in great abundance in the post-exilic literature. There is no reference to exile or the rebuilding of the city. Unlike Isaiah 2, Isaiah 4 does speak of the divine activity that will be necessary in order to bring about the new era, the cleansing of Jerusalem by a spirit of judgment and a spirit of burning (4:4). This is distinctive language that owes nothing to the actual experiences of 587 B.C., and it might date from any period. Its tone is characteristic of pre-exilic prophecy in at least one respect, in that it offers not a hint that there is any way to avert that spirit of judgment. The remnant in 4:3 is thus not a group that may be expected to escape the judgment because of its faithfulness (a theme appearing in post-exilic, but not pre-exilic, prophecy), but the group that can qualify to be God's people only after it has gone through the judgment.

The promises of Isa. 4:5–6 are puzzling at first. Is Jerusalem to be the first city to have a Superdome covering the entire municipality? A close look at the text makes things clearer than one might have expected, however. The cloud by day and fire by night are certainly a reference to the wilderness experience. Originally they were given for guidance (Exod. 13:21), but when they are associated with the Tabernacle their significance is different. In Exod. 40:34 the glory of the Lord filled the Tabernacle when the cloud covered it, indicating that it has become a sign of the immediate presence of God in the midst of his people. The same thing is said of Solomon's temple; at its dedication the cloud and the glory filled the temple (1 Kings 8:10–11), so now the wilderness sign of God's presence is associated with Zion. So the promise of a cloud by day and a fire by night in Isaiah 4 is clearly a promise of the permanent presence of God himself in the midst of his people. Similar imagery appears in the picture of the new Jerusalem in Rev. 21:22–23; God will be eternally present in its midst and "the glory of God is its light."

There is also a protective quality about the cloud and the fire, which is a bit more puzzling, but which can also be easily explained by reference to other OT materials. Psalm 105:39 refers to the wilderness tradition in this way: "He spread a cloud for covering and fire to give light by night." What sort of covering could they have been talking about? How literally should we take it? The answer is to be found in other psalms:

> The Lord is your keeper;
> the Lord is your shade
> on your right hand.
> The sun shall not smite you by day,
> nor the moon by night.
> (Ps. 121:5–6)

> For he will hide me in his shelter
> in the day of trouble;
> he will conceal me under the cover of his tent,
> he will set me high upon a rock.
> (Ps. 27:5; cf. 31:20)

It is thus the certain, never failing, all-sufficient, caring, and protecting presence of God "in that day" which this text promises. Its central concern is the future existence of a holy people enjoying the presence of God in their midst.

One more Zion text that is typical of Isaiah·1—39 deserves attention. In Isa. 33:17–24 we encounter a fairly comprehensive picture of the new age. Kingship appears in connection with Zion for the first time in the texts we have dealt with. In 33:22 it is clearly the kingship of Yahweh that is expected, but there is debate over whether 33:17 makes the same reference or speaks of the ideal human king of the future, who will eventually be called Messiah.[21] The familiar and repeated threats against Jerusalem will be a thing of the past (33:18–19) and the security of the city will be perfectly assured (33:20). The tent imagery in 33:20 is a not surprising reference to Israel's pastoral traditions, now urbanized, but the linking of the majesty of Yahweh, in 33:21, with a place of "rivers and Niles" that are not navigable is not so clear. It may be an example of the marvelous stream associated with the mountain of God in Ps. 46:4 and Ezek. 47:1–12,[22] or, it has been suggested, it may be a claim that God's presence will compensate for the absence of the great rivers that enhance other cities, such as Babylon.[23] A new element of considerable interest is the promise in Isa. 33:24 that "No inhabitant will say, 'I am sick'; the people who dwell there will be forgiven their iniquity," one of several texts describing the people of Zion in the days to come.

Isaiah 33:17–24 contains a contrast between the coming time of security and the threats posed by foreign peoples, and between the times of sickness and forgiveness. The promise of peace is not very different from the hopes that apparently were expressed regularly in the cult, as the Psalms indicate.[24] The river imagery also is not greatly different from the way it is used in cultic language, if we understand these verses correctly. But Isa. 33:24 introduces something truly eschatological, indicating that this is more than an idealizing of the Jerusalem of the present. This picture of the future city of God can be presented without any reference to judgment, destruction, or exile, however, indicating that it belongs with the distinctive Zion tradition preserved in Isaiah 1—39, and is not typical of post-exilic Zion eschatology.

Most of the passages that deal with the future of Jerusalem are promises of restoration. Two examples of this type will suffice to illustrate the principal concerns that are expressed. The first is ascribed to 2 Isaiah (Isa. 49:14–26; mid–sixth century B.C. in Babylonia), and differs from the texts just considered in describing Jerusalem as a desolate place (Isa. 49:19; cf. vv. 14, 17). The emphasis throughout is on assurance that despite the catastrophe which has befallen Jerusalem and her people, God has not forgotten and intends to restore everything, to make it better than ever before. A new element is the tendency to personify Jerusalem. The passage begins with a lament of Zion, and Zion is addressed by the prophet. By this time it has become possible for that city to be used as a symbol for the people of God, so it is beginning to transcend its spatial origins. Note that Zion is metaphorically the mother of Israel. The prophet speaks of "the children born in the time of your bereavement" (Isa. 49:20), and alludes to the returning exiles as her sons and daughters (49:22; cf. v. 25). Since Zion has become a symbol for the people themselves, the prophet's impressive assurances of the intimate relationship that exists between God and his city represent another way of promising a permanent relationship between God and his people in the days to come:

> But Zion said, "The Lord has forsaken me,
> my Lord has forgotten me."
> "Can a woman forget her sucking child,
> that she should have no compassion on the son of her womb?"
> Even these may forget,
> yet I will not forget you.
> Behold, I have graven you on the palms of my hands;
> your walls are continually before me."
>
> (Isa. 49:14–16)

The symbol has become more than merely spatial, but it has not lost its original significance; for Zion also is a real city. It has walls, it has builders, it will even expect a housing shortage when the ingathering of the exiles begins (Isa. 49:19–20). It may be claimed that this passage has nothing in it that could not be hoped for in the normal course of human history—only the dimension of the divine will that assures it will indeed happen has been added. Hence it is on the borderline of our definition of true eschatology. It is an important passage, however, because it develops with fervor and imagination a single theme, that of the restoration of Zion, which will be combined elsewhere with all the expected transformations we call "eschatological."

A second example comes from the conclusion to the Book of Zephaniah. The passage begins like the hymns in the Psalter, with a call to praise:

> Sing aloud, O daughter of Zion;
> shout, O Israel!
> Rejoice and exult with all your heart,
> O daughter of Jerusalem!
> (Zeph. 3:14)

The relationship between Zeph. 3:14–15 and the psalms of the enthronement of Yahweh (Psalms 47, 93, 95—99) has been observed by several scholars,[25] but in this case a prophet has projected himself and his listeners into the immediate future as he calls on them to sing praises for what he expects to occur very soon. The succeeding verses begin with a word of assurance concerning the presence of God in the midst of Zion (Zeph. 3:16–17) followed by an oracle of the Lord promising deliverance from oppressors (vv. 18–19a), reversal of fortune for the lame and the outcast (v. 19b), and restoration and exaltation of Zion's people (v. 20). The word of assurance is introduced by "on that day" and the oracle uses "at that/the time" three times. The passage as a whole provides a good illustration of how the Zion theme has moved from the cult into eschatology and of the way it tended to gather around it a broad array of hopes for the future.[26] The reversal of fortune, God's promise to make right all that has gone wrong with this world and human life,[27] the essence of OT eschatology, is well represented in this short collection of assurances and promises focused on Zion. God's people will be gathered, unfortunate individuals (lame and outcast) will have shame turned into praise, and there will be no more cause to fear evil, for God will cast out their enemies. As usual, what will make all this possible, and permanent, is that "the King of Israel, the Lord, is in your midst" (Zeph. 3:15b).

This important biblical theme—the presence of God[28]—takes on an eschatological form with the promise of God's immediate and continuing presence with his people on Mt. Zion. As Jerusalem is described in both the cultic and eschatological passages of the OT, it is a perfect example of the "holy place" as defined by historians of religion.[29] It is the center of the world, the point from which creation began, the highest place on earth and thus the point of contact between heaven and earth; its holiness has been manifested by supernatural phenomena; and it is the place around which all of life is organized. As noted, one of the triumphs of Judaism, wrought by the exile experience, was the discovery that Yahweh could be encountered everywhere. Yet that discovery and its eventual realization in synagogue worship did not diminish the honor paid to the Jerusalem of the present and the future, as the post-exilic literature amply reveals.

A persistent theme that runs through the Old and New Testaments is the assurance "I am with you" and the promise "I will be with you." The tension between the belief that God may be found anywhere and the expectation of his immediate presence in Jerusalem is partly relieved by the tendency for all hopes to be centered in Zion. The expected glorification of that place is not exclusive, but inclusive; all that needs to be said about human destiny and the future of the world can be expressed in terms of Zion, the source from which all blessings flow.

It is of considerable interest that in the book of the prophet Ezekiel, who encountered a mobile God enthroned on a fiery chariot moving about the plains of Babylonia, who saw the glory of the Lord leave the doomed city (11:23), there are promises that God will once again be found in Jerusalem. Having described at length the new Jerusalem, Ezekiel 40—48 concludes with a new name for that city: *YHWH Shammah*. "And the name of the city henceforth shall be, The LORD is there" (Ezek. 48:35).[30]

This remarkable concentration of hope on a single point of the earth's surface will have its effect on each of the themes to be discussed in subsequent chapters, and it has had far-reaching consequences for the faith and worship of Judaism and Christianity, and for world politics as well (see the concluding sections of this chapter).

Subsequent Development of the Zion Tradition

Jewish religious literature from the period ca. 200 B.C.—A.D. 200, commonly called the Apocrypha and Pseudepigrapha, continued to express hopes for the establishment of a glorified Zion in the last days. The addition of new themes to the eschatological drama presented by apocalyptic books, such as heaven and hell, angelology, Satan, and resurrection, does mean that Jerusalem tends to be overshadowed somewhat in the elaborate schemes that are presented, but it does appear regularly. The theme has not been studied as intently in this literature as in the OT, but at least one scholar has concluded that eschatological hopes for Jerusalem were central to Judaism of this period.[31] It is still a real city in Palestine; the concept of a heavenly Jerusalem only appears late in the period now under consideration. Return from exile is typically represented as return to Jerusalem (Bar. 5:5–6; Tob. 13:8–18; 14:5–7), and the city is expected to be rebuilt in unearthly splendor (Tob. 13:16–17; 14:5; *1 Enoch* 90:28–29; *Sib. Or.* 5:250–55, 414–33; *2 Apoc. Bar.* 32:2–4). This literature may speak of a new temple not identified with the structure built by Zerubabbel and actually standing in Jerusalem during this period (Tob. 14:5; *Jub.* 1:29; *T. Benj.* 9:2; *Sib. Or.* 5:414–33; cf. 2 Macc. 2:4–8). The Temple Scroll from Qumran distinguishes between the new temple described therein and that which God himself will build on the Day of

Blessing.[32] The Messiah, who is not an eschatological figure in the OT, does play that role in this literature, and he is expected to participate in the re-establishment of Jerusalem and its sanctuary (*Sib. Or.* 5:414–33; 4 Ezra 13:35–36; *Pss. Sol.* 17:25, 33). The relationship of the Gentiles to Zion is reaffirmed, especially with new descriptions of the pilgrimage of the nations (Tob. 13:11; 14:6–7; *Sib. Or.* 3:702–31, 772–84; negative: Bar. 4:31–35). Other aspects of the appearance of the new Jerusalem appear in *Jub.* 1:29; 4:26; *T. Dan* 5:12; and *Sib. Or.* 5:250–51.

The shock produced by the destruction of Jerusalem in A.D. 70 was dealt with by two apocalyptic writers of the latter part of the first century in 2 Esdras (4 Ezra) and *2 Apocalypse Baruch*. A significantly new feature in Jewish thinking about Jerusalem appears in these books; without in any way giving up their hope for the restoration of the earthly Jerusalem—once more in ruins—they now speak of a heavenly city that has existed since the creation of the world and that corresponds to some extent with the city of this world. In 2 Esdras, probably the earlier of the two, Ezra sees a vision of a mother mourning her dead son and speaks to her of the tragedy of Zion until suddenly she is transformed and he sees a great city (9:38—10:27). The angel who interprets his vision tells him the woman is in fact the Zion of history, and in witnessing her transformation Ezra has seen the true city of the Most High (10:40–56; cf. 7:26). In *2 Apocalypse Baruch* the earthly Jerusalem is declared not to be the city said to have been engraved on the palms of God's hands in Isa. 49:16. That transcendental city was revealed to Adam, to Abraham, and to Moses and is now preserved, along with Paradise, in God's presence (4:2–7).

At about the same time these books were produced, a Christian writer developed more fully the concept of a new Jerusalem that would in the last days come down from heaven to take its place on the re-created earth (Revelation 21—22). The transcendentalizing of Jerusalem thus appears to be related to the historical occurrence of the destruction of the earthly city with its temple. The author of the Book of Revelation also created a most unusual triad: God, Christ, and the new Jerusalem (Rev. 3:12).

Paul also speaks of a heavenly Jerusalem several decades earlier than the writing of Revelation, but in quite a different way. In Gal. 4:21–31 he develops an allegory in which the present Jerusalem stands for the law of Judaism and the heavenly Jerusalem represents freedom. Another use of the heavenly city appears in the letter to the Hebrews, where it represents the goal of the Christian pilgrimage (Heb. 13:14). Already Abraham and Sarah sought it and God has "prepared for them a city" (11:16). As for Christians, "You have come to Mount Zion and to the city of the living God, the heavenly Jerusalem . . . and to Jesus, the mediator of a new covenant" (12:22, 24).[33]

Aspects of the earthly and heavenly Jerusalems are elaborated and reaffirmed in a variety of ways in Judaism and Christianity throughout the centuries that followed. The earthly city will be rebuilt by God and he will restore all its joy (*Exod. Rab.* LII.5), it will be built with sapphire stones (*Exod. Rab.* XV.21), and precious stones will mark its borders (*Pesiq. Rab Kah.* 18.6), which will extend to Damascus and Joppa (*Pesiq. Rab Kah.* 20.7). It will become the Metropolis of the whole earth (*Exod. Rab.* XXII.10), and all men from Adam to the resurrection will be assembled there (*Midr. Tanhuma* III 19.21).[34] God will bring either Sinai, Tabor and Carmel, or those three mountains plus Hermon together and bring down Jerusalem from heaven to rest on their tops (*Pesiq. Rab Kah.* 21.4; 55.4). When that happens the mountains will sing and the mountain of the Lord's house will be leader of the chorus (*Pesiq. Rab Kah.* 21.4). On the other hand there is a heavenly Jerusalem that already exists. In one manuscript of *2 Enoch* 55:2, a very late apocalypse, the seer says, "tomorrow morning I shall go up to the highest heaven, into the highest Jerusalem, into my eternal inheritance." Some rabbis spoke of a celestial Jerusalem located in the fourth heaven, where there is a temple in which Michael ministers as high priest (*Ḥag.* 12b).[35] Moses was permitted to see both Jerusalems in a vision (*Beth Hamidrash* VI Intro 22).[36] But Judaism did not follow the tendency, which appeared prominently in Christianity, of replacing their hope for a restored and glorified earthly Jerusalem with hope for a heavenly home. Rabbi Joḥanan said, "The Holy One, blessed be He, said, 'I will not enter the heavenly Jerusalem until I can enter the earthly Jerusalem' " (*b. Ta'an.* 5a). And the Eighteen Benedictions *(Amidah)*, which may be the oldest part of synagogue worship in use to this day, contain prayers for the restoration of Jerusalem (14th and 17th petitions).

The eschatological Zion took on a wider range of meanings in Christianity. As background for eschatology proper, it is instructive to note the legends that grew up concerning the present, earthly Jerusalem, reflecting a "mythologizing" tendency. According to the Syriac "Cave of Treasures," Adam was created and buried at the center of the earth, namely Jerusalem, on the exact spot where the cross of Christ would be erected, so the blood of Christ physically washed away the sins of Adam.[37] Jerusalem was also considered to be the navel of the earth and the highest point on earth, as Pope Urban II asserted in his famous speech, credited with instigating the First Crusade.[38] There was an aura about the existing city which inspired, and still inspires, pilgrimages, and which aroused at one period the crusading fervor.

The literal fulfillment of Revelation 21—22 by the descent of a heavenly city to remain on earth during the millennium was taught by the early Christian writers Justin and Tertullian,[39] and there is no doubt that such expectations may still be found to this day.[40]

Two other uses of the concept of the new Jerusalem have tended to predominate, however. One is a kind of realized eschatology; the heavenly Jerusalem has been identified with the church. Paul's statement that "our commonwealth is in heaven" (Phil. 3:20) was repeated and elaborated in a variety of ways.[41] Early interpretations of the scriptural Jerusalem as the church may be found in Origen, Augustine, and Eusebius,[42] and the idea was even given material expression by the architects of church buildings, who attempted to make the structure itself reflect the glories of the new Jerusalem.[43] To this day, in hymnody, Zion regularly functions as a symbol for the church.

The second use is the equation of the new Jerusalem with heaven. This also appears in Eusebius[44] and has been a regular feature of Christian hymnody throughout its history. There has been an extensive transcendentalizing of the new Jerusalem in Christianity, so that it most often represents Christian hopes for the coming of the kingdom of God on earth, already foreshadowed in the church, or for a blissful life of the believer in heaven. The expectation of a future restoration of the physical city of Jerusalem as the center of the new world has not disappeared, but it holds a much less significant place than in Jewish eschatology.

Contemporary Manifestations

The occurrence of prayers for the restoration of Jerusalem in synagogue worship continues to this day. The centrality of the real, earthly Jerusalem for the hopes of Jews throughout the world can be documented in a great many ways. What comes first to the minds of many is surely the conclusion of the Passover Seder: "Next year in Jerusalem." When the political movement to establish a homeland for world Judaism came into existence in the nineteenth century, its name almost from the beginning was taken from the subject of this chapter: Zionism.[45] The fact that there are both religious and non-religious Zionists and that among the religious Zionism is a mixture of vigorous, human effort to secure the immediate future and continuing hope for a divinely established time of peace provides a fascinating example of the influence of biblical eschatology in the modern world, and of the ways eschatology can be transformed—into calls for action and into completely secularized forms of hope.

In modern Christianity the place of Zion in future expectations is much less clear than in Judaism, but it is by no means absent. For many the concept is significant only in its transcendentalized form, most often as a symbol for heaven, or sometimes as a way of referring to the spiritual kingdom of God on earth. Some forms of Christianity, which devote great attention to discerning the signs of the end, include the restoration of Jews to the promised land and the rebuilding of the temple in their scenario for the last days, and debate the way in which the new Jerusalem of Revelation will be related to the millennium. Although this might seem to be pure speculation, it does have ethical implications, since these beliefs have often led to fundamentalist

Christian support for Zionist causes, for quite different reasons from those held by the Zionists. For Christians whose eschatology is different from the kind just described, who are deeply concerned about their relationships with the Jews, Jerusalem is one of the most difficult problems they must face. Christians may prefer to look at the city as a negotiable subject, involving populations, political advantage, access to holy places, and the like. If, however, their Jewish counterparts are to be understood, the theology of Jerusalem, with its intimate relationship to most Jews' hopes for their future, must be taken into account even though it may not be fully accepted.

CHAPTER 2

PEACE IN ZION

The Transformation of Human Society

The new city that Israel hoped God would establish on earth "in that day" was described in such a way as to include radical changes in human nature itself as well as renewal of social institutions and the natural world. Instinct or logic suggests to the modern author that the appropriate place to begin a discussion of the major eschatological themes ought to be with those inner changes in the lives of individuals. A careful consideration of where the emphasis lies in the OT itself, however, leads to the conclusion that it is more appropriate to begin with those institutions of the future that were expected to enable human beings to live in harmony. These are the eschatological themes that appear most regularly and are most fully developed.

That most of the eschatological material in the OT presupposes the experience of exile is indicated by the prominence of the re-establishment of the people of God in their homeland. In many texts it is the return of all the exiles to the promised land that is understood to be the necessary first step in the establishment of the new society of peace that Israel hoped for. The existence of a people in a land is thus the first promise. The harmonious society hoped for in that place at that time is sometimes described in terms of the rule of the righteous king, and because that king eventually becomes Messiah (in post–OT literature), a central figure for Jewish and Christian eschatology, we shall devote a section to him. Finally, the future involves many peoples, not just one, and the problems and conflicts created by that diversity also need to be solved; and so we shall see that the OT has a great deal to say about the future of the nations.

Restoration to the Promised Land

"Therefore, behold, the days are coming," says the Lord, "when it shall no longer be said, 'As the Lord lives who brought up the people of Israel out of the land of Egypt,' but, 'As the Lord lives who brought up the people of Israel out of the

> north country and out of all the countries where he had driven them.' For I will bring them back to their own land which I gave to their fathers." (Jer. 16:14–15; also 23:7–8)

No better introduction to the theme of this section could have been provided. Two discrete eras are contemplated, each of them constituted by a mighty, redemptive act of God. For the faith of Israel, its past and present existence have been given their character by the exodus, and so the text points us immediately to the tradition on which this aspect of eschatology was built. That the hope it expresses is appropriately called "eschatology" is revealed by the radical nature of the change that is expected, however. A new exodus is anticipated, but it will be so much greater than the former that the fundamental expression of Israel's faith, "As the LORD lives who brought up the people of Israel out of the land of Egypt" (cf. Exod. 20:2), will be replaced by a new one that celebrates the return of the diaspora to the promised land. Nowhere does the OT suggest that any other aspect of its hopes for the ideal future will have so fundamental an effect on Israel's confession of faith. But in fact, this prediction has not yet come true. Judaism still celebrates the exodus, not the return from exile, as its constitutive event. And so the text not only serves as an introduction to the theme as eschatology and to the tradition on which it is based but it also raises the question of fulfillment (of great importance in tracing the subsequent history of the theme).

History of the Promised Land Tradition

According to Israel's memory, God's promise to give them the land of Canaan to be their homeland antedated the exodus; indeed it antedated their existence as a people. It was offered to Abraham when he first set foot in the land (Gen. 12:7). The Pentateuch documents Israel's conviction that the possession of that land was inseparably connected to their relationship with Yahweh.[1] It may be read as the story of how the fulfillment of the promise was delayed and put into jeopardy in various ways over a period of many generations (e.g. Gen. 12:10–20; Exodus 2; 32:7–14; Num. 14:11–35). The triumphalism of the Book of Joshua, as it describes a thorough and complete conquest of Canaan that never actually happened, according to the rest of the OT, is clearly motivated by the strong need to affirm that God did indeed keep his promise (cf. Josh. 1:1–9 and 11:23). For all practical purposes it was fulfilled in the reigns of David and Solomon, when the borders were approximately those cited in the patriarchal materials and when Israel lived in relative peace and security. Although these parts of the OT deal with promise and fulfillment, there is nothing in them that needs to be called eschatology, for the possession of the land comes about through God's direction of the events of history and without any radical break in its normal course.

With the appearance of the prophet Amos the imminent arrival of a radical break was announced, however, and it was a change for the worse. "Israel shall surely go into exile away from its land" (Amos 7:17b). This threat of removal from the promised land struck at the very heart of Israel's relationship with God, as the pre-prophetic materials of the OT understood it. And so the question must be considered whether there was any place in the tradition for such a threat, or whether Amos was really attacking the roots of the Israelite faith.[2] In the patriarchal materials the promise of the land is completely unconditional (Gen. 13:14–17; 48:4; Exod. 6:6–8; 32:13); the land is to belong to Israel forever. But elsewhere in the Pentateuch, especially in Deuteronomy, conditions are imposed for maintaining Israel's existence in the land. There are apparently early threats against *security* in the land, but nothing is said about losing it completely (Exod. 23:33b; 34:12; Num. 33:55b; Deut. 7:16b; Josh. 23:13; Judg. 2:3). Threats of thoroughgoing destruction, ending the covenant relationship, also appear (Deut. 4:26; 6:15 and frequently in this book; Josh. 23:13, 15, 16; Jer. 9:15–16). But the concept of exile and restoration, a temporary loss of the land followed by return, does not appear with any prominence in materials that can claim to be earlier than the eighth century. The promises of restoration in Deut. 30:1–10; Isa. 11:11–16; Amos 9:14–15; Mic. 2:12; 4:6–7; Zeph. 3:19–20 are worded in such a way as to make it clear they are addressed to people who are already in exile. Only Hos. 11:5–11 projects into the future both exile and return. Furthermore, even the idea of exile itself seems to have been so inconsistent with Israelite theology that despite its prominence in Amos and Hosea (who develop it in two different ways) it produces no consistent tradition that can be traced through eighth- and seventh-century literature. Standard ways of speaking about exile only appear when the experience itself has become a reality for Judah.[3] There is some evidence to suggest that the pre–sixth-century materials dealing with exile are all related to the end of the Northern Kingdom in 722 B.C., and do not seriously contemplate the possibility that the whole people of God might be cut off from the promised land.[4]

The threat of exile and its realization for Judah in 597 and 587 B.C. was thus a blow to the heart of Israel's understanding of itself as a people of God. Israel possessed no theology that could justify its continuing identity in another country. "How shall we sing the Lord's song in a foreign land?" (Ps. 137:4) was their initial response to exile. It was crucial to their continuing existence that some basis for a future could be provided them, and in just that setting two important prophetic traditions concerning exile as an interim period, to be followed by a restoration to the land, may be found. Whether any or all of these words, attributed to Jeremiah and Ezekiel, actually came from the prophets themselves is another debated subject, but in this case the date of the materials is not so much in question. There is general agreement that prophetic promises of restoration appeared among the Babylonian exiles shortly after 587. Raitt's *Theology of Exile* avoids some of the psychologizing and building on presuppositions that is common in much of this work and makes a strong case for attributing some of the restoration promises to Jeremiah and Ezekiel themselves, but there is nothing approaching a consensus on the subject.[5] The Jeremiah tradition, at any rate, found a way to speak of a future for the exiles in this way:

The letter to the exiles (Jeremiah 29) contains first a warning against premature expectations, condemning false prophets in Babylonia who are promoting hope for an imminent return (29:4–9, 15–23), and counseling acceptance of life in exile. Jeremiah does promise that restoration will come in seventy years (29:10), but the practical effect of that for every adult who heard it was "You're not going back." The promise in Jeremiah 24 is also brief and modest, but moves a significant step in the direction of eschatology. God promises to "regard as good the exiles from Judah"(24:5b) and to "bring them back to this land" (24:6a), and the restoration will be accompanied by internal changes: "I will give them a heart to know that I am the Lord; and they shall be my people and I will be their God, for they shall return to me with their whole heart" (24:7). But this is the extent of the promise, and in its brevity and modesty it is quite different from the glorious pictures that appear elsewhere.

We have reached the turning point in the promised land tradition, the point at which history itself called the entire promise into question and seemed to be the fulfillment of those dire early threats that connected the loss of the land with the death of Israel. We can imagine two possible ways in which hope for some kind of future for Israel as the people of God might have been expressed. A theology of "sojourning" might have developed, abandoning the familiar association of peoplehood with a given piece of property (as Christianity eventually succeeded in doing), or one's hopes for Israel might have been tied to hope for return to the land of Canaan. It was the latter that prevailed.

Restoration as an Eschatological Theme

Judeans who were taken into exile in Babylonia believed that when Jerusalem fell it was the end of Israel as the people of God. The city that Yahweh had chosen for himself had been destroyed, his temple lay in ruins and its cult had been abandoned, and the people had been rooted up from the land he had promised them. "Our bones are dried up, and our hope is lost; we are clean cut off" (Ezek. 37:11b) became a proverb in their midst. Israel was dead, and as the prophet Ezekiel ministered to those exiles his message concerning new life inevitably involved a promise of return to their land.

The vision of the valley of the dry bones and its accompanying interpretation in Ezekiel 37 contain most of the important concepts associated with the theme of return to the land in OT eschatology. The resurrection of Israel from the death of exile is immediately associated with restoration:

> Behold, I will open your graves, and raise you from your graves, O my people; and I will bring you home into the land of Israel. . . . And I will put my Spirit within you, and you shall live, and I will place you in your own land. (Ezek. 37:12, 14)

For Israel to *live*, according to this text, is to return to the land of Canaan.

Added to this vision is a symbolic action and an extended oracle concerning restoration. The prophet is to take two sticks and label them "Judah" and "Joseph" (Ephraim), then join them in his hand, with the accompanying message that the Northern Kingdom will also return from its exile, to be reunited with Judah under one king (37:15–23). This is a concern that also appears in the Book of Jeremiah (3:18; 30:3), and that reappears from time to time in Judaism's hopes for the future (cf. Zech. 10:6–12). Although the twelve tribes of Israel were actually united politically for only a short period in all of history, under the reigns of David and Solomon, in the minds of the people there clearly existed the conviction that despite their political and religious differences, the "people of God" consisted of the twelve tribes, and this feeling was expressed in passages such as this, which promised reunion one day.

Ezekiel 37 continues with the promise of a new David (to be discussed in the next section) and the gift of an everlasting covenant of peace (37:24–26). Finally, God's sanctuary will be established in their midst forever (37:26–28). For obvious reasons, the Book of Ezekiel is cautious about its positive statements concerning Jerusalem. We and the exiles would understand that the holy city has been alluded to here, but only in its function as a center, a holy place where God's presence is evident.

Ezekiel has made use of covenant traditions (note the language of 37:23b, 24b, 26–27) and of traditions associated with the monarchy, including the uniting of the twelve tribes, in this chapter. In Ezekiel 20 a retelling of Israel's history from Egypt to the exile appears, written as a history of thoroughgoing rebellion from beginning to end, with only the patience of God allowing it to last as long as it did. So the prophet justifies the exile on the basis of a "history of salvation" which is really a history of human rebellion and divine forbearance. In the second half of chapter 20, a future is contemplated that will be the result of a new, redemptive act of God, but the prophet (or one of his followers) finds it possible to talk about the new, the unknown (because it is expected to be a time of obedience) by means of an appeal to the way God has dealt with his people in the past. History thus provides a pattern for the prophet's projection of the future, and this is of great importance for our appreciation of the validity of OT eschatology. This makes it possible to say more than merely "A better day is coming," since it appeals to the acknowledged consistency in God's dealings with his people in the past, providing some basis in the community's faith for its projections of hope; and it also serves as a check on the imagination, which might be tempted to introduce all sorts of products of wishful thinking, if the acts of God in the past were not accepted as providing legitimate language for talking about the future.

So the prophet finds the situation of his people to be comparable to that of Israel in captivity in Egypt long ago. And since Yahweh is known to be a God who sets captives free and leads them through the wilderness to a land that he gives them, it seems fair to promise that will happen once again (Ezek. 20:33–34, 41–42). Given the tone of the first part of Ezekiel 20, with its emphasis on Israel's rebelliousness, it is not surprising that the wilderness traditions concerning judgment (e.g., the golden calf, Korah's rebellion) are projected into the future wilderness experience, which is described as a time of purging (20:35–38). But for the people as a whole, only the act of grace—which is the new gift of the land—will produce the ultimate result of wholesale repentance (20:40–44). Jerusalem is not missing from Ezekiel's ideal future ("on my holy mountain," 20:40), but is de-emphasized in favor of possession of the land as the key to Israel's future life.

The re-use of Israel's saving history by a prophet had already occurred long before in the Book of Hosea. Amos had threatened exile without finding any way to connect it with the sacred traditions, but Hosea suggested God might, in effect, reverse the process of saving history and take Israel out of the promised land and back to the wilderness (2:14–15) or all the way back to Egypt (8:13; 11:5). In Hosea 11 the possibility of a new exodus is first intimated. Having threatened return to the land of bondage in v. 5, the prophet speaks of the possibility of restoration in v. 11: "They shall come trembling like birds from Egypt, and like doves from the land of Assyria; and I will return them to their homes, says the Lord."[6]

This concept of a new exodus as a way of projecting how God might work out a positive future for Jews in exile had as its natural conclusion a purely material outcome, emigration from the countries of the diaspora and resettlement in Palestine, and that expectation is reiterated many times in the OT. There are diaspora materials that do not bother to affirm it, such as Esther and Daniel, but nowhere is it spiritualized or made merely a symbol for some other kind of "return." That will have profound implications for the later history of Judaism, as we shall soon see. Spiritual content could be added to the promise of physical return, however, as Ezekiel 20, with its concern for repentance, has already shown us (cf. Jeremiah 24). Second Isaiah's extensive use of the new exodus theme carries different spiritual connotations.[7] God's marvelous care for his people in the wilderness is the part of the tradition this prophet wishes to emphasize, and for him the new exodus will be a triumphal procession across a transformed land (Isa. 49:10–11). Throughout Second Isaiah there is rejoicing because God has already forgiven (Isa. 40:2; 43:1) and because all obstacles, spiritual and material, are in the process of being overcome.

> And the ransomed of the Lord shall return,
> and come to Zion with singing;
> everlasting joy shall be upon their heads;
> they shall obtain joy and gladness,
> and sorrow and sighing shall flee away.
> (Isa.51:11)

Among the triumphs to be celebrated when the exiles are restored to their homeland are the vindication of Israel in the sight of the nations, who will acknowledge the supremacy of Yahweh by assisting in the restoration (Isa. 45:14–17; 49:22–23), and the completeness of the gathering of the dispersed (43:5–7). The latter theme had already appeared in one form in the concern shown by Jeremiah and Ezekiel for the northern tribes, and it reappears frequently throughout Jewish history.[8]

Second Isaiah was partly right in his announcement of an imminent return to the promised land; his words were probably spoken shortly before the decree of Cyrus (Ezra 1) made it possible for some exiles to re-establish themselves in Jerusalem. But the wilderness did not blossom beneath their feet, the cooperation of the nations in the grand project was negligible, Zion was not glorified but remained a minor city, and there remained more Jews outside the promised land than within it. The way one of those early returnees dealt with the question of fulfillment is thus a matter of considerable importance. We have already dealt with the passage once, because of its emphasis on Zion, but will find it helpful to look once again at Zechariah 7—8.[9] Behind the question about whether fasts commemorating the fall of Jerusalem should still be kept (Zech. 7:2–3) surely lies the issue of whether the returnees in those early days ought to believe that *this* was the answer to their expectations.

Zechariah's answer was that they were just then in the midst of fulfillment (8:9–13). The laying of the foundation of the temple seems to have been, for him, the sign that the days of full restoration were upon them. So he does not interpret the return from exile which has already occurred as a major event, nor those presently living in Jerusalem as the true eschatological community; the promise of ingathering "from the east country and from the west country" is repeated in very much the form it had taken in earlier prophetic books (Zech. 8:7–8).[10]

Subsequent Occurrences of the Theme

There is an understandable ambiguity in the eschatological uses of the theme of return to the land in the Jewish literature produced during the Second Temple period. On the one hand, exiles had returned and established a slowly growing Jewish community in the homeland. The temple had been rebuilt and with its services functioned as a spiritual center for world Judaism. But on the other hand, the ingathering was far from complete and the experiences of Jews who lived in Palestine between 520 B.C. and A.D. 70 were hardly literal fulfillments of the OT's expectation of the ideal future. So we find the actual historical return dealt with in different ways in the apocalyptic schematizing of past, present, and future, which becomes typical of the eschatology of this period.[11]

Sometimes the restoration that had occurred in history is affirmed as part of God's work, but Israel's actual situation is then accounted for by speaking of an ensuing period of tribulation preceding the eschaton (*Adam and Eve* 29:5–10; *T. Zeb.* 9:6–9; *T. Naph.* 4:2–5). In these cases a full ingathering at the end is not mentioned. A second pattern judges the restoration that has already occurred to be flawed and expects the perfection of it in the last days. For example, Tobit says:

> But God will have mercy on them, and bring them back into their land; and they will rebuild the house of God, though it will not be like the former one until the times of the age are completed. After this they will return from the places of their captivity, and will rebuild Jerusalem in splendor. (Tob. 14:5; cf. *1 Enoch* 89:72–73; 90:28–33)

Most frequently we encounter a repetition of the OT pattern, which simply moves from exile to an eschatological restoration without attempting to account for the present state of affairs (*Jub.* 1:15–18; *T. Levi* 16—18; *T. Dan* 5; *T. Benj.* 9; *T. Jos.* 6; *T. Ash.* 7; *T. Jud.* 23—25; *T. Jos.*[Arm] 19). The concern about reunion of the twelve tribes reappears in interesting ways in several of these texts (*T. Jos.*[Arm] 19; *As. Mos.* 3:3—4:9; *2 Apoc. Bar.* 78—87).

As would be expected, rabbinic Judaism, after the fall of Jerusalem in A.D. 70, frequently takes up the question of the meaning of exile, but the subject cannot be pursued further in this context.[12] The continuing eschatological quality of the hope for return, in rabbinic thought, is nicely illustrated by this saying from the Babylonian Talmud:

> Whoever goes up from Babylon to the Land of Israel transgresses a positive commandment, for it is said in Scripture, They shall be carried to Babylon, and there they shall be, until the day that I remember them, saith the Lord. (*b. Ketub.* 110b–111a)

In early Christianity, the Jewish concern about re-occupation of Palestine is simply not a subject of interest.[13] To cite a few examples, the author of Hebrews takes up the theme of "rest," which in the OT means prosperity and security in the promised land, and uses it to refer to the ultimate relationship of believers to the Lord, without feeling any need to discuss the original meaning of the promise (Heb. 3:7—4:13). And the "homeland" that the patriarchs sought is redefined as a heavenly country (11:13–16). Later, Tertullian used Ezek. 37:1–14 as evidence for the doctrine of resurrection of the flesh and did note in passing that some read the passage as referring to the restoration of the "Jewish polity," but he dismisses this as of no real interest.[14] Augustine's retelling of the history of Judaism finds nothing of fulfillment of prophecy in the restoration of the Second Temple period, but affirms the importance of the diaspora in the divine plan in order that the prophecies of Christ in Jewish Scriptures might witness to the world of the truth of Christian claims.[15] This early disinterest in the idea that in the last days the Jews would be gathered from the diaspora and returned to Palestine has tended to remain characteristic of much subsequent Christian thought, but there are types of Christian eschatology in which it plays an important role. Therefore, we now turn to the variety of views on this subject in modern Judaism and Christianity.

Contemporary Manifestations

No OT theme has more obvious contemporary relevance for international affairs than the promise of return to the land. One of the reasons for the appearance of the modern state of Israel is surely the persistence in Judaism of the hope that one day the Jews of the diaspora would be able to return to Palestine and make it their national homeland once again. There is no single "Jewish view" of the promised land, however, and because of the brevity that is called for in this section, the risk of distorting things must be taken by simply listing a variety of points of view.[16] Some Orthodox Jews take a thoroughly eschatological position with reference to the promises of return, and believe that will occur only when Messiah comes. As a result, they do not accept the modern state of Israel as a legitimate expression of their faith at all. Other Jewish thinkers have turned away from religious hopes and affirmed the validity of a cultural Judaism that accepts diaspora existence.[17] The opposite point of view is taken by other, non-religious Jews, the secular Zionists who have moved in this century to create a homeland for themselves. Their arguments have focused on the inherent need for a people to have a land, and in the early days some of them were so little influenced by the promises of Scripture as to consider other countries, such as Argentina or Uganda, as possibilities for a Jewish homeland.[18] The continuing influence of the promised land on the Jewish mind is revealed by the fact that those suggestions were scorned, and the Zionist movement refused ever to take seriously any potential homeland but Palestine. It should be noted that these political efforts to establish a modern Jewish state normally appeal more to the promises of the land to the patriarchs as establishing their legitimate claim to the place than to the eschatological hope of ingathering, since in this movement eschatology has been taken into human hands. Some Zionists, however, appeal to the biblical promise of full restoration of all Jews to the land as the basis for their call for a wholesale emigration to the land of Israel.[19]

From this sketchy statement one can see that despite the predominance of Zionism in the twentieth century, there are differences within Judaism, and there also exist anti-Zionist points of view.[20] For Christians, then, it is not simply a question of whether to affirm and support "the Jewish hope," since that is not the same for everyone. To take seriously both the biblical promises concerning the land and the real needs of contemporary Jews calls for some very difficult theological and ethical thinking on the part of Christians, precisely because the NT provides so little guidance.[21] For most of Christian history the promises of return to the Holy Land have been reaffirmed as applicable to Christians, but only in a spiritual or theological sense, following the lead of the letter to the Hebrews. The ingathering has been taken as a type of the unity of the mystical body of Christ.[22] The promised land has regularly been taken as equivalent to heaven, as a great many hymns reveal. In the spirituals of black Americans, Canaan represented heaven on the surface, but at the same time served as a code word for physical freedom from slavery.[23] Some of the crusaders may, of course, have believed in transferring the literal promise of the land to Christian recipients, but fortunately that point of view has seldom had much appeal. In some forms of modern fundamentalism the attempt has been made to put together all the eschatological materials of both Testaments in order to make one coherent, comprehensive plan for the last days. These schemes vary among the interpreters, as would be expected by one who views the Bible historically. Some of them are inclined to take literally the promise of the full ingathering of the Jews and to make it one of the stages near the end of the eschatological drama. In their enthusiasm for discerning the signs of the times they tend to see the rise of the modern state of Israel as the beginning of the fulfillment of that promise, and so Zionism has received considerable support from this type of fundamentalist Christianity. It should be noted, however, that the support seems to be motivated not so much by concern for the Jewish people themselves as by enthusiasm for finding oneself very near the Second Coming of Christ, a motive that would hardly be shared by Jews.

Can Christians find solid exegetical grounds for taking seriously the intense Jewish concern with the land of Canaan? Recent efforts to engage in such a dialogue have yielded only tentative conclusions. But we must see what we can say. For instance, already in 1904 A. B. Davidson took the subject seriously. He devoted the last chapter of his book *Old Testament Prophecy* to "The Restoration of the Jews."[24] He concluded from his studies of the NT, especially Romans 9–11, that the original promise of Canaan to Abraham has been widened to become a promise of the whole world to the people of God (Jew and Gentile). Such a broadening of the promise already begins to appear in the later Prophets, who speak of new heaven and new earth as God's gift to his people. So without rejecting the place of the Jews in the divine economy, Davidson found evidence in Scripture that Christians ought not to expect a literal ingathering at the end of time, but ought to accept those promises as the first step in God's intention to offer the transformed world to his people.[25]

Other readings of the two testaments, somewhat more literal than Davidson's, have been offered. The return of the exiles that already had occurred in the sixth century B.C. is sometimes said to be the literal fulfillment of OT prophecy, so that nothing further of that kind is to be expected. Others emphasize that in the NT the preoccupation with land is replaced by a corresponding promise of a new kingdom, a new people of God (including Jews and Gentiles as one), in a new creation.[26] Yet another reading of the NT claims that its silence concerning the land implies that the OT promise has not been nullified. The beatitude "Blessed are the meek, for they shall inherit the earth" broadens the promise but does not negate its earlier form. Since all God's promises are fulfilled in Christ, the state of Israel may be understood as a part of realized eschatology.[27]

Some tentative conclusions:

1. The OT affirms that the attachment of a people to their land is not unimportant in the sight of God.

2. The exilic materials in the OT also show that Jews learned in practice that it is possible to be a faithful member of God's people no matter where one lives. But this experienced truth never became an explicit part of OT theology important enough to rival the promise of the land.

3. This truth was made explicit in the NT's double affirmation that the whole world belongs to Christians, as a sojourning place, while their true home is in heaven.

4. Despite the freedom offered to Christians from ethnic and territorial constraints, the NT nowhere rejects peoplehood and homelands as wrong. Government, for example, is affirmed (Rom. 13:1–7; 1 Pet. 2:13–17), and there are still nations involved in Revelation's picture of the ideal future (Rev. 21:24–26; 22:2). Although the rest of the NT shows little interest in the OT picture of peoples and nations living peacefully in their own territories, it contains no argument against that.

5. The ultimate loyalties of Christians thus transcend loyalty to any one nation or place, but they do not ignore the legitimate needs of their own people and other peoples in these times before the end comes; hence the

desire of peoples (Jews and others) for a secure place of their own is a concern of Christians.

6. No one can know just how God will dispose of the problem of Palestine in the last days; Scripture does not present the kind of detailed blueprint for the future which we might desire for that subject, or any other. In the meantime, however, Christians' appropriate recognition of their special relationship to the Jews must surely be to take seriously the special attachment of many of them to Palestine and their legitimate desire for a national homeland, and to seek a *just* response to that desire. It must be emphasized that to find a *just* response may not necessarily mean agreeing wholeheartedly with the proposals of any one particular Jewish group.

The Righteous King (Messiah)

The King has played a significant role in only a few of the texts discussed so far. This elementary observation is actually responsible for one of the major differences between this presentation of the OT message concerning the future and traditional Jewish and Christian expositions of what has usually been called "messianic prophecy." The familiar way of using the OT, in scholarship and piety of all varieties, has been to go to it with a predetermined interest—the Messiah—and then to look for messianic texts. With such an approach, scholarship and piety have been able to identify a great deal that for one reason or another might be called "messianic," to the extent that what is now generally called eschatology has through most of Christian history been called messianism. But this figure—Messiah—and all that is associated with him in both Jewish and Christian eschatology are to a great extent the product of the hopes of post–OT Judaism and of the Christian identification of Jesus as the fulfillment of the whole OT promise. This is not at all to say that those generations were wrong in what they expected of Messiah, nor to say that it is improper for Christians to apply that name to Jesus. My approach, in agreement with other recent studies, aims to look first at the OT simply on its own terms, beginning with the Hebrew word *mašiaḥ*, which we have anglicized as Messiah, and then trace the concepts associated with that word in a strictly historical way. Eventually we shall end up where traditional studies have begun.

The word *mašiaḥ* means "anointed" and occurs in the OT only thirty-nine times. The physical sense of rubbing with oil or having oil poured over the head is never far removed from any of its occurrences. Four times it is used of priests, suggesting that at one period priests were anointed, but there is insufficient evidence to conclude that was always the case (Lev. 4:3, 5, 16; 6:22). Nearly all the other occurrences refer to kings. Saul is called the Lord's anointed twelve times (1 Sam. 12:3, 5; 16:6; 24:6 [2x], 10; 26:9, 11, 16, 23; 2 Sam. 1:14, 16) and David is given that title seven times (2 Sam. 19:21;

23:1; Ps. 18:50 = 2 Sam. 22:51; Ps. 132:10; 132:17 = 2 Chron. 6:42). The other named king so favored is, remarkably enough, a pagan, Cyrus the Persian (Isa. 45:1). Where, then, are the messianic prophecies, predictions of the coming savior? Here are the remaining texts: Hannah's song concludes by saying of God, "He will give strength to his king, and exalt the power of his anointed" (1 Sam. 2:10). A prophet announces to Eli that God will raise up a faithful priest (Samuel) who will "go in and out before my anointed forever" (1 Sam. 2:35). Part of the description of the disaster of 587 reads, "the breath of our nostrils, the Lord's anointed, was taken in their pits, he of whom we said, 'Under his shadow we shall live among the nations' " (Lam. 4:20). Habakkuk and one of the Psalms speak of God's people as anointed (Hab. 3:13; Ps. 28:8). Another psalm refers to Abraham, Isaac, and Jacob as God's anointed ones, his prophets (Ps. 105:15 = 1 Chron. 16:22; cf. Isa. 61:1 where a prophet uses the verb "anoint" of himself). Some of these texts no doubt may be interpreted as prophecies of the eschatological redeemer, if one insists, but the natural reading of them does not suggest any such thing.

We are left, then, with seven more debatable occurrences, in Pss. 2:2; 20:6; 84:9; 89:38, 51, and Dan. 9:25, 26. Critical scholarship understands these psalms to be references to the currently reigning king in Israel and the anointed ones in Daniel to be the high priests, Joshua of the sixth century B.C. and Onias III, who was removed from office around 175 B.C. So we are left without any eschatological Messiah in the OT! But the roots of messianic hope are present in the OT; it is the legitimate offspring of an important strand of Israelite theology—that of kingship, which is the tradition out of which messianic hope grew.[28]

History of the Theology of Kingship in Israel

While anointing was done for various purposes in ancient Israel, it is clear from the uses of the noun *mašiaḥ* which have been cited that ordinarily when an Israelite referred to "the anointed one," he meant the king. Anointing was how one got to be a king, as 1 Sam. 10:1; 16:13, and 2 Kings 9:1–3 indicate. And since the line of Saul and all the royal families of the Northern Kingdom died out, it is the family of David which possessed the only royal ideology of lasting importance. The meaning of Davidic kingship is another major tradition in OT theology which can be studied at length in other works, but it must be outlined here in order to show the roots from which the hope for a future righteous king grew.

The foundation document for the royal ideology of the house of David is the prophecy attributed to Nathan in 2 Samuel 7. It announced God's choice of David to be the ruler of his people and established a special relationship between God and David which included the promise to maintain his dynasty forever. Other references to this oracle describe that relationship as a unique covenant between God and David (Pss. 89:3, 28; 132:12). The personal successes of David and the glories of the reign of Solomon, including the establishment of a temple in which the royal ideology could be preserved and celebrated, gave this new element in the faith of Israel a permanent place and a growing importance. Although interpreters of the Psalms prior to the twentieth century had always agreed in taking them to be "prophetic" eschatological expressions of hope for the coming of the Messiah, the form-critical approach to the Psalter has made a strong case for understanding them as present-tense celebrations of what Israel believed about kingship in their own day. So, Psalms 2 and 110 are taken to be coronation songs, Psalm 45 a song for a royal wedding, and Psalm 72 to be a prayer for the king. When one looks at them without thinking about the traditional Christian uses, this seems to be a perfectly natural reading, except perhaps for two verses: "I will tell of the decree of the Lord: He said to me, 'You are my son, today I have begotten you' " (Ps. 2:7), and v. 6 of Psalm 45, which seems to say to the king, "Your throne, O God, endures for ever and ever." It has been argued that these lines only make sense if taken to be prophecies of Jesus, the incarnate Son of God. But it is clear from other texts that the historic David and his descendants were believed to stand in a very special relationship to God which might have been expressed as adoptive sonship.[29] Israelites did not believe in divine kingship, but it was possible for them to think of human beings as sons of God their heavenly Father, much as we do today. So it is not difficult to explain these verses as slightly extravagant language that might very well have been used to express Israel's hopes that were fixed on a king whom they believed God had chosen to rule over them.

There were two flaws in Israel's kingship ideology. The first was spelled out at length by the Prophets; although *kingship* might be a marvelous thing and the work of God, actual kings were usually quite another matter. They seldom lived up to the ideals expressed in the Psalms (cf. Jeremiah 22). The second was the shocking break in the continuity of the Davidic dynasty brought about by the Babylonian triumph over Judah in 587 B.C. (cf. Psalm 89, which may reflect that event, and Lam. 4:20). From that point on kingship could not be celebrated, for it no longer existed. It might be commemorated, as the Chronicler seems to do in his idealization of the work of David, or it might become the basis of hope for a better future. Although the word Messiah itself is never used in a futuristic way in the OT, the hope for the coming of a righteous king in that day does appear, with terms other than Messiah being used to denote that king.

The Eschatological King in the Old Testament

A famous "messianic prophecy" from Isaiah may be taken as a transitional text between Israel's practice of glorifying the present king and the tendency to look into the future for the coming of a king who would really live up to the divine intention for Israel's ruler. This is Isa. 9:2–7: "For unto us a child is born." It is not at all clear from the form of the passage that it is intended to be a prediction, for it sounds like an announcement. As we compare it with the royal psalms it seems more and more likely that the setting of this text was either a coronation or the time of the birth of an heir to the throne. The names to be given to the child: Wonderful Counsellor, Mighty God, Everlasting Father, Prince of Peace, are not too exalted to be ascribed to an ordinary Israelite king, as has been argued, but are good examples of the kind of extravagant language typically used in the throne names of oriental potentates.[30] Furthermore, there are several possibilities for the translation of these names, so it is not as certain that the king is being called "Almighty God" as many English translations would suggest. If this reading of the passage is correct, Isa. 9:2–7 may then represent a prophetic affirmation of traditional kingship ideology.

The other famous text from Isaiah is clearly futuristic, however. Chapter 11, vv. 1–5 speak of a shoot that will come forth from the stump of Jesse, referring presumably to a time when the tree that is the Davidic dynasty has been cut down. That this new offspring of David is expected to be a human being is indicated by vv. 2 and 3. The Spirit of the Lord will rest on him, as on others in Israel whom God had chosen to carry out his work (Bezalel, Exod. 31:3; Balaam, Num. 24:2; Gideon, Judg. 6:34, etc.), and his obedience is described in familiar language: "His delight shall be in the fear of the Lord." He does possess supernatural gifts, however, due to the grace of God. His wisdom is emphasized very prominently, with a clustering of typical wisdom terms: *ḥokmah* (wisdom), *binah* (understanding), *'eṣah* (counsel), and *da'at* (knowledge), but his capacities surpass those even of the greatest wise man, for his powers of judgment are not limited by what he can observe (Isa. 11:3b). His work and character are described briefly, but emphatically; he is essentially to be the establisher and maintainer of justice (11:4–5). His nature and work are thus no more than would be expected of the ideal king, and the message of the prophecy, in our way of putting it, is that the day is coming when God will see to it that his people have good government.[31]

There is a fascinating passage in the Book of Jeremiah which remains one of the least known of the OT's so-called messianic prophecies, probably because it makes the unparalleled move of linking the house of David with the house of Levi and making the eternal covenant applicable to both. This creates something of a problem for Christians, who are interested in the promise to David because of Jesus' Davidic ancestry but who have no stake at all in the perpetuation of the levitical priesthood. The passage has a somewhat doubtful textual history; Jer. 33:14–26 is completely missing from the Septuagint, which preserves a much shorter recension of the Book of Jeremiah. Internal evidence also raises questions about whether it is as old as Jeremiah himself, since 33:14–16 is a citation of 23:5–6, and the whole text may be understood as a commentary on that passage. The oracle in Jeremiah 23 follows his condemnation of the worthless rulers who have afflicted Judah and promises in contrast that the days are coming when God will raise up a Branch (cf. the *shoot* of Isa. 11:1) who will be wise, just, and righteous. There are good reasons for thinking that passage may have been the work of Jeremiah himself and that 33:14–26 comes from a later time, but that does not make the latter text of any less interest to us. If it is later than Jeremiah it comes from a time when the functioning of both houses, David and Levi, was either non-existent or greatly altered, and its attempt to deal with that situation was simply to reiterate the promise of an eternal covenant, and to make it stronger than ever. "Thus says the Lord: If you can break my covenant with the day and my covenant with the night, so that day and night will not come at their appointed time, then also my covenant with David my servant may be broken . . . " (33:20–21a). No explanation is offered, just reaffirmation. As to the nature and functions of this heir of David, nothing new is added to the picture we have already gained of the good king. The same may be said of other texts such as Isa. 32:1; 33:17; Jer. 3:15; 30:9, 21; Ezek. 34:23–24; 37:22–25; Hos. 3:5; and Amos 9:11–12.

It will be seen that although the Davidic king is mentioned fairly often, he plays a limited role in each of these descriptions of the ideal future, and in no sense can he be called a "savior." It is Yahweh who saves his people, and the gift of a righteous king is sometimes mentioned as a part of that salvation. Before looking at three slightly different appearances of the king, one should pay attention to a series of eschatological texts where no need is felt to mention the king at all. He does not appear in Ezekiel 40—48 (which speaks of a prince who has a few limited rights and responsibilities, 45:7—46:18), and is missing from all the exilic and post-exilic Isaiah materials (Isaiah 24—27, 34—35, 40—66). Neither does the king appear in the futuristic parts of Joel, Zephaniah, or Malachi. This non-monarchical eschatological tradition will be seen for many generations beyond the OT period when we turn to the intertestamental literature.

Two other famous texts must be discussed, then we will conclude the OT section with a historical note and an important excursus. Much of Mic. 5:2–4 is familiar to us by now: the reference to Bethlehem assures us that the subject is the son of David, that he is a ruler who will feed his flock (continuing the ancient Near Eastern tradition of calling the king a shepherd; cf. Jer. 23:1–6 and Ezekiel 34), and that his rule will be associated with the restoration of his people, as in Ezekiel 34 and 37. There is one intriguing expression in the passage, however: "whose origin is from of old, from ancient days" *(miqqedem mime 'olam)*. Does this mean no more than that his ancestry can be traced all the way back to David, or does it introduce into the concept of kingship a mysterious aspect that we have not seen elsewhere?[32] Whatever its origin, it will be important for the later development of belief in a Messiah to whom will be ascribed supernatural qualities that transcend the original OT concept.

The king in Zech. 9:9–10 is also a figure with somewhat mysterious qualities. Just in the midst of a chapter filled with warfare and bloodshed there appears, for two verses, a king who is triumphant and victorious, all right, but not in the normal sense. He is no soldier, but is "humble" (the word may even mean "afflicted") and riding on an ass—the domestic burden-bearer and no beast of battle. There is something surprising here, not adequately accounted for by tradition, and this is the kind of passage which may have to be explained as much by what follows it in history as by what precedes it.[33]

The historical note mentioned earlier has to do with the apparent conclusion by the prophets Haggai and Zechariah that Zerubbabel, a member of the family of David and in charge of rebuilding the temple in 520–516 B.C., was the fulfillment of the promise to establish David's throne forever. The hopes of those prophets that they might be living "in that day" were tied at least in part to that identification, as Hag. 2:23 and Zech. 3:8; 4:5–10; 6:12–13 reveal. It has often been suggested that the obvious incorrectness of that assumption may have had something to do with the disappearance of any references to a future king from Jewish literature for several centuries thereafter.

If we now survey what has been gleaned from a study of those eschatological texts in which the righteous king appears, we may draw these conclusions: He plays an important though limited role in many pictures of the ideal future, but there are a good many texts in which he does not appear at all; he is not the agent by which God saves his people but is one of God's gifts of salvation, and he is a purely human figure, responsible for good government. This is "Messiah" in the OT, but that is not the end of the story.

Excursus: The Suffering Servant and the Son of Man

The reader who is familiar with Christian tradition will have noticed that my survey did not include such famous "messianic prophecies" as Psalm 22, Isaiah 53, or Daniel 7.[34] There were valid reasons for that, from within the OT perspective, but in order to account for the later development of Christian messianism, some comment must be made here on those texts. This matter is treated as an excursus because there is no inner–OT reason for calling Psalm 22 or Isaiah 53 eschatological. The psalm plays an important role in the way the Gospels interpret the death of Jesus. The whole theme of the "righteous sufferer" in the OT is, in fact, fulfilled and transformed by Jesus. But in the

Hebrew Scriptures the righteous sufferer had nothing to do with the future righteous king. It is true that an effort has been made to identify an aspect of kingship ideology which was not mentioned earlier, taking a hint from the ritual humiliation of the king in the Babylonian New Year festival.[35] It has been suggested that psalms such as the twenty-second were actually ritual texts describing how the Israelite king also suffered in place of his people, and so, it is argued, the concept of a suffering Messiah can actually be traced all the way back to pre-exilic Israel. The idea is intriguing, but it has two major flaws. Although it may very well be true that the king was the original speaker in many of the laments in the Psalter, the evidence for a ceremony of ritual humiliation or a theology of a suffering king is simply not to be found outside those psalms. And if one insists that they are sufficient evidence for the existence of such a concept during the period of monarchy, then it will be necessary to account for its complete eclipse in post-exilic Judaism—only to reappear centuries later in the Gospels.

As for Isaiah 53, it is my position that Jesus was indeed the fulfillment of those words, but the words themselves do not take the form of a prediction and they originally had nothing to do with Messiah. The Songs of the Suffering Servant (Isa. 42:1–4; 49:1–7; 50:4–9; 52:13—53:12) stand in a class by themselves, and from the perspective taken by this book it does not seem appropriate to call them eschatological—a part of the Jewish people's hopes for an ideal future. It has been pointed out by others, for example, that Isaiah 53 produces no growing, ongoing tradition of its own in Judaism. Those who sought to find a suffering king in the OT have pointed out the royal elements that do appear in the Servant Songs, but they are combined with other traditions and the question of the identity of the Servant is by no means solved as easily as that.[36] None of this is in any way intended to downgrade the importance of Isaiah 53; rather, it may be that we better understand and appreciate it the more its uniqueness is acknowledged.

The Son of man does appear in an eschatological passage, Daniel 7, but is in no way connected with Messiah. This is an apocalyptic vision making use of extravagant symbolism. Four great beasts come up from the sea, composite animals unlike anything on earth, and they are interpreted as symbols of four world empires (7:3–8, 19–24). In contrast to them there appears "one like a son of man" (7:13); in other words, understanding the Aramaic idiom, a human figure. The identity of that figure is not left a mystery at all, for an interpretation of 7:14, "and to him was given dominion and glory and kingdom . . . ," follows in 7:27: "and the kingdom and the dominion and the greatness of the kingdoms under the whole heaven shall be given to the people of the saints of the Most High." As beastly figures represent the pagan nations, then, a human figure represents the people of

God. So much for Daniel, but once again that is not the end of the story for the Son of man, who reappears in surprising ways in the Gospels.

The Servant of the Lord and the Son of man, studied historically, are revealed to be separate strands of tradition in the OT, never combined with one another or with the Messiah. That this was also true of Judaism in the intertestamental period has been carefully documented and supports our conclusion that the rich potential of all these different ideas is first realized in a single figure only in the Gospels, in the figure of Jesus.[37]

The Appearance of the Full-Fledged Messianic Hope

Hope for the ideal future could be expressed very nicely in post–OT Judaism without a Messiah. No such figure appears in the eschatology of *Jubilees; 1 Enoch* 1—36; 91—104; *Assumption of Moses; 2 Enoch; Sibylline Oracles* IV; the War Scroll, Psalms Scroll, or Habakkuk Commentary of Qumran; or in any of the books of the Apocrypha except 2 Esdras. Messiah does appear in other documents from Qumran, but does not play a major role in them (1QSa II.11–22; The Patriarchal Blessings; 1QS IX.11).[38] A royal figure who might fairly be said to represent the messianic hope, although the word itself is not used, appears in the *Testaments of the Twelve Patriarchs* (*T. Sim.* 7:2; *T. Jud.* 24:1–6; *T. Dan* 5:10–13; *T. Jos.* 19:8–11), in company with an eschatological priest. A white bull who presumably represents the Messiah appears in the dream-vision of Enoch (*1 Enoch* 90:37), but plays no significant role. The only extensive pre-Christian description of the Messiah that we possess is in *Psalms of Solomon* 17, dated in the middle of the first century B.C. It is still familiar OT language; Messiah is the king, the son of David, but he is a bit more active now. It is he who will defeat Israel's enemies, gather the people, and settle the tribes in the land where he will be their judge. The nations will come under his yoke and he will rule in righteousness, for he is sinless and wise because of God's holy spirit. But he is still a purely human figure and his functions are exclusively political.

Messiah is thus not at all a common figure in Jewish eschatology down to the first century B.C. But the Gospels leave the impression that there was a ferment of messianic expectations among the Jews of Palestine in the first century A.D., and there is no reason to think that is not an accurate account of a changed situation. The new element apparently was the appearance of the Romans and the aggravated political problems produced by the rule of the Herods and then the procurators. Evidence for the connection between hatred of the Romans and the rise of the messianic hope already appears in the *Psalms of Solomon*.

There is an abundance of scholarly literature dealing with Messiah and Son of man in the NT and tracing the messianic hope in later Christianity and Judaism. That extensive and continuing discussion cannot even be summarized here, but some bibliographic references will be offered, together with a way of looking at the messianic hope different from the traditional Christian reading of the Scriptures.

As Jesus is presented in the Synoptic Gospels, he is not at all comfortable with the title "Messiah" (translated into Greek as "Christ"). He never uses the term of himself, and when he allows others to call him Christ he either cautions them to say nothing to anyone about it (Mark 8:29–30) or he seems to correct them by changing to his own preferred terms, which are drawn from the Son of man and Suffering Servant traditions (e.g., Matt. 16:13–23; Mark 14:61–62). "Son of man" is, in fact, a term that is never used by anyone but Jesus in the Gospels. This expression remains something of a mystery, largely because evidence for the pre-Gospels Son-of-man tradition is so sparse. But Jesus' reticence to use the term Messiah is easily explained by the history of its tradition which we have been tracing. It is clear that in Jesus' lifetime the messianic hope was completely political in content; it was a hope that he did not in fact fulfill, and according to the Gospels he had no intention of fulfilling it but came to understand his ministry in terms of other OT themes.[39] In spite of all this, his followers insisted on Messiah/Christ, above all other titles, as the proper designation for him *after* his resurrection, and that calls for some explanation.

It seems likely that messianic hope had grown so intense in first-century Palestinian Judaism that "Messiah" was the inevitable title to be applied to any savior. What the followers of Jesus then found it necessary to do, once they understood the difference, was to redefine the word Messiah in terms of the kind of savior they perceived Jesus really to be. We see them in the act of doing just this in the early chapters of Acts (Acts 2:22–36; 3:12–26; 10:34–43). It is of interest to note how the NT uses the royal psalms and the prophecies of the future righteous king with respect to its affirmations that Jesus is the Messiah. The political aspects of those passages are largely ignored, for they are of little relevance for explaining the work of Jesus. However, Christians found other elements in those texts, which everyone at that time accepted as messianic prophecies and which could be said to have been fulfilled in the life and times of Jesus, and these are emphasized.[40] The royal aspects of Jewish messianism have been translated into the heavenly rule of the Risen Christ (as in Eph. 1:20) and projected into the future once again in connection with the Second Coming (as in 1 Cor. 15:25 and throughout Revelation).

In Judaism from late in the first century of the Common Era the coming of the Messiah became a standard part of hope for the ideal future, and the nature and functions of that figure were changed little from that of the ideal king in OT times.[41] In the Aramaic Targums he is always called King Messiah, for example. He is a thoroughly human, purely political figure who will defeat Israel's enemies and gather the diaspora to the promised land, where the temple will be rebuilt and he will rule over a realm of peace and abundant prosperity. Those *other* OT promises, such as the forgiveness of sins and the transformation of the human person, which Christians came to associate with Messiah because they found the promises to be fulfilled in Jesus, have remained for Jews the business of God, not Messiah. And so the major difference between Jew and Christian has been over the Christian insistence on redefining his nature and functions in terms of their identification of Messiah as Jesus.

Contemporary Manifestations

Hope for the coming of the Messiah remains a part of the Jewish faith to this day, as the prayer book shows in several places:

> Speedily cause the offspring of David, thy servant, to flourish, and let his horn be exalted by thy salvation, because we wait for thy salvation all the day. (*Amidah*, petition 14)

One change has occurred among those Jews who find the expectation of a personal Messiah to be too supernatural for their beliefs; in Reform Judaism one may encounter affirmations of hope for a messianic age of world peace which is awaited, without any longer looking for an individual Messiah.

Christian eschatology has been greatly complicated by the conviction that Messiah has already come in the person of Jesus, although it is not possible to affirm the arrival as yet of the messianic era in its fullness. So it deals with a first and second Advent, with the latter fully eschatological, but with a desire somehow to redefine "eschatology" so as to make the word applicable to the former as well.[42] Questions about supernaturalism arise in Christianity as well as in Judaism, and this means that what the second coming of Christ means to individual Christians will vary greatly, from the most important aspect of the faith to something that is not really anticipated in any literal way at all.

If Jesus did not literally fulfill the OT hopes for a righteous king, and if Christianity has transformed those hopes into spiritual, heavenly, or existential forms, then it should be asked whether that OT material itself, expressing the hope for a just ruler on earth, should be expected to have any contemporary relevance for the Christian. If Christianity is a purely spiritual affair, as some in each generation have indeed maintained, then the answer must be no. But many Christians believe that the gospel has a worldly as well as a spiritual relevance, and are not so ready to admit that hope for good government is unimportant theologically.[43] That point of view may be supported scripturally in two ways: 1. Accepting the OT as fully a part of the Christian canon means taking all its concerns seriously, even though some of them may be ignored or slighted or presupposed or modified by the NT. 2. In this case, the NT does take seriously good government in our own era (Rom. 13:1–7; 1 Pet. 2:13–17; 3:13–17), and on occasion thinks of a time when the will of God will be fully expressed through human society (Matt. 25:31–46; Revelation 21—22).

The question of the identity of the Messiah continues to be the main theological issue dividing Christians from Jews, and in history that theological debate has had some appalling sociological consequences. A recent development that is of special interest both because it is virtually unprecedented in Christian history and because it offers hope that those sociological excesses may never again recur is the willingness of some Christians today to consider whether there may not in fact be a legitimate continuing identity for the Jewish people—as Jews—defined by the gospel of Jesus the Messiah. The major text that has led to such reconsiderations of the traditional Christian attitude is Romans 9—11, which is now being taken very seriously, and none too soon.[44]

The words Messiah and messianic are no longer the personal property of the religions that originated and first adopted/adapted them, for they are now widely used to denote any kind of would-be savior and/or plan for a transformed world.[45] Their currency reveals the extent to which eschatologies of various kinds have permeated the world of the twentieth century, from the cargo cults of Melanesia to the pseudo-religious cults that flourish in America. Once again, we encounter abundant evidence of the longevity and the potency of a symbol of hope formulated long ago—in ancient Israel.

The Nations

Eschatology could not ignore the non-Israelite population of the earth—"the nations"—if for no other reason than the roles they had played as the agents responsible for Israel's present predicament. But the OT has more than that to say about the nations, and we shall encounter a remarkable spectrum of concerns and hopes for them, reflecting attitudes that range from hatred to full acceptance.

There is a corresponding spectrum of needs which can be detected as the motivation for the variety of hopes expressed concerning the nations, and it may be helpful to begin by identifying them. 1. There is the material problem of living in the midst of a foreign nation, in exile and without any nationhood of one's own. The nations had produced Israel's predicament, and if the promise of restoration to their own land was to be meaningful, it would have to include the victory of God's will over the will of the great empires. 2. A theological issue also appears in direct connection with Israel's dilemma, and that is theodicy. If God is really in charge, how is it that Assyria and Babylonia—and even the Edomites!—seem to be able to do as they please? It became essential to affirm something about the future of the nations in order to continue to believe that the future was really in the hands of the God of Israel. 3. The first two needs grew out of the hostility that existed between Israel and the other nations, but another concern appears, one that ordinarily would be labeled "universalism." Long before any explicit monotheism is expressed in the literature of the OT, indications already appear that Yahweh is a universal God who is involved not only with his chosen people, but with all others as well. In the midst of the very natural expressions of hostility toward those foreigners who are so often one's enemies, then, there appear some fascinating responses to a contrary impulse, which acknowledges that all people are the creations of the same God.

The tensions already apparent among these needs have produced a complex set of traditions in the OT concerning the nations. In the small body of scholarly literature on this subject the tendency has been to trace one strand or another: for example, God as warrior, separatism, or the trend toward proselytism. I find it necessary, however, and potentially helpful to sort through the great amount and variety of material concerning the nations in the OT in order to clarify the several sometimes conflicting traditions.[46]

Old Testament Traditions Concerning the Nations

Israel owed its very existence to a victory over one of the world's great nations. "We were Pharaoh's slaves in Egypt; and the Lord brought us out of Egypt with a mighty hand" (Deut. 6:21). The Israelites remembered that they were different from other peoples in having been constituted a nation only after God chose to intervene in the affairs of Egypt, to wrest from it forceably a part of its slave population and to give those former slaves a land by taking it away from the city-states of Canaan (Exod. 3:7–8). Hence Israel always understood itself as existing over against the other nations, and most of the time in spite of their activities. Exodus became the archetype celebrated in song (Exodus 15, Psalm 105) which influenced the telling of later history (Josh. 3:7–17) and accounts of battles that were won by divine intervention (e.g. Josh. 10:10–14). It was projected into the future in pictures of the final victory of the divine warrior (e.g. Isaiah 34).[47] The conception of divinely given victory over enemy nations which had been learned from the exodus strongly influenced Israel's memory of its settlement in Canaan, especially as recounted in the Book of Joshua, even though historical evidence was preserved to indicate that reality was something far less sensational.[48] Next to the exodus tradition with its message of thoroughgoing triumph over a great nation, then, stood the traditions of conquest and settlement, which bore a mixed message reflecting the realities of a precarious life in Canaan.

When the Philistines began to push from the coastal plain into the hill country of Canaan where the Israelites had settled, the latter's continuing existence as an independent people was seriously threatened, and so the city-states of Philistia were added to the growing tradition of nations hostile to the people of God (Judg. 13:1; 1 Sam. 13:19–23). Except for the time when David and Solomon ruled, Israel was seldom at ease, since it had the misfortune to occupy that narrow, fertile corridor connecting Asia with Africa. Egypt was occasionally involved with Israelite affairs, and for a long time after the division of the monarchy the Northern Kingdom suffered under repeated attacks from the Syrians. Then the great empire-builders appeared on the Mediterranean coast, and Assyria and Babylonia took the place of Egypt and Philistia as the political world's challenge to the continuing existence of the people of Yahweh. With the fall of Jerusalem to the Babylonians, one of the old neighbors also gained for itself a special place as an enemy of Israel. The Edomites seem to have taken every advantage possible at that time: capturing Judean refugees and selling them into slavery (Obad. 10—14; Ezekiel 35); eventually moving into the southern part of Judah and taking over that territory. So Edom also became a classic example of the nations who have been, from beginning to end, a continuing threat to the security and even to the existence of Israel.

Given this precarious national existence, beginning with nothing, gaining a little and then losing everything, it is not at all surprising to find that the nations play a prominent role in the OT. Moreover, they are often represented as hostile to both Israel and Israel's God, so that God will have to do something about them if there is to be any future for Israel. That is only natural and to be expected. What is not so natural among human beings is the appearance within that same group of tormented people of a conviction that their God was also the God of the enemy, of a willingness to accept proselytes from other nations into their community, and (just once in a while) of a desire for a future in which Israel and her enemies would live peaceably as equals. Both these attitudes have long histories that must be sketched before their eschatological forms are studied.

An early way of dealing with the nations as a threat to Israel's existence is the tradition that Yahweh is a warrior. This is associated with the exodus itself ("Yahweh is a man of war," Exod. 15:3), and it took on a virtually institutionalized form in the practice of what some have called "holy war" and others have called "Yahweh war" in the early period after the settlement in Canaan.[49] This tradition makes God virtually the sole combatant against the enemy nations, as in the exodus materials where Israel is simply a spectator; or in some accounts of the battles of the conquest, such as Jericho; and as in Isaiah's advice, "In returning and rest you will be saved; in quietness and in trust shall be your strength" (Isa. 30:15; cf. Ps. 44:1–8). It has a long history, since it reappears in eschatology in passages such as Isaiah 34 and

Ezekiel 38—39. Behind the Ezekiel text lies another form of expression of the conviction that Yahweh and the nations are natural enemies, best known by the German terms *Völkersturm* or *Völkerkampfmythus*. This is the threatened attack on Jerusalem by a coalition of nations, alluded to several times in the Psalter (Pss. 2:1–3; 33:10; 46:6–10; 48:4–6; 76). The apparent fact that this theme does not represent anything that had actually happened in Israel's history, but was a universalization of its recurring problems with enemy nations and a localization of the theme at one place—Jerusalem—probably made it especially useful for eschatological development.

A second theme, not always as violent in its forms of expression as the first, is that of the kingship of Yahweh. It is a universal and a rightful kingship over the nations which is celebrated especially in the Psalms, and so the note of hostility is less prominent than in the warrior tradition.[50] It may be associated with war and annihilation, as in Ps. 10:16 and Psalm 149, and the "judging" that is associated with divine kingship may involve conflict and not merely a court scene,[51] but often the Psalms simply call on the nations to acclaim their rightful and righteous king and the language has strong forensic overtones (Pss. 7:7–8; 22:27–31; 47:8–9; 82; 96:10–13; 99:1–5). The point of it all is of course the exposure and destruction of the wicked, but they are not so necessarily identified with the entire nation as in the warrior tradition. The court scene is not prominent in OT eschatology but it does reappear later, and the judgment of the nations in Matt. 25:31–46 is an especially striking example.

Behind both the warrior and kingship traditions lay the conviction that Israel was Yahweh's elect nation (Exod. 19:4–6), so that harm done to Israel by other nations should rightfully be punished. A shocking modification of this nationalistic theology appeared in the teachings of the canonical Prophets, who announced that Israel itself was to be numbered among the enemies of Yahweh. The nations had been considered worthy of punishment not only because they were threats to Israel's existence, but also on moral grounds. Certain standards of humanity were considered applicable to everyone, and as the upholder of those standards Yahweh judged the nations (Gen. 18:20–21; Deut. 9:4–5; Amos 1:3—2:3). But the prophets saw that when those same standards plus the higher requirements of the law of Sinai were held up against Israel's behavior, God's own people also stood under judgment, and they concluded that Israel was as much the enemy of God as any of the other nations (Amos 2:4–3:2). But this brought the nations into the picture in a new way. Israel's misfortunes at the hands of Assyria and Babylonia were interpreted as the will of God, and therefore he was depicted as using the nations to carry out judgment against his own people (Isa. 10:5–6; Jer. 25:8–11), much as Israel had been instructed to carry out his judgment of the Canaanites earlier (Deut. 7:1–5; 9:1–6; 12:1–4).[52] It was not that all the cruelties inflicted by those nations were the very will of God himself, but he did have the power to use even evil forces for his own purposes, and then, eventually that evil would also have to be punished (Isa. 10:7–19; Jer. 25:12–14).[53] So a measure of equality under judgment between Israel and the nations was achieved in prophetic teaching, but without ever giving up the conviction that there was a unique relationship available only to Israel. That uniqueness might be expressed in the accusation that Israel was in fact worse than any other nation. "Has a nation changed its gods, even though they are no gods? But my people have changed their glory for that which does not profit" (Jer. 2:11; cf. Ezek. 5:5–6).

The result of this outlook was likely to be a picture of forthcoming world-wide judgment (Jer. 25:15—38). Judgment of both the nations and Israel on moral grounds continues to appear throughout the Prophets (Nah. 3:1; Zech. 9:7; Isa. 14:4–21; Ezek. 28:1–19; 29:1–5, 9b–10; 31:1–18), but the old conception of Yahweh as the champion of Israel against its enemies does not disappear. After the fall of Judah the excessive harm done by other peoples to God's people is seen to be an evil that must be punished (Jer. 51:24; Ezekiel 25; Joel 3:4–6; Obadiah 10; Zeph. 2:8). But most of the oracles against the nations are not yet fully eschatological, as we are using the term. They involve judgment in the pre-eschatological sense (see introduction, n. 3). Before turning to eschatology proper, however, it is necessary to trace the OT's positive traditions concerning the nations.

Despite its focus on Israel as the chosen people, the OT story does not begin with Israel but with the human race. The first eleven chapters of Genesis are a kind of universal history extending from the creation of human beings to their dispersal throughout the world as a great variety of linguistic groups following the episode of the Tower of Babel. Just before that story appears the "Table of Nations" (Genesis 10), which attempts to account for all nations as the descendants of Noah. Israel is given no special place in the genealogy; without reading on to the end of chapter 11 one could only guess in which part of the family tree it will eventually appear. The history of salvation begins in chapter 12, with Abraham, the father of Israel, and the patriarchal stories contain a breadth of outlook which had a continuing influence on Israel's understanding of its relationship to the nations. The promise to Abraham, as first reported, is:

> And I will make of you a great nation, and I will bless you and make your name great, so that you will be a blessing. I will bless those who bless you, and him who curses you I will curse; and by you all the families of the earth shall bless themselves. (Gen. 12:2–3; cf. 22:17–18)

Abraham and his descendants were thus not only to be blessed but also were to become a blessing, a source of blessing for all the families (nations, in Gen.

22:18) of the earth. How that was to come about is not specified, except by saying that those who bless Abraham will be blessed, but other roles for Israel as a source of blessing were eventually imagined.[54]

If the stories in Genesis are correctly understood as reflections of Israel's self-understanding, then it is of considerable importance that they formulated and preserved stories concerning the Ishmaelites and the Edomites.[55] In both cases the sagas deal with younger sons (Isaac and Jacob) who achieve pre-eminence over the elder and become the ancestors of Israel, so they are affirmations of Israel's sense of election, but in neither case is the ancestor of the other nation left without a blessing of his own. Although Ishmael was sent away into the desert, Israel affirmed that God had offered promises to him which were parallel in remarkable ways to those that he gave to Isaac (Gen. 21:13, 18, 20). Esau, who was remembered to be the ancestor of the Edomites, lost the blessing that he should have received as firstborn, but did receive another blessing of sorts (Gen. 27:40). The Edomites were considered important enough by Israel that a lengthy genealogy of Esau was preserved in Genesis 36.[56] Despite the hostile attitude that Israel felt toward these two peoples, then, they were also willing to acknowledge that they held a relationship of their own to Yahweh.

Although Israel had a family tree and called itself the sons of Jacob (Israel), it also possessed a keen enough historical memory to be able to acknowledge that not every member of the covenant people was descended from the patriarchs. It was a "mixed multitude" that came out of Egypt (Exod. 12:38), and Israel made a covenant with the Gibeonites when they arrived in Canaan (Joshua 9). It is not uncommon for people with Yahwistic names to be identified as having come from some other ethnic group. Uriah the Hittite is a good example. The story of Ruth, the Moabite woman who became an ancestor of King David himself, does not even argue the question of whether a Moabite could become a member of an Israelite community; it simply takes that possibility for granted.[57]

These fragments of evidence from narratives are supported by legal materials that make explicit provisions for sojourners, i.e., aliens residing within Israel. They are not to be oppressed because they are foreigners, but on the contrary special care is to be taken to be sure that justice is available to them (Exod. 22:21; 23:9; Lev. 19:33; Deut. 24:17; 27:19). The great principle of neighborliness, "You shall love your neighbor as yourself" (Lev. 19:18), is extended to include more than just one's fellow Israelites: "The stranger who sojourns with you shall be to you as the native among you, and you shall love him as yourself; for you were strangers in the land of Egypt" (Lev. 19:34). This acceptance of non-Israelites who were living in Israelite communities not only included matters of justice and mercy (Lev. 19:10; 23:22; Num. 35:15; Deut. 14:29; 24:17–21; 26:11) but also provided ways for them to participate in the Yahwistic cult, if they wished.[58] OT law never quite prescribes a full procedure for the acceptance of proselytes, but requires circumcision before eating the Passover, and Deuteronomy's provisions for the participation of sojourners in covenant renewal (29:11; 31:12; cf. Josh. 8:33) certainly contain the basic elements. The one famous proselyte in the OT is, of course, Naaman (2 Kings 5), but there must have been a good many others. Although Israelites experienced strong feelings of hostility toward other nations as political entities that regularly threatened their security or their very existence, this did not make them entirely xenophobic; individuals living in their midst were to be treated as neighbors, and the law summed up this attitude with the principle "You shall have one statute, both for the sojourner and for the native" (Num. 9:14; 15:14–16, 29–30; Lev. 24:22).[59] The tensions between hostile feelings and the conviction that all humanity stands before the same God continued to be reflected in post-exilic Judaism, which at the same time was adopting a disciplined life that set Jews apart from Gentiles, and also was becoming a religion actively involved in seeking proselytes.[60]

The Nations in Eschatology

A series of examples has been chosen to demonstrate the continuing tension in Israel's attitudes toward the nations, even as hopes for an ideal future were expressed. We begin with the hostile attitudes that seem to be content with hoping for nothing more than the total destruction of the nations, then move toward various kinds of expectations of world peace which allow for the continuing existence of other peoples.

Since it has sometimes been suggested that the main function of the oracles against the nations in the prophetic books is to provide the intermediate step between the judgment of Israel and its restoration, we begin with an example where such a relationship is indeed clear: Isa. 11:11–16. The oracle contains the promise of a thoroughgoing restoration of the diaspora, beginning with a detailed listing of the places from which its members will come, and concluding with a comparison with the exodus, as two ways of emphasizing the greatness of the event. In the middle are two expected components of the restoration: the elimination of the old rivalry between the Northern and Southern Kingdoms (v. 13) and a series of campaigns of the new united kingdom against the old enemies: Philistia, Edom, Moab, and Ammon (Isa. 11:14). It is assumed that the return will not be peaceful and that the new Israel will be established in its place by means similar to those used by David in founding the original kingdom. The occupation of those neighboring territories by a victorious Israel is also contemplated in Zephaniah 2 and Zechariah 9.[61] The picture of Israel as the conqueror of surrounding nations in God's future is a disquieting one for us, but it cannot be ignored since it was put into effect by the Hasmoneans as one of the results of the Maccabean revolt and appears to be acceptable to some strains of modern Zionist thought as well.

That a final, decisive battle between God and the nations will occur in the vicinity of Jerusalem is a tradition with a broader (and potentially less harmful) effect, and we turn now to the classic example of that type, the prophecy concerning Gog of the land of Magog: Ezekiel 38—39.[62] This is one of the most unusual eschatological passages in the OT since it adds a new act to the final drama as it was usually conceived. The battle between God and the nations which is depicted here has nothing to do with the re-establishment of exiled Israel, for we are assured that already will have happened before Gog makes his appearance. His intention will be to attack "the land that is restored from war, the land where people were gathered from many nations upon the mountains of Israel, which had been a continual waste; its people were brought out from the nations and now dwell securely, all of them" (38:8; cf. 38:11, 14). This takes us to a period in the future that is of no interest to any other prophet, considering as it does the possibility of a new threat to Israel after the restoration. These chapters have appropriately been identified as an early stage in the development of apocalyptic thought, for they contain the materials for the division of history into a series of periods, one of the favorite techniques of that later form of eschatology.[63]

But what is the need to which such a message is responding? If the author was Ezekiel, the answer is not so obvious; if these chapters come from a later author it would not be hard to think of them as a response to the dilemma experienced by returnees who were depressed by the maneuvers of the great nations around them, manipulating their destiny and leaving them without any evident control over it. The concern that is made explicit in the passage, however, is one mentioned at the beginning of this section, and that is theodicy. Although the destiny of Israel cannot be ignored, that is not the major emphasis here; for the divine intention in bringing Gog and his allies to their doom in Palestine is to demonstrate something about God himself to the other nations: "In the latter days I will bring you against my land, that the nations may know me, when through you, O Gog, I vindicate my holiness before their eyes" (38:16; cf. 38:23; 39:7, 21–24). This conception of the nations as spectators who will learn something about the true God from his works in history ("then they will know that I am Yahweh") is a theme that recurs throughout the Book of Ezekiel.[64]

In addition to their chronological separation from reality, there are other elements of remoteness about these chapters. Gog is an unknown king from an unknown land, associated with places in "the uttermost parts of the north,"[65] and it will not help us here to survey the efforts to identify him.[66] Perhaps this is another step in the direction of apocalyptic, in addition to the move toward periodizing. As in apocalyptic literature, the nations mentioned here really function as a symbol for all those historical forces that work in opposition to the will of God, but note that the passage is by no means to be taken as a universal condemnation of all the nations, for the *real* nations, we suggest, are those spectators who will be brought to a knowledge of Yahweh by observing what he does to that great coalition of evil forces (Ezek. 39:21–23).

The first re-use of this theme of the last great battle between God and evil appears in Zechariah 12 and 14, and eventually it will become Armageddon, in the Book of Revelation. Here the last judgment has become an event that is inflicted on the wicked and vindicates the righteous, unlike the prophetic judgment messages, which involved the whole people of God. Perhaps an early form of the true last judgment tradition may be discerned in Ezekiel 38—39.

A helpful example of the transition from oracles against the nations to an eschatological promise concerning the future of one of the nations appears in Ezek. 29:6b–9a. It contains a familiar type of oracle, an announcement of judgment on Egypt (29:8–9), coupled with a reason (29:6b–7) that concerns their complicity in the fall of Judah. This is inserted into another oracle (29:3–5, 9b–12), addressed to the king of Egypt, using mythological materials common to the ancient Near East to make its point at first, and condemning the king for *hybris,* that is for a sin against Yahweh, with Israel not in the picture at all. Comparable oracles also may be found in Ezek. 28:1–19; 31:1–18; 32:1–16; Isa. 14:4–21; and Daniel 4.[67] This is a vigorous example of the Israelite belief in the accountability of all peoples, including the kings of the world's greatest nations, to their God Yahweh.

Destruction, death, and desolation are threatened, but this is not the end. "At the end of forty years I will gather the Egyptians from the peoples among whom they were scattered; and I will restore the fortunes of Egypt" (Ezek. 29:13–14). The language is identical to that used for Israel; Egypt will also experience exile and restoration! Here is evidence that at times the prophets projected a future for other nations the same way they did for Israel, by using the history of salvation as their guide.[68] And their breadth of understanding of the universality of the role of Yahweh was such that they did not hesitate to apply salvation history to the nations. Now of course the sentence ends, "and there they shall be a lowly kingdom." Ezekiel stops short of a full restoration of Egypt to its former glory, presumably because of his concern for Israel's future, but not necessarily for purely chauvinistic reasons. Egypt had always been a source of trouble to Israel, and the prophet merely wants reassurance that such will never be the case again (29:15–16). Note that unlike Israel, Egypt is not necessarily expected to repent and be converted as a part of its restoration; just, "then they will know that I am the Lord God" (29:16; contrast 16:53–54, 59–63; 20:42–44). Similar brief promises of the restoration of other nations after they have been judged appear in Jer. 46:26; 48:47; 49:6, 39; and something like a seventy-year exile is predicted for Tyre in Isa. 23:15–18.

Another example of the prophetic willingness to introduce the Gentiles into the history of salvation is 2 Isaiah's identification of Cyrus the Persian as Yahweh's shepherd, his anointed one (Isa. 44:28; 45:1), the one chosen to make possible the restoration of Jerusalem, whose work would result in all knowing, "from the rising of the sun and from the west, that there is none besides me; I am the Lord, and there is no other" (Isa. 45:6). The prophet knows that Cyrus has never even heard of Yahweh (45:4–5), but that makes no difference, since he can be used for blessing just as Sennacherib and Nebuchadnezzar were used earlier for judgment. The prophet apparently feels no need for Cyrus to be "converted," and the immediate effects of his work are to bring a blessing to Israel, but we shall soon see that 2 Isaiah is not satisfied to stop there and does have a truly eschatological outlook in expecting that Israel will become a source of blessing to the nations, as promised to Abraham.[69]

The hopes for a fully peaceful relationship between Israel and the nations which are often expressed in the OT take on several forms that reflect varying degrees of chauvinism. It was not always enough to be assured that Egypt would be too weak ever to cause trouble in the future. It is natural for human beings to want the best and to be the best, and those feelings appear in the Bible. It would be surprising if so realistic a book did not also reflect that aspect of what the people of God is really like. Amid the sweeping statements about the uniqueness of Yahweh and the universality of this work which appear in 2 Isaiah are some expectations of subservient roles for the nations which have puzzled exegetes because they do not seem to correlate well with the rest of his theology. The reversal of fortune is the pattern that is used prominently in these texts. As the nations carried Israel into exile, so they will carry them back to their homeland (Isa. 49:22; cf. 60:4–9). As the nations removed the wealth of Israel, including the temple treasures themselves, so the day will come when the world's treasures will be lavished on Jerusalem (Isa. 45:14; cf. 60:6–7, 13; 61:6). As Israelites served the nations, so one day the nations will serve Israel (Isa. 49:23; cf. 60:10, 12, 14; 61:5). If such hopes seem unworthy of the prophets, and of redeemed Israel, perhaps they can be explained away as largely oriental hyperbole. However, since such attitudes have never completely disappeared from among the people of God, they should be left to stand as expressions of natural human feelings in the hope that we may be all the more surprised and impressed by the other kinds of hope that appear, and that are not so natural.[70]

That the Jewish communities in exile in Babylonia had begun to succeed in making proselytes from among their pagan neighbors is strongly suggested by the interest shown in the conversion of the nations by exilic and post-exilic prophets (Isa. 45:22–23). The post-exilic prophets expect that the one true God of all people will be found and acknowledged in Jerusalem by the nations.

> Many peoples and strong nations shall come to seek the Lord of hosts in Jerusalem, and to entreat the favor of the Lord. Thus says the Lord of hosts: In those days ten men from the nations of every tongue shall take hold of the robe of a Jew, saying, "Let us go with you, for we have heard that God is with you." (Zech. 8:22–23; cf. Isa. 45:14–15; 56:3–8; 66:18–19, 23)

Note that Israel remains central to all of this; the true God is to be found in Jerusalem, and the Israelites will in truth become that "kingdom of priests" promised at Sinai (Exod. 19:6; cf. Isa. 61:6).

Israel will be a light to the nations (Isa. 60:2–3). Light, in 2 and 3 Isaiah, appears in parallel with healing and righteousness (58:8), with law and justice (51:4), and when the Servant of the Lord is called a light to the nations in 49:6 it is so that "my salvation may reach to the end of the earth." In Isaiah 40—66 the fulfillment of the promise of blessing to all the families of the earth through the offspring of Abraham is imminent. Whether Israel is to engage in any kind of missionary activity, or is just to become a witness to the nations by being the willing recipient of God's grace, has been debated; Isa. 66:19 appears to be the nearest thing in the OT to an expectation of active testimony.[71]

A rather cryptic text in the so-called Isaiah apocalypse (Isaiah 24—27) also seems to express a universalistic outlook, as it promises a feast for all peoples, to be offered "on this mountain" by the Lord of hosts (25:6–7). The passage is less important for what it says in its original context than for its inception of the idea of the messianic banquet, which appears in later Jewish literature and in the NT in Matt. 8:11; Luke 13:29; and Rev. 19:9.

That Jerusalem will be in the future the source of full knowledge of the one true God remains without question in these sources (cf. Isa. 66:20), and since Israel will be found in its completeness dwelling in and around the holy city there is no compromise with the continuing conviction of election to a special place in the saving work of God. But the finest of these texts hold universalism and particularism in a remarkable balance. In that great picture of world peace in Isa. 2:2–4 and Mic. 4:1–4 (see chap. 1) a surprising willingness to remain in the background may be noticed. Zion is central, and certainly we know that Israelites are there, but it is not necessary to mention them, as it is in the post-exilic materials. Peoples and nations make their pilgrimage freely and willingly, "that he may teach us his ways and we may walk in his paths. For out of Zion shall go forth the law, and the word of the Lord from Jerusalem." No doubt it is assumed that Israelites will do the teaching, serving in a priestly function, but the text does not have to specify special responsibilities or privileges for them; neither does it have to provide for pre-eminence of Israel in the peaceful community of nations which it foresees, as other OT texts have been careful to do. This is one of those surprising texts which goes beyond the hopes that are natural to human beings. If we do not see that at first, think about your own patriotic feelings and about the histories of the League of Nations and the United Nations. Ordinary visions of world peace are quick to make special provisions not to lose the privileges and prestige that "rightfully" belong to one's own country. But beginning already in the eighth century B.C., Israel had sometimes dared to go against the grain of all that is natural and to consider another way.

Perhaps too much has been deduced from what is missing from this oracle, but the existence of such an openness to the nations cannot be denied once we look at Isaiah 19. It may be compared with Ezekiel 29, since it begins with a traditional oracle against Egypt (Isa. 19:1–15), but then it continues with a series of eschatological affirmations. The first promises that Judah will become a terror to the Egyptians (19:16–17), that unsurprisingly human kind of hope which we have found elsewhere. The second does surprise, for it seems to speak of a continuation of the Jewish diaspora in Egypt in that day (19:18). Are these to be Jews or Hebrew-speaking Egyptian converts? We cannot be sure, since the third oracle goes even further than Ezekiel did in using Israel's saving history as a basis for predicting Egypt's future. There will be an altar to Yahweh in the midst of the land of Egypt—functioning for Egypt as Jerusalem did for the land of Israel. There will be a pillar to the Lord at its border, reminiscent, perhaps of the stones set up by Joshua at the borders of Canaan (Josh. 4:20). "When they cry to the Lord because of oppressors he will send them a savior and will defend and deliver them" is an echo of the language the Book of Judges uses to describe Israel's history (Judg. 3:9, etc.). The Egyptians will participate in a sacrificial cult dedicated to Yahweh (Isa. 19:21) and their continuing history will be like Israel's: "and the Lord will smite Egypt, smiting and healing, and they will return to the Lord, and he will heed their supplications and heal them" (19:22).

If possible, the fourth and fifth oracles are even more surprising, for now Assyria joins Egypt in friendship (19:23), and Israel will not be the great world power ruling over the other nations, but will just be an equal, having fulfilled God's promise to Abraham.

> In that day Israel will be the third with Egypt and Assyria, a blessing in the midst of the earth, whom the Lord of hosts has blessed, saying, "Blessed be Egypt my people, and Assyria the work of my hands, and Israel my heritage." (Isa. 19:24–25)

This is as far as the OT can go. Nowhere else does Yahweh call any nation but Israel "my people," but now some Israelites, at least, hope for a day when he will so speak to that old enemy, Egypt, and for a day when that nation whose atrocities terrorized the world, Assyria, can rightfully be called "the work of my hands."[72]

It is easy to criticize the OT for its expressions of hatred for Israel's enemies such as we find in Nahum, Obadiah, and Psalm 137. We may be thankful that we live in an age where some people, at least, see something wrong in hating one's enemy, for the spirit of Obadiah has been a fully acceptable thing throughout most of history, and still is for many people today. If we set the OT against that realistic background, then, and acknowledge that Israel's expressions of hope for victory, for the destruction of evil powers, and for the gift of national security in a position of pre-eminence are natural hopes among human beings, then we are ready to be properly surprised that sometimes it was able to break out of that normal pattern; to find ways of accepting strangers, to hope for a world united in the worship of Yahweh, and to dream of a time when the old enemies, under whom they had suffered so much, would not be destroyed but would become friends. We then understand that we are not to take the natural and the commonplace in Israel's experience as normative, using it to excuse our own holy wars, but that we need to listen to what is radical and truly visionary, daring to take seriously a promise that seems simply foolish in the light of real politics.

The conditions that produced apocalyptic literature added a new perspective on the nations; it appears in the Book of Daniel. Note that although Zion, return, and Messiah become important subjects in later apocalyptic works, they do not play a prominent role in the eschatology of Daniel. The nations provide the main structural element for this book's approach to the future. Israel's history appears only in 9:24–27; elsewhere the book takes us repeatedly through the history of the great world empires, as a way of showing its readers where they stood in the course of God's plan for the world. Typical of apocalyptic is the conviction that the nations are political manifestations of the cosmic forces of evil which God must overcome in order to save his people (Dan. 10:13, 20–21), and thus it is "overcoming" that is the climax of each of Daniel's presentations (2:44–45; 7:26–27; 8:25; 11:45). In Daniel 2 and 7 the "kingdom of heaven" is promised as the replacement of the human empires over which God will triumph, and so the concept of a great world empire in which the "people of the saints of the Most High" (Dan. 7:27) will be pre-eminent takes on a prominence in apocalyptic that it never achieved in earlier OT literature.

The Nations in Post–Old Testament Eschatology

Each of the surveys of history in the Book of Daniel brings one to the time of Antiochus IV Epiphanes, the king who attempted to eradicate the Jewish religion in 167–165 B.C.[73] It is generally agreed that this date and this book mark the beginning of the flowering of apocalyptic literature, and the special place given to the nations in these works is surely due to their character as persecution literature and to their efforts to provide a comprehensive explanation of the problems they faced as part of the cosmic battle between good and evil. As the first known king to persecute a people for their religion alone, Antiochus became the model of the wicked king who is the agent of evil on earth, the archenemy of the people of God. There was no conceivable way of describing him as the instrument of God raised up to judge his rebellious people when it was precisely the most faithful who suffered the worst under Antiochus' edict. That persecution, followed by the sufferings of Palestinian Jews under Herod and the Romans, resulted in a tendency to equate the nations with the forces of Satan on earth and to look for their destruction as an essential part of the initiation of the new age. So the last assault of a great coalition of nations against the Holy Land reappears in apocalyptic texts such as *1 Enoch* 90:13–19; *Sib. Or.* 3:660–68; 4 Ezra 13:30–34; and in the War Scroll from Qumran (1QM). The destruction of the nations by God, or God's people, or the Messiah appears even more frequently, and it is not surprising to find that in the Targums, Gog appears in several other parts of the Bible in addition to Ezekiel.[74] The judgment scene also reappears, with God himself (*1 Enoch* 90:20–27; 4 Ezra 7:33–44) or the Messiah (*2 Apoc. Bar.* 72:2–6) or the Son of man (*1 Enoch* 62:1–16; 69:27–29) seated upon the throne, with the nations brought before him.[75]

In spite of the bitterness produced by the sufferings undergone by the Jews during the Hellenistic and Roman periods, the hope for the conversion of the nations which was occasionally expressed in the OT did not die out. This period was, in fact, the one part of Jewish history in which enthusiastic missionary activity was undertaken.[76] The tensions between universalism and particularism which we found in the OT were preserved, if not heightened, in subsequent Jewish experience. Around 190 B.C. Jesus ben Sirac wrote of the oneness of humanity under God, but could not fail to add "but Israel is the Lord's own portion" (Sir. 16:24—17:32). Acknowledgment by the nations of Jerusalem as the place where the true God is to be found is still one of the Jewish hopes, as Tob. 13:11; *1 Enoch* 90:33; *Sib. Or.* 3:710–19, 772–76; *T. Benj.* 9:2; *Pss. Sol.* 17:30–31; and *2 Apoc. Bar.* 68:5 reveal. And the conversion of the nations is predicted in texts such as Tob. 14:6–7; *1 Enoch* 10:21; 50:1–3; *T. Levi* 18:9; and *T. Naph.* 8:1–4.[77]

Rabbinic literature preserves the tension. It was decided that Gentiles have their own rightful relationship to God under the covenant made with Noah, and seven commandments were identified as having been given to Noah, comprising the entire responsibility of non-Jews to God. The righteous Gentile could thus be saved without having to convert to Judaism. Proselytes were still accepted, and there is a large body of regulations on that subject. But at the same time the periodic sufferings of Jews at the hands of Gentiles, along with the idolatry and immorality of the pagans among whom they lived during the early period, continued to produce expressions of doubt about the salvation of the nations and hopes for victory over them in the last days.[78] On the one hand, a prayer from the Passover Haggadah says:

> Pour out thy wrath upon the heathen who will not acknowledge thee, and upon the kingdoms who invoke not thy name, for they have devoured Jacob and laid waste his dwelling. Pour out thy indignation upon them. Pursue them in wrath and destroy them from under the heavens of the Eternal.

But on the other hand, the Daily Service concludes with this prayer:

> We therefore hope in thee, O Lord our God, that we may speedily behold the glory of thy might, when thou wilt remove the abominations from the earth, and the idols will be utterly cut off, when the world will be perfected under the kingdom of the Almighty, and all the children of flesh will call upon thy name, when thou wilt turn unto thyself all the wicked of the earth. Let all the inhabitants of the world perceive and know that unto thee every knee must bow, every tongue must swear. Before thee, O Lord our God, let them bow and fall; and unto thy glorious name let them give honor; let them all accept the yoke of thy kingdom, and do thou reign over them speedily, and for ever and ever.

Christianity considers itself to be the fulfillment of that old promise to Abraham, the first step toward that acknowledgement by all nations that there is but one God, who is the God of Abraham, Isaac, and Jacob. As Paul put it, "I tell you that Christ became a servant to the circumcised to show God's truthfulness, in order to confirm the promises given to the patriarchs, and in order that the Gentiles might glorify God for his mercy" (Rom. 15:8–9; cf. John 8:56). The NT not only reaffirms with enthusiasm the OT promise of the eventual conversion of the nations but it also asserts that with the coming of Jesus the time had arrived for that to happen and repeats the old themes with interesting new twists. The teachings of Jesus, reported in the Synoptic Gospels, take up both the positive and negative statements of the OT and contemporary Judaism, but often to use them in new ways. He spoke of the attack on Jerusalem by that mighty coalition of nations in the last days, but as he foresaw it there would be no divine intervention to save the holy city; it would fall (Luke 21:20–24). He spoke of the great judgment scene, in the end of days, when all the nations will be gathered before the throne of the Son of man, and provided his own definition of those who would be declared "righteous Gentiles" (Matt. 25:31–46). He confined his own ministry to the Jews (Matt. 15:24), and during his lifetime sent his disciples to preach to Jews only (Matt. 10:5–6), but in his eschatology he shared the Jewish expectation for the conversion of the Gentiles in the last days, and even dared to speak of the possibility that Gentiles might be at an advantage in that time, a distinctly non-Jewish thought (Matt. 8:11–12; 11:21–24;

12:41–42). One of many indications that Jesus believed his ministry was heralding the coming of the eschaton is his commission to the disciples to begin doing the work of the last days: "Go therefore and make disciples of all nations . . ." (Matt. 28:19).[79]

Thus one of the relatively minor themes of the OT became a definitive element for the Christian church because of its conviction that the fulfillment of that hope for the conversion of the nations had begun. For a Jew, different opinions about the future of the nations could be held, but for a Gentile it was a personal matter. Gentile Christians have accepted the Jewish judgment of the religions of their pagan ancestors—that they were abominations in the sight of the one God—and have welcomed the assurance they found in the OT that the God of the Jews also welcomes all who repent and come to him. In Christian apocalyptic, however, the Gentile found it appropriate to reaffirm the Jewish hope for a divinely given victory over the nations, continuing to use the term to denote the powers of evil manifested on earth and excluding themselves from the nations, as the Jews had done. Persecution of Christians by Rome made the adoption of apocalyptic thought as natural for them as it had been for Jews. In the Book of Revelation, Babylon becomes the symbol for the great God-defying world empire of the last days, and the final battle of God against all the nations, resulting in their annihilation, is retold again (Rev. 16:12–21; 20:7–10). Yet, as a warning to us not to take apocalyptic language too literally, the final scene of the book shows us the new Jerusalem with the glory of God as its light, and "By its light shall the nations walk; and the kings of the earth shall bring their glory into it . . ." (Rev. 21:24). In that city grows the tree of life, and "the leaves of the tree were for the healing of the nations" (22:2).

Contemporary Manifestations

For most Jews, from the end of the Hasmonean period to the founding of the state of Israel, present reality has meant living as a minority group within one of the gentile nations. What the OT promised about the time when Israel—as a nation—would live in peace with the other nations has entirely been a matter for the future. In the meantime, the theology that motivates the members of most American synagogues in their relationships with non-Jews seems to be the old rabbinic teaching that a Jew ought to live in such a way that the nations will be led to give honor to the Name. The Holocaust has raised questions in the minds of Jews, however, which even apocalyptic outlooks have not been able to handle, although one effect of the horrible event has been to make the apocalyptic equation of the nations with the forces of evil arrayed against God's people an easily believable idea.

Christians, except for those few who are converts from Judaism, are members of the gentile nations, but they are also the products, they believe, of realized eschatology, so that they are a third force, neither the idolators of which the OT spoke nor citizens of the OT's Jewish state. Having received the benefits of the promise of blessing for the nations, they have taken seriously its ethical implications by engaging in a missionary movement that has literally carried the name of the God of Abraham to every nation. But they also have been tempted to appropriate those triumphalistic parts of OT eschatology for themselves and to see the church or their conception of the Christian nation as the new Israel that will be victorious over all earthly enemies in the last day. Unfortunately, the ethical implications of this attitude have not always been so fortunate. Studies of the influences of Christian eschatology on American life have suggested, for example, that a kind of civil religion has become widely accepted which includes a nationalistic form of millennialism. The implications of that are alarming; it was relatively harmless to expect a last great battle against Gog and his cohorts when God was going to do the fighting, but in a secular state there is nothing but the Bomb to take on the forces of evil in what might then well be the world's last battle—but brought about by human initiative and with no redemptive results that can seriously be hoped for.[80]

The alternative is to reaffirm another OT hope, and that is for internationalism and world peace brought about by cooperation and the acceptance of others. We cannot expect to see that pilgrimage of the nations to Zion before the eschaton, but in the meantime the dream it represents can be a powerful motivating force, as those who know how to use such dreams have already shown in the past. One can scarcely find a better example of eschatology's potential to motivate human action—for great good or great harm—than the one provided by the various roles of the nations in the OT's depictions of the future.

CHAPTER 3

THE PEOPLE OF ZION

The Transformation of the Human Person

The Bible contains promises concerning needs that are less easy to describe than the material things—a place to live, a just ruler, and peace—just described in chapter 2. These needs involve personal relationships, parts of which are visible, and also the inner sense of being related to God, something that is not accessible to observation at all. Along with the "materialism" of the OT is to be found the conviction of the reality of these emotional and spiritual needs; indeed, of the absolute necessity of being assured of personal and corporate harmony with God. The eschatological texts of the OT affirm that both individual human beings and the institutions of human society need redemption if there is ever to be peace, justice, and joy on earth.

Fewer passages are dealt with in this chapter, but the relevant themes reappear throughout the eschatological texts, and some of those texts have had a profound influence on later generations. The parts of this chapter are related in a way somewhat different from those of the preceding chapter. Where exile or injustice is involved the changes that are needed are obvious, but when the problem is sin, the procedure for improving things is not so clear. So the way to make things right is discussed in the OT perhaps as much as the results are. In the first section, then, we will deal with the question of what can be done about the effects sin has had on the individual—erasing the past. Canceling the negative effects of sin is by no means sufficient to produce the ideal life, however, and so the OT turns to transformation itself, to the re-creation of new people who will finally be able to live the blessed life, the nature of which will be described in the final section.

Erasing the Past: Eschatological Forgiveness

We come now to the personal feeling that there is something wrong within one's life which cannot be blamed entirely on outside forces, that is, the sense of shame, or defilement, or guilt. Israelites, like all other peoples, had found structured ways of dealing with such feelings so that life might ordinarily continue with a minimum of disruption from those powerful inner forces. But the appearances in eschatological texts of promises of forgiveness and of the re-creation of humanity so that no further occasions of forgiveness would ever arise reveals an underlying sense of the inadequacy of the restorative powers of forgiveness in the present. It will not be necessary to discuss the entire OT tradition concerning forgiveness, since materials such as details of the sacrificial cult do not reappear in the eschatological texts. We will focus on the definition of the personal problem which requires an eschatological solution. It will be sufficient to examine the "vocabulary of confession" in the light of the insights shed on this kind of language by the phenomenologists.[1]

Forgiveness of Sin in Old Testament Tradition

Israel rejoiced in having a God who would not permit himself to be limited by his just rule of the world, but who in his good pleasure chose to remit the punishment due to sinners who repented and asked his mercy. This attribution of the forgiving spirit to the essential nature of Yahweh appears in a creed-like statement that is now generally thought to be archaic and that is cited numerous times in the OT. At Mt. Sinai, God introduced himself as follows:

> Yahweh, Yahweh, a God merciful and gracious, slow to anger, and abounding in steadfast love and faithfulness, keeping steadfast love for thousands, forgiving iniquity and transgression and sin, but who will by no means clear the guilty, visiting the iniquity of the fathers upon the children and the children's children, to the third and fourth generation. (Exod. 34:6–7)[2]

In the Psalms Israel both celebrated the forgiveness of God (Ps. 103:2–3) and appealed to it as they asked once again for help (Ps. 130:3–4; cf. vv. 7–8). The present possibility of forgiveness may be taken as a firmly held part of the Israelite faith in Yahweh. So we turn our attention to the kind of help for which they were asking. Note that in Psalms and the Prophets forgiveness is not ordinarily connected with concerns about undoing the harm one's sins have done to others. There were institutional ways of making things right with others, through the law and the cult, but Israelites sensed that making restitution and finding reconciliation with neighbors by asking their forgiveness were not the end of the matter. Infringement of the law of God was an offense against God which had to be made right somehow, and the feelings that are described in texts concerning forgiveness are those that phenomenologists have identified as among the most elemental aspects of human experience.

The consciousness of sin made them feel "unclean." "Purge me with hyssop, and I shall be clean; wash me, and I shall be whiter than snow" (Ps.

51:7; cf. Isa. 4:4). This has nothing to do with physical dirtiness; although the symbolism is drawn from the physical world it describes an entirely inner feeling. Comparable to that is shame and self-loathing (Ezek. 16:54, 61–62; 20:43; 39:26), and the crushed and depressed spirit (Isa. 57:15; 66:2). One of the fundamental needs Israelites expressed in their desire for forgiveness thus was the need for restoration of a sense of self-worth, which had been destroyed by the consciousness of sin.

A somewhat more objective awareness that sin had done harm to one's person could be expressed in language concerning health and more outward aspects of well-being:

> When I declared not my sin, my body wasted away
> through my groaning all day long.
> For day and night thy hand was heavy upon me;
> my strength was dried up as by the heat of summer.
> (Ps. 32:3–4; cf. Ps. 25:15)

Although the OT made great progress toward a deeper understanding of distress than the popular one, which attempts to explain all trouble as the result of having done something to anger God (Job; Psalms 49, 73; Isaiah 53, Habakkuk), the tendency to think of illness and other afflictions as the effects of sin still appears throughout the literature, and of course that is partly right. So healing is connected with forgiveness.

The sense of having damaged an essential personal relationship because of sin is expressed in language concerning estrangement from God and the hope for reconciliation. Words for anger and for distance are normally used to express these feelings.

> Because of the iniquity of his covetousness I was angry,
> I smote him, I hid my face and was angry,
> but he went on backsliding in the way of his own heart.
> I have seen his ways, but I will heal him.
> (Isa. 57:17–18a; cf. Ps. 51:11; Isa. 59:1–2; Mic. 7:18)

The Israelites' personal plight, then, which the history of religions has shown to be shared by people everywhere, was the inner sense of defilement, a lack of physical well-being, and the dread feeling of estrangement from God himself—and all of it deserved because of things they had done. How could that be overcome?

Some deeds can be undone—if one has taken property belonging to another it can be returned—but many cannot be. The effects of some deeds can be nullified—an angry neighbor might be placated by an act of friendship—but not all of them can be. Especially when one has harmed another human being, there are always residual emotional effects on both sides which may not be touched by deeds or words. The past cannot really be erased. But the

Israelite cult attempted to provide assurances that one could go on without being completely crippled by the past. God had offered to accept the sacrifices of repentant people as a sign that he did not hold unwitting transgressions against them.[3] Those sacrifices probably were always accompanied by confession, as a sign of true repentance. In the case of deliberate sins, forgiveness also was possible, but the prior sign of repentance, before a sacrifice could be offered, had to be restitution. Texts such as Psalms 25, 32, 51, and 130 ought to be read along with the ritual instructions in Leviticus 1—7 in order to obtain the fullest possible picture of what Israel believed God had done in order to make forgiveness possible for them.[4] But there were two hitches in this system.

The first was that it could not guarantee the future; repentance may involve the sincere intention never to commit that sin again, but backsliding does occur, and even true repentance concerning one sin doesn't inoculate a person against other temptations. And the second problem is that the system doesn't fully deal with the past, either. Even if one's relationship with God has been restored and God doesn't hold the deed against the sinner, if the evil effects of the deed itself still are being felt in the world, then the problem isn't fully solved. Israel sometimes spoke of sin as a kind of infection or pollution that would continue to work in the world until some purgative measures were taken in order to counteract it. We are not likely to use the same imagery, but still may be willing to acknowledge that it does reflect an unnerving aspect of truth about certain kinds of evil. Israel's belief in a forgiving God and the assurances provided by prayer and sacrifice did not make forgiveness a matter simply to be confined to the present tense. Something more needed to be done, and if the analysis made of Israel's situation by the canonical prophets was correct, it desperately needed to be done.

Repentance and confession ordinarily are considered to be matters within the powers of the individual. Ezekiel's theology was fully orthodox when he said: ". . . when a wicked man turns away from the wickedness he has committed and does what is lawful and right, he shall save his life" (Ezek. 18:27). It has been commonplace to take such a text as exemplary of the preaching of the prophets, understanding them to be preachers of repentance of a kind that Israel had always believed to be possible. But a study of the use of the word *shuv* ("turn," "return"; thus sometimes "repent") in the Prophets brings to light a different message:

> Why then has this people turned away
> in perpetual backsliding?
> They hold fast to deceit,
> they refuse to return.
>
> (Jer. 8:5)

There are indeed a few admonitions and appeals for change in the canonical Prophets, but the main use of *shuv* in these books is to describe the predicament Israel is in.[5] They haven't repented, it is very unlikely that they will repent, and Jeremiah even begins to wonder if they can repent (13:23). So the dilemma of initiative is raised. If the fault is human, as it certainly is, then for repentance to be meaningful the initiative ought to arise on the human side. Then if it doesn't arise, is everything lost? The predominance of judgment messages in the pre-exilic prophets suggests that for Israel as they knew it, everything was indeed lost; no more than a remnant might be expected to "return" (Isa. 10:21), and that really meant the end of Israel (Isa. 10:20–23; 22:14; Jer. 5:7–9; Amos 3:12; 5:15). The question is, what role will forgiveness play in Israel's hopes for an ideal future? Can the past simply be forgotten by those who have passed through the judgment of exile, or is there more to be done? And who is to do it? That is, what is the appropriate place of the human initiative, repentance, in a future that is ordinarily depicted as entirely the work of the will of God? We need to see if the OT really speaks of something that can appropriately be called "eschatological forgiveness."

Forgiveness in Old Testament Eschatology

The fall of Jerusalem and the exile so impressed those who were left alive with the certainty that they had fallen under God's judgment for a longstanding and thoroughgoing series of acts of rebellion against him, that they understood that only an unprecedented, gracious act of forgiveness could make possible any future for them as the people of God. And so almost every text we here deal with concerns the exile.

The letter of Jeremiah to those Judeans who were deported to Babylonia in 597 takes up the question of when and how a restoration may become possible (Jer. 29:10–14). After the unusual date-setting (seventy years), which as we saw earlier had the practical effect of telling the exiles they might as well give up hoping for an imminent return, the Lord says through Jeremiah that he intends to visit them, fulfill his promise and bring them back (29:10). "Then you will call upon me and come and pray to me and I will hear you" (29:12, continued in vv. 13–14a). Here the word *shuv* is used of God's actions in restoring them from exile (29:10, 14; translated "bring back" in the RSV), not of the actions of the people, but verbs used elsewhere of repenting, "call upon me" and "seek me with all your heart," are ascribed to the people *after* the restoration occurs. Is the true repentance of the future, then, understood to be the *result* of God's forgiving act, rather than one of its causes? The OT is not unequivocal on this subject, but there are other texts that speak even more explicitly about that order of things. This is especially true of Ezekiel, who says that God's re-establishment of the covenant will lead Jerusalem to remember her ways and be ashamed and confounded (Ezek. 16:49–63), and that the restoration of Israel to the promised land will finally lead them to remember and to loathe themselves for all the evils they have committed (20:43).[6] Similar ideas appear in Jer. 24:4–7; Ezek. 36:31; 39:25–27; and Isa. 44:22. These texts surely express in the most striking ways a sense of the desperateness of Israel's situation in exile and of the radically new thing they sometimes believed God would have to do if they were to become his people again.

In other texts the familiar insistence on human responsibility for one's own future puts repentance prior to restoration. This is very obviously the case in an unusual passage, Deut. 30:1–10, one of the few texts outside the prophetic books which qualifies to be called eschatological. It deals with a time in the distant future (from the book's perspective; perhaps not so distant from the actual time of writing these verses), when Israel will be in exile and return to the promised land will become possible. There is no compromise with typical Deuteronomistic theology, for the return together with God's blessings that go with it are conditional upon repentance (Deut. 30:2, 10). But this attitude is not so common in the Prophets. Hosea makes repentance the result of a disciplining experience, rather than of redemption (Hos. 3:5), and God is once said to be the redeemer of those who turn from transgression, but that is already within a description of the new era (Isa. 59:20). Once forgiveness is connected with Israel's paying for its sins, but that is poetic hyperbole, and must not be taken too literally (Isa. 40:2). As Israel connected the process of forgiveness with the experiences of exile and restoration there was a definite tendency to eschatologize something that had been a normal part of the faith, due to the unparalleled nature of the events that had occurred and the enormity of the sins they confessed to be responsible for them. In their radicalizing of forgiveness, at times they reversed the normal order in which repentance comes first, for the future they hoped for was not one that could be expected tò grow out of normal processes.

The imagery of cleansing, mentioned earlier as a virtually universal part of human language concerning sin and forgiveness, appears in connection with restoration as the bridge that makes it possible to leave the past behind and enter into a new era (Jer. 33:7–9a; Ezek. 36:24–25a, 29; 37:23). Certainly these are the corporate sins of Israel which will be washed away, according to these promises, but the needs of individuals are also close at hand, as Ezekiel 36 shows, in moving immediately from restoration and cleansing to the new heart and new spirit. In the exuberant language of 2 Isaiah, the thoroughness of that new kind of forgiveness which is celebrated is described by the verb *mḥh* ("wipe away"), among others (Isa. 43:25; 44:22). As far as God is concerned, then, those sins are just gone, disappeared without leaving any more trace than yesterday's mist.

A corporate result of that thoroughgoing forgiveness was to be the re-establishment of the relationship between God and Israel which the prophets insisted had been broken as a result of their perennial rebellions and God's eventual decision to put them under judgment. So we hear the covenant promise projected into the future:

> They shall not defile themselves any more with their idols and their detestable things, or with any of their transgressions; but I will save them from all the backslidings in which they have sinned, and will cleanse them; and they shall be my people, and I will be their God. (Ezek. 37:23; cf. 36:28; Jer. 24:7; 31:33; Zech. 13:9)

Here is a promise that presumably was fulfilled along with the partial fulfillment of the restoration promise, for the Jews continued to live as the people of Yahweh. This confronts us with the difficulty of the expectations of future forgiveness in the OT, that they tend to focus on one situation: overcoming the causes of the exile. With the rebuilding of the temple in 516 B.C. the sacrificial cult was re-established, and once again the traditional means of assurance that God would forgive sins, individual and national, were available and believed to be efficacious. Eventually there appeared a new eschatological dimension to the forgiveness of sins in post-exilic Judaism, in discussions of how repentance and the mercy of God determined the fate of individuals after death, but the one, sweeping, unique act of forgiveness in the OT remained tied to the prophetic interpretation of the exile as the evidence of Israel's complete failure. As the people viewed the future, before new life could come out of that ultimate punishment for sin, there had to be an unprecedented outpouring of God's grace—forgiveness of Israel's apostasy so as to do away with its past that had brought it to such a hopeless state. The fact that restoration did occur and that the Jews saw evidence for the renewed legitimacy of the promise "I will be your God and you shall be my people" probably meant that they believed the returnees had entered the new era. "But now I will not deal with the remnant of this people as in the former days, says the Lord of hosts" (Zech. 8:11). But, as in other cases, the affirmation that an eschatological promise has been fulfilled leads to some tensions with reality. The fact that sin and guilt offerings were once again being sacrificed in Jerusalem stands over against the promise:

> In those days and in that time, says the Lord, iniquity shall be sought in Israel, and there shall be none; and sin in Judah, and none shall be found; for I will pardon those whom I leave as a remnant. (Jer. 50:20)

For the most part, however, post-exilic Judaism seems to have accepted the great action of national forgiveness promised by the exilic prophets as an accomplished fact, and to have thought of the eschatological aspects of forgiveness in connection with the destiny of individuals after death.

Forgiveness in Later Eschatologies

In post-exilic Judaism, repentance and divine forgiveness took their normal place in the lives of pious Jews, much as they were understood earlier in the OT period, but they do occasionally appear in an eschatological context.[7] The experience of exile and restoration continued to be a great watershed in Jewish experience, as the large number of references in post-exilic literature indicate,[8] but the misfortunes of subsequent generations seem to have dampened the enthusiasm that led OT authors to connect the restoration with so great an act of forgiveness that it was appropriate to speak of it in eschatological language. Occasionally we encounter familiar expressions, as in the *Book of Jubilees:*

> And after this they will turn to Me from amongst the Gentiles with all their heart and with all their soul and with all their strength, and I will gather them from amongst all the Gentiles, and they will seek me, so that I shall be found of them, when they seek me with all their heart and with all their soul. (*Jub.* 1:15; cf. *As. Mos. 4:5)*

In the Apocrypha, 1 Baruch contains confessions and reminders of God's mercy, but reflects quite a different attitude from the Prophets; although written long after restoration became possible, it speaks from the perspective of Jews in exile, suggesting that the problems created by 587 B.C. were not yet thought to be ended. The eschatologizing of forgiveness, which began in sixth-century literature, did not produce a strong and continuing tradition, and we can see two reasons for that. Forgiveness remained very much a daily affair, not to be put off until some distant time; and as for the restoration, it brought with it so many problems of its own that the tendency to see it as God's unique act of forgiveness was bound to diminish with time.

Forgiveness does appear in some eschatological contexts in Jewish literature, however. The *Book of Jubilees* speaks of another time of rebellion in Jewish history, after the restoration, then uses OT language to speak of a final act of mercy (*Jub.* 1:23). The *Assumption of Moses* also speaks of "the day of recompense when the Lord will surely have regard for his people" (*As. Mos.* 1:18), but the apocalyptic spirit of this period tends to think of the future in much more rigid terms than the OT and to look forward to the vindication of the righteous and the condemnation of the wicked at a time when it is too late for repentance and forgiveness.[9]

Rabbinic Judaism put a strong emphasis on repentance and forgiveness in this life, with the former becoming more prominent than ever once the sacrificial system was no longer in operation.[10] To the question raised by the OT whether the initiative must lie on the human or the divine side, a typically rabbinic answer was provided:

> A king had a son who had gone astray from his father a journey of a hundred

days; his friends said to him, 'Return to your father'; he said, 'I cannot.' Then his father sent to say, 'Return as far as you can, and I will come to you the rest of the way.' So God says, 'Return to me, and I will return to you.'[11]

The rabbinic view of judgment, especially of Israel, was much more merciful than that found in earlier apocalyptic, so that along with the familiar statements about justice being done to the wicked may appear expectations of forgiveness, even in the next world.

Even when, for their sins, God slays Israel in this world, there is healing for them in the world to come, as it is said, 'Come, let us return unto the Lord, for it is He who has torn us, and He will bind us up. After two days He will revive us; on the third day He will raise us up' (Hos. 6.2). The two days are this world and the days of the Messiah; the third day is the world to come.[12]

Since continued repentance for Judaism is the key to a healthy relationship with God in this life, it was not appropriate to put too strong an eschatological emphasis on forgiveness.

The coming of Jesus added such a radically new dimension to the understanding of forgiveness that the use of the term "realized eschatology" can scarcely be avoided in our discussion of the matter. The preaching of John the Baptist and Jesus concerning repentance and forgiveness has a familiar Jewish ring about it, but added to John's call for changed lives is the announcement of the coming of Messiah (Luke 3:3–17). Jesus also connected the demand for repentance with the proclamation that the kingdom was at hand (Mark 1:15). That his mission was more than announcement but was actually the realization of the coming of the kingdom was the claim of the stories in which Jesus himself offered the forgiveness that every Jew believed could come only from God (Luke 5:17–26; 7:36–50). The NT thus sees the OT promises of eschatological forgiveness as having begun to come true in the earthly ministry of Jesus. Because the sacrificial system was still being practiced and it was believed God's way of offering forgiveness involved his acceptance of the blood of a victim shed in the place of the sinner, the apostolic church quickly came to a sacrificial understanding of Jesus' death, adding a new and even more unprecedented element to Jesus' own claim to be able to mediate divine forgiveness. But they believed this to be the fulfillment of OT promise, despite its unexpected qualities: "God exalted him at his right hand as Leader and Savior, to give repentance to Israel and forgiveness of sins" (Acts 5:31).[13]

One of the problems with these new claims was that Judaism already seemed to provide very nicely for repentance and forgiveness. A primary reason for the appearance of this understanding of Jesus' death among his followers, alongside the personal impact that his claim to have the authority to forgive sins may have had on them, seems to have been their conviction that the resurrection did indeed mark the beginning of that new era the OT promised. This understanding is most clearly expressed in Hebrews, which presents a detailed interpretation of Christ's death as a sacrifice, insisting that "without the shedding of blood there is no forgiveness of sins" (Heb. 9:22), and using the promise of the new covenant in Jer. 31:31–34 as the key to the announcement that an entirely new era had begun. Forgiveness is the turning point of his argument; having quoted Jer. 31:34, "I will remember their sins and their misdeeds no more," he continues, "Where there is forgiveness of these, there is no longer any offering for sin" (10:17–18). The author of Hebrews thus found it possible to connect the OT promise of forgiveness under the new covenant with his sacrificial interpretation of the death of Christ in order to announce that the new covenant was now in effect.

Other NT authors made less use of the traditional language of repentance and forgiveness in their interpretation of Jesus' death and developed a broader vocabulary, speaking of ransom, atonement, justification, reconciliation, and sanctification, but this survey cannot discuss that very large and complex subject.[14] For the first Christians that comprehensive act of forgiveness which the OT promised for the last days had come to pass on the cross, and so what had been eschatological became past tense and, as one experienced it, present tense. Truly futuristic thought is not so different from that of Judaism, then, in its omission of a great act of forgiveness in the last days and its emphasis on the importance of repentance in the present, but in its teachings about sanctification earliest Christianity did preserve something of the OT hope. A realistic assessment of the lives of forgiven Christians made it necessary to introduce some tension into their declaration that the eschatological hope had been realized, and to look forward to the day when the past would fully be overcome and what they were now experiencing in part would be perfected.

Contemporary Manifestations

In a world where the problem of sin—hence the need for forgiveness—is regularly downplayed if not denied, it is ironic that efforts to erase the past are more prominent than they probably have ever been before. Psychoanalysis has made the individual's past (and in some cases the collective past) determinative for the present, has found ways of uncovering that past, and attempts (with only modest success, it would seem) to guide patients in finding ways to overcome it. The problem for which the OT partially provided an eschatological answer is one of which a great many people are acutely conscious, but it is seldom expressed in eschatological terms. A modern form of eschatology has appeared in the naive hope that some day social planning will bypass the problem of human sin so that it will not have to be solved.

They constantly try to escape
From the darkness outside and within
By dreaming of systems so perfect that no will need to be good.[15]

The popularity in certain Christian circles today of the expression "born again" is surely a contemporary manifestation of that old need to do away with the past. It is not a common expression in the NT and seems to have come to special prominence only with the appearance of revivalism in modern history, but the idea it conveys of being able to start all over again from the beginning is a very effective one. Once again, the emphasis is on the present, not the future, but in reality it is found that no matter how impressive the triumphs over the past may be, if thoroughgoing cleansing and renewal is desired, that still remains future tense.

The Means of Re-Creation: New Heart, New Spirit, New Covenant

The conviction about the radical wrongness of life which underlay OT eschatology extended to human nature itself, so that the prophetic hope for a better future also included anthropological changes, a transformation of human beings which would finally make obedience possible. It must be acknowledged that this pessimistic attitude concerning human potential, appearing for the most part in the sixth-century prophets, stands in some contrast with the rest of the OT, which tends to be generally optimistic about the possibility of obedience. But there are historical reasons for the appearance of that attitude, and without it there might not have developed a full-fledged eschatology, since by our definition it does not grow out of situations conducive to optimism. The transformation of human beings involves a re-creation of our presently distorted condition—a new heart; requires a gift from God which is more than simply a restoration to an uncorrupted state—a new spirit; and calls for the establishment of a relationship between God and humanity on different grounds from those of the present—a new covenant. Essential background for dealing with these texts will thus be found in Israelite anthropology and the covenant traditions.

Human Nature and the Divine Covenant

"Heart is the most important word in OT anthropology."[17] Here we turn to the promises that God will give a new heart to his people, will give them one heart, will put the fear of him into their heart, will give them a heart to know him, and will circumcise the heart. Thus it is essential to understand what the OT is saying about the human condition when it uses that word.

The palpitations of the heart in times of excitement did lead Israelites to associate it with the emotions at times (Jer. 4:19; 23:9; Ps. 25:17; 38:10), but it did not become the metaphorical seat of feelings such as love, sorrow, joy, and compassion to the extent that it has in the Western world. The OT tends to locate those emotions lower in the abdomen, and not without some accuracy (Cant. 5:4 and Lam. 1:20 use *me'ah*, "inwards"). Israelites spoke of the heart pre-eminently as the seat of the rational will. One thinks with the heart, in Hebrew (Isa. 10:7; cf. Ps. 16:7). It is the seat of wisdom (Ps. 51:6; Prov. 2:2; 10:8; 16:21) and of the memory (Isa. 65:17). Plans are made with the heart (Ps. 140:2; Prov. 6:18; 16:9), and as the seat of the will it is the location of moral decisions: obedience, loyalty, deceit, and the intent to do evil (Prov. 26:24; Ps. 40:8). The righteous, the obedient, then are those who have the law of God in their hearts; they know it (Ps. 37:31; 119:11) and have chosen to do it (Prov. 3:1). They are the upright of heart (Ps. 64:10), the pure of heart (Ps. 24:4). Ordinarily, human beings are thought to have both the intelligence and the decision-making powers to enable them to live in accordance with God's will (Deut. 30:10, 14, 17; even Ezek. 18:31).

What if all appeals and threats to the human decision-making capability seemed to fail? Was everything lost? This was the dilemma that faced Jeremiah and Ezekiel as they lived through the decay and collapse of all that was rational and upright and pure, and so it is that a different and far more pessimistic attitude concerning the human heart appears in their books. "The heart is deceitful above all things, and desperately corrupt; who can understand it?" laments Jeremiah (Jer. 17:9; cf. 5:22–24; 18:12). Evil has become as much a part of human nature as spots are to the nature of the leopard (Jer. 13:23).

Ezekiel's outlook is no more pleasant. The account of his call contains the warning, "But the house of Israel will not listen to you; for they are not willing to listen to me; because all the house of Israel are of a hard forehead and of a stubborn heart" (Ezek. 3:7). It is not at all surprising, then, that in precisely these two prophetic books the conviction appears that if the future is ever to be any better, God will have to do something about the heart.

Ezekiel called for a new heart and a new spirit, in 18:31, and later promised them as the transforming work of God (36:26). Although the Bible may speak of the spirit of a person, it never fully belongs to one the way the heart does. The same word, *rûaḥ*, means wind or breath and also something even less tangible.[18] The gift of God's spirit is virtually identical with breath, for it brings the body to life, and when it is withdrawn, death comes (Job 34:14–15; Ps. 104:29–30; Ezek. 37:9–10). But it is more than just an animating force. There may be additional, special gifts of the spirit, which induce ecstasy (1 Sam. 10:6, 10–13), convey messages from God to prophets (1 Kings 22:24), turn ordinary people into leaders (Judg. 6:34), give artistic talent (Exod. 28:3), and make possible the perception of truth (Isa. 11:2). These latter gifts bring us near the capacities of the heart, and it will be noted that as the heart may will to do either good or evil, so the human use of the spirit may also be morally right or wrong. God may even be said to send an "evil spirit' in order to accomplish his will (1 Sam. 16:14), but what is more important for our purposes is the observation that although God may be the source of those spirits that empower human beings, they take on their ethical quality from the free choice of the individual.[19] Hans Walter Wolff compares the heart and spirit by saying that if the heart represents the will, then the spirit represents the power to carry out the decisions of the will. This corresponds to the way Ezekiel speaks of the new spirit, but other benefits of the gift of the spirit will also be predicted for the new day.

It is probably not an overstatement to say that Israel's basic understanding of the relationship between God and human beings was expressed in terms of covenants. The subject is thus one that can by no means be surveyed in any comprehensive way in this context, so an outline will be offered and the reader will be referred to other works for additional background.[20] The OT speaks of four covenants in which God is involved, and they appear to have been of two different types. The best known and most extensively discussed is the covenant concluded between God and Israel at Mt. Sinai (Exodus 19—24; 32–34), establishing a relationship that is now compared with the suzerainty treaties imposed by ancient Near Eastern emperors upon their vassal kings. [21] This has been called the covenant of "human obligation," for it not only establishes a relationship based on divine promises; it also makes that relationship conditional on human obedience to a set of requirements, and so law is based on covenant.[22]

The covenant with Noah (Genesis 9) contained the promise to all flesh never again to destroy the world by a flood; the covenant with Abraham (Genesis 17) promised that his seed would come a great nation that would inherit the land of Canaan, be blessed and become a blessing; and the covenant with David promised that he would never lack an heir to sit on his throne in Jerusalem (2 Samuel 7). These have been called covenants of divine obligation. But it was the Sinai covenant that constituted Israel as a nation belonging in a special sense to Yahweh (Exod. 19:4–6). And this covenant, due to its conditional nature, provided a theological explanation for national failure. The standards were so high for their time that seldom could Israel as a whole be said to have been faithful to them. Hence it was easy to explain disaster on ethical grounds and with reference to the exclusivism of the Yahwistic cult, as we find in Judges 2, 1 Kings 17, and many other places. Although the covenant material in Exodus contains no curses, at some point in the development of the Sinai tradition a series of curses was added, threatening the most severe consequences imaginable for covenant-breaking, and we have examples of them in Leviticus 26 and Deuteronomy 27 and 28.[23] As we have seen in tracing the relationship between the covenant promise of land and threats against that promise, however, the non-prophetic references to covenant do not suggest that Israel ever thought of the possibility that Yahweh might actually abrogate that relationship. Even the experience of the exile itself was not interpreted as a rupture of the covenant by every Israelite. Two very interesting texts of this type are usually dated after 587: Lev. 26:40–45 and Deut. 4:25–31. Whether they are early or late, they are representatives of the belief that Yahweh would remain faithful to the Sinai covenant no matter what Israel did, but if they are late they also reveal that even after exile had occurred it was possible for some to affirm the continuation of the covenant, and thus to hold to a non-eschatological kind of hope which did not anticipate truly radical changes (Lev. 26:44).

The canonical Prophets, however, do not appeal to the covenant as a ground for hope, for they see the predicament of Israel as much too desperate for that. Perhaps they seldom used the word because they thought the covenant had functioned too effectively as a ground for assurance. They found ways of attacking covenant theology and of declaring it to be no longer effective, making use of other terminology, however. Amos alludes to Israel's belief in election in a new way:

> You only have I known of all the families of the earth; therefore I will punish you for all your iniquities. (Amos 3:2)

He finds a variety of ways to declare that the old relationship between Yahweh and Israel is no longer in force (Amos 5:1–2, 18–20; 8:1–3, 11–12; 9:1–4, 7–8).

Hosea did use the word covenant, to announce that Israel had broken it (Hos. 6:7; 8:1–3), and struggled with the tension between Israel's continual faithlessness and Yahweh's covenant love in Hosea 11, but the burden of his message also seems to be that the old certainties can no longer be appealed to (13:4–11). The same case can be made for the other pre-exilic prophets, that the radically different element in their message is their conclusion that the provisions of the Sinai covenant no longer hold true. For a long time Yahweh has been faithful despite Israel's continuing unfaithfulness, but the time is imminent when God will abrogate that covenant.[24] When eschatological passages speak of a new future for Israel, beyond the time of suffering which the breaking of the relationship made at Sinai must inevitably bring, they find various ways of overcoming the embarrassment of the failure of Sinai. Second Isaiah speaks of Noah, Abraham, and David, but not of Moses. We have traced the importance of Zion in eschatology, and its associations were with the Davidic covenant. The unconditional covenants continued to offer assurance that under any circumstances whatsoever there might still be, in God himself, some basis for a new relationship with Israel, but they offer no answer to the anthropological questions raised especially by Jeremiah and Ezekiel. When the Prophets consider what kind of future God might create, they find that the Sinai type of covenant, with its requirement of human response, cannot simply be bypassed. Ezekiel will speak of the changes necessary to make it possible for human beings to be able to obey God's statutes and ordinances, and Jeremiah will go so far as to speak of a new covenant.

The Transformation of Human Beings

The OT never suggests that the freedom of choice which God gave to human beings at creation ought to be done away with or that obedience should be ensured by turning people into automatons. But the prophets did conclude that the problem of sin is a fundamental one, for as long as the same kind of people populate the world there can be no ideal society or peace in nature, and so they speak of divine intervention to make a change in human nature itself. Among the promises contained in Deut. 30:1–10 is this: "And the Lord your God will circumcise your heart and the heart of your offspring, so that you will love the Lord your God with all your heart and with all your soul, that you may live" (v. 6). "Circumcision of the heart" is hardly a transparent term for us, but it appears to have been a fairly common expression in Hebrew, and other references to uncircumcision show us that the term was used metaphorically to denote a blockage of some sort, offering resistance to good influences.[25] So the Deuteronomist appeals to Israel: "Circumcise therefore the foreskin of your heart, and be no longer stubborn" (10:16; cf. Jer. 4:4). But in that unusual promissory text in Deuteronomy 30, the circumcising is to be done by God himself. The primary result will be to make it possible for Israel to love God without qualifications or restraints. Love for God means far more than to have warm feelings about him, for it is intimately connected with obedience, and conversely, to hate or despise God means to disobey him.[26] The context of that which is to be remedied by circumcision of the heart is provided by the Sinai covenant (Deut. 30:8).

The promise of human transformation in connection with restoration also appears as a part of Jeremiah's interpretation of the vision of two baskets of figs, in chapter 24. As we have noted in discussing repentance, the initiative is with God; there is something like "imputed righteousness" in 24:5: "Like these good figs, so I will regard as good the exiles from Judah," and for all we know it is purely God's free choice to bless them and restore them to the land, as he promises in 24:6. Then follows the internal change: "I will give them a heart to know that I am the Lord; and they shall be my people and I will be their God, for they shall return to me with their whole heart" (24:7). The heart is appropriately associated with knowledge, as we have seen, but it is important not to restrict the Hebrew concept of knowledge to the way the English word is ordinarily used. "Now Adam knew Eve his wife, and she conceived" (Gen. 4:1) may be evidence enough to reveal the relational, intimate, and personal overtones of knowledge in Hebrew, so this also is covenantal knowledge.[27] Two other restoration passages speak of the gift of "one heart" for the people, "that they may fear me forever" (Jer. 32:37–41) and "that they may walk in my statutes" (Ezek. 11:17–21). Here also the change is entirely the result of divine initiative.

There is one more reference to the change of heart in Jeremiah, and that is in the new covenant passage (31:31–34). It will be discussed in a preliminary way here. The one thing that is identified as *new* about that covenant is that it will be written on their hearts, and parallel to that is, "I will put my law within them." The beginning of the passage makes it clear again that obedience is the concern of the prophet, and it concludes with a surprising promise about the extent of the knowledge of God which writing the covenant on the heart will provide.

Finally we come to the only passage that uses the expression "new heart and new spirit," Ezek. 36:24–32. Here we shall consider just this portion of the longer text that includes almost all of Israel's hopes for a better day. Like all other passages discussed in this section, it moves from restoration to the promised land to the internal changes of those who will return.[28] Ezekiel describes those changes in more detail. First, forgiveness is depicted in ritual terms: "I will sprinkle clean water upon you, and you shall be clean from all your uncleannesses, and from all your idols I will cleanse you." Next, the gift of a new heart and new spirit is promised, but more of an explanation of that change is offered here than anywhere else. "I will take out of your flesh the heart of stone and give you a heart of flesh." Although there can be a dichotomy between flesh and spirit in the OT, that appears only when the difference between God and his created world is being stressed, as in Isa. 31:3. As this passage clearly reveals, Israel saw nothing inherently wrong with the material world. It was a heart of flesh which God put into the human breast at creation, and nothing better is needed for the good life to be possible. He creates no automatons, then, according to Ezekiel, for the heart of flesh is that free, rational will that is part of uncorrupted humanity. The problem is that in history the responsive, truly human heart has turned to stone; something of humanity has been lost so that love, obedience, and knowledge of God are no longer possible. This is more appropriately called re-creation than new creation. To become truly human again, able to make the choice to follow God, must also be accompanied by the gift of the spirit to empower one to act on those choices. "And I will put my spirit within you, and cause you to walk in my statutes and be careful to observe my ordinances." This passage by no means resolves the problem of divine determination and human free will; rather it shows us one of the several helpful ways the OT holds them in tension. Self-help is no longer possible, Ezekiel says, but the divine initiative is expected to produce responsive people somehow freed from their inability to hear God speaking to them and to act for their own good.

As the new spirit makes it possible to walk in the statutes and ordinances of the Lord (in Ezekiel), and the new covenant writes the law of God on the heart (in Jeremiah), in Isa. 59:21 the effect of the gift of covenant and spirit is an internalizing of the divine word, expressed in terms of putting God's word in their mouth forever—not so puzzling if we recall that as Israel encountered the word of God it was normally in oral form (Deut. 30:14).[29]

The universality of the work of the spirit in the last days is emphasized in Joel 2:28–29. The reasons for the changes promised are not so immediately evident as in the other passages dealing with heart and spirit, but they can be located within the OT tradition. It had, of course, always been believed the spirit might bestow special gifts on certain individuals, including that of prophecy. It is this belief, and that expressed in Num. 12:6, "If there is a prophet among you, I the Lord make myself known to him in a vision, I speak with him in a dream," which lies behind Joel's promise:

> And it shall come to pass afterward,
> that I will pour out my spirit on all flesh;
> your sons and your daughters shall prophesy,
> your old men shall dream dreams,
> and your young men shall see visions.
> Even upon the menservants and maidservants
> in those days, I will pour out my spirit.
> (Joel 2:28–29)

This "gift of universal prophecy" is another way of responding to a need that other texts in this section have dealt with; what we might call the internalization of the will of God. Israel had prophets to speak the word of God to them, but that was external and subject to reception by uncircumcised ears, stony hearts, and stubborn spirits. Joel promises that the democratization of prophecy which Moses once hoped for will in fact one day occur: "Would that all the Lord's people were prophets, that the Lord would put his spirit upon them!" (Num. 11:29). This is what Joel now promises. No longer will one have to depend on someone else to learn the will of God, for all will have the same access to revelation. Joel's choices of subjects make sure that no one will be left out. Young and old, male and female, free and slave—all are to be included, and once the slave is mentioned one cannot say that Gentiles are excluded, even though they are not specifically mentioned. There is considerable debate over the scope of "all flesh" in 2:28, with some scholars insisting it means all Israel, not all humanity, but the reference to slaves surely means some Gentiles might be included.[30] It is a time in which an entire community will enjoy direct access to God, and if the verses that follow are to be associated with these, Joel connects this anthropological change with great cosmic disturbances—"portents in the heavens and on earth"—and makes the community in Mount Zion the center of his interest (2:32).[31]

Despite the difference in language and some variation in the choice of themes, then, the needs to which this passage responds and its essential message are very closely related to the other texts concerning the changes of heart and spirit in the new day.[32]

Although covenants are social documents and Jeremiah's new covenant (Jer. 31:31–34) will have its effects on human society, the fundamental change in the new covenant which he promises is anthropological. The inescapable relationship between individual and social righteousness is nicely expressed by Jeremiah's choice of a concept such as a covenant that is to be written on the heart.[33] The passage stands within a group of promises which has been labelled "The Book of Consolation," Jeremiah 30–31. It is not unimportant for its interpretation to consider these other promises with which it is associated. We are dealing with another restoration text and one in which the return of the Northern Kingdom plays a prominent role (30:3, 10; 31:7–11, 16–17). A second theme, the nations, also appears in passing; those who oppressed Israel will in that day be punished for it (30:11, 16, 20). Zion is present, even though the people are called Ephraim and Jacob. The city will be rebuilt and apparently will be the center of the new life (30:17–18; 31:12, 23, 38–40). The new community will have a king (30:21), servitude will be at an end (30:8), their numbers will be multiplied (30:19–20), and they will be blessed with abundant fertility (31:12). The note that resounds throughout these chapters is one of rejoicing (30:19; 31:4, 7, 13). Now, it may very well be that this is a compilation of materials from various authors and dates, but each element that has been added has been appropriate, for the result is a view of the ultimate purpose of God which almost completely represents the repeated hopes of the OT. The text that immediately concerns us (31:31–34) stands as a complete unit without any close relationship to what surrounds it, but it does pick up the theme of the broken covenant which appears elsewhere in Jeremiah (especially chapter 11). This broken covenant is identified clearly: ". . . not like the covenant which I made with their fathers when I took them by the hand to bring them out of the land of Egypt" (31:32). The "newness," then, is something that will distinguish it from the relationship made at Sinai. What will be different? The parties will be the same: Yahweh and Israel. It will also be a covenant with stipulations, not unconditional, for the *torah* of Yahweh is central to it (31:33). What is new, according to 31:33–34, is the location of the stipulations, which will be written on the heart. This can be nothing but a change in the mind and will of the people. The emphasis in the next verse is on knowledge, but the OT does not permit that to be divorced from the will. This is a more explicit and extreme way of promising the eventual internalization of the will of God than was expressed in Ezekiel 36 or Joel 2, for teaching and admonition, the very ways commended by Deuteronomy for internalizing the law (Deut. 4:9–10;

6:6–9), will no longer be necessary! To a teacher and preacher this remains one of the most surprising of the OT's promises, but it is a natural conclusion for Israel to draw from its tendency to democratize the processes of revelation. If all are prophets, as Joel says, then there will no longer be an office of prophet, and if God communicates his will directly to everyone, then teachers will not be needed, either. Then the question of free will arises again. If the *torah* is written on the heart, does the will of God then overpower the human will, so that choice is no longer in the picture? We cannot offer a confident answer, for the text does not discuss it, but there are two facts that suggest an approach to the question which seems in keeping with the Book of Jeremiah. We have noticed that this book is pessimistic about obedience and about repentance; they may be humanly impossible. Perhaps the writing of the law on the heart simply makes it possible to make a right choice, and when it is possible the prophet assumes it will be done. Support for this approach may be offered by the way the passage concludes: ". . . for I will forgive their iniquity, and I will remember their sin no more." It is the removal of that barrier to the knowledge of God, their iniquity, which may thus make obedience once again an option for human beings.

The covenant of the future appears in other passages as well, although it is qualified by an adjective other than "new." This is the *b^e^rith 'olam*, usually translated "everlasting covenant." The word *'olam* never can be proved to mean "eternal," that is timeless, but it is ordinarily understood to designate a very long time, in either the past or the future. A recent study concludes that its basic meaning has to do with limits, so that the expression should perhaps be translated "exclusive covenant," but without having to decide the merits of that suggestion we can find evidence in several of the relevant contexts that the long-lasting qualities of this covenant are in mind.[34] The expression occurs in several non-eschatological passages to designate the unconditional covenants; with Noah (Gen. 9:6), with the patriarchs (Gen. 17:7, 13, 19; 1 Chron. 16:17; Ps. 105;10), and with David (2 Sam. 23:5). In Isa. 24:5, however, we discover that Israel has broken the everlasting covenant, by transgressing the laws and statutes! This is obviously a reference to Sinai, and the fact that *b^e^rith 'olam* can be broken forces the question on us whether "everlasting" is the correct translation in every occurrence.[35]

If the prophets really did proclaim the scandal of an abrogated covenant, as scholarship has concluded, then it begins to appear that exilic and post-exilic Israel ordinarily preferred not to take on that scandal directly. It might have made a great deal of the promise of new covenant, but as we shall see, it did not. Or it might have challenged the prophetic interpretation of history by emphasizing the Sinai covenant as an eternal covenant, but the texts just surveyed do not show that much progress was made in that direction. The post-exilic community seems just to have assumed, for the most part, that the Sinai covenant was still in effect for the faithful remnant, so that "covenant" does not become for them a central eschatological term.

The Means of Re-Creation in Post–Old Testament Eschatology

The OT materials that have been discussed in this section became much more important for Christianity than for Judaism, and this seems clearly due to the differences in the anthropology of the two faiths. Post-exilic Jews believed the Sinai covenant still to be in effect, that repentance was humanly possible, and that divine forgiveness was thus always available.[36] Hence there was little reason for further development of the hope for a radical change in human nature which appeared in the Books of Jeremiah and Ezekiel. Christianity, on the other hand, found sin to be a deeper problem than Judaism ordinarily did and believed the human predicament to be one which would require profound changes in order for communion with God and healthy human community to become possible. There is thus a considerable development of these OT ideas in the NT, and they contribute to important aspects of Christian theology.

Jewish literature does cite the promises of new heart, new spirit, and new convenant as scriptural grounds for the hope that one day all will be righteous; the difference is that the ideas concerning drastic internal changes are not extensively developed. At the beginning of Moses' vision of Israel's future history, in *Jub.* 1:23, God promises:

> And after this they will turn to Me in all uprightness and with all (their) heart and with all (their) soul, and I will circumcise the foreskin of their heart and the foreskin of the heart of their seed, and I will create in them a holy spirit and I will cleanse them so that they shall not turn away from Me from that day unto eternity.

The combination of Ezekiel 36 with Deuteronomy 30 is evident here, and the latter's opinion that repentance must precede restoration has also influenced Baruch's version of Jeremiah's promises in 1 Bar. 2:30–35, which includes a heart that obeys, ears that hear, and an everlasting covenant.[37]

Two themes reappear in the rabbinic literature, both connected with the central Jewish emphasis on study of the Torah. Learning is imperfect because all human beings forget, and that is something God is expected to correct in the days to come.

> For in this world a man learns and forgets but, as for the time to come, what is written there? I have given my Law in their inward parts. (*Midr. Qoh.* 2:1)[38]

The second theme is that God himself will become Israel's teacher (*Pesiq. R.* 12:21; *Tg. Isa.* 12:3; *Tg. Cant.* 5:10; and *Yalq.* on Isaiah 26).[39] These expected changes are hardly radical enough to be called true eschatology, except that they are located in the days to come. The closest thing to the Christian teaching about inner transformation is to be found in teachings about the Evil Inclination, the source of human temptation, which, quoting Ezek. 36:26, include the promise that God will eradicate it in the last days.[40]

The idea of a new covenant appears to have been not at all attractive to most Jewish groups, but there were two movements that broke away from the rest of Judaism and found the concept to be very useful as an explanation of their present existence. As sectarian Jews who believed they alone were living in accordance with the law of Moses, the authors of the Qumran community speak of themselves again and again as the people of the covenant. Having summarized briefly the history of Israel as an abandonment of the covenant, resulting in the cutting off of the monarchy and the ravaging of the land, the Damascus Document continues:

> But because of those who clung to the commandments of God (and) survived them as a remnant, God established His Covenant with Israel forever, revealing to them the hidden things in which all Israel had strayed. (CD III.12–14)[41]

Several times in this document the expression new covenant is used (VI.19, VIII.21, XIX.33–34, XX.12), in one case in connection with a reference to Jeremiah (VIII.20–21), but for Qumran the new covenant is realized eschatology, if indeed we should call it eschatology at all. The covenant community has been brought into existence by the instruction of the Righteous Teacher and is living now in full accordance with the will of God, as properly instructed. The community itself has a strongly eschatological character, but the kind of hope for an inner transformation of the individual which we have been tracing does not appear prominently. So, despite the occurrence of the term new covenant, the Qumran community does not play a very important role in the history of this eschatological tradition; first, because it is not used in a strongly eschatological way, and second, because Qumran had no heirs.

Early Christianity does not appear to have been at all sectarian in its outlook, but it does share a certain similarity of attitude with the Qumran community in its use of the term new covenant as a way of upholding the validity of a movement which differed from other Jewish groups of the time. The anthropology of the NT is strongly influenced by the early church's consciousness of living in the last days, so that once again the term "realized eschatology" is a useful one, even though it does not really resolve the tensions in the NT between present reality and what is yet to come. The subject of the internal, personal change in the lives of individuals brought about by the work of Christ introduces us to a major component of NT theology. Here I will briefly comment on texts that are obviously related to the OT passages that have been discussed.[42]

That the church already believed itself to be living in the era of the new covenant is indicated by many NT passages. The oldest form of the words of the institution of the Lord's Supper, as preserved in 1 Cor. 11:25, attributes to Jesus himself the identification of that meal with the establishment of the new covenant: "This cup is the new covenant in my blood." Since new covenant is mentioned only once in the OT, this is almost certainly a claim that Jer. 31:31 has been fulfilled, and so the church understood it, as other references reveal. The allusion to blood points back to the Sinai covenant, to which Jeremiah also referred, since it was the only one sealed with blood (Exodus 24). The conviction that Christians live under the new covenant and have thus received that changed heart promised by Jeremiah and the gift of the spirit foreseen by Ezekiel was a significant influence on the thinking of Paul. In his earliest letter, 1 Thess. 4:1–12, he alludes to Ezek. 36:26 and/or 37:6 as the basis for ethical instruction.[43] The existence of a new human condition marked by the presence of the spirit is simply taken for granted here, but in 2 Cor. 3:1–11 language taken from Jeremiah 31 and Ezekiel 36 is used as evidence by Paul to counter an attack on his credentials as an apostle.

The contrast of covenants, surely suggested to early Christian writers by Jer. 31:31–34, is developed even further by Paul in Gal. 4:21–28, where a series of opposites (antitheses) is presented: Hagar/Sarah; slavery/freedom; flesh/promise; Sinai/Jerusalem; flesh/spirit. Later in the same letter Paul says that those who are spiritual should "fulfill the law of Christ" (Gal. 6:1–2), which is presumably Jeremiah's law written on the heart. Such an expression probably came from thinking of Christ as the mediator of the new covenant, filling a role analogous to that of Moses at Sinai.

That is clearly the view of the author of Hebrews, who quotes parts of Jeremiah 31 twice in explaining the differences between new and old covenants. The first time it is only to show that there was something inadequate in the first (Heb. 8:6–13), but shortly thereafter, having introduced the concept of new covenant, he speaks of Christ as its mediator whose death made possible the forgiveness of sins (9:15–22). The sufficiency of that sacrificial shedding of blood is emphasized in 10:14–18 with another quotation from Jeremiah 31, and once again the contrast between the covenants appears in 12:22–24, where Zion (the heavenly Jerusalem), Jesus as mediator, and sprinkled blood are the major features of the new covenant which are identified. It should be noted that for Hebrews, forgiveness and the establishment of one's relationship with God take precedence over the transforming power of the spirit on this life, which is emphasized elsewhere.

The Johannine writings speak of a "new commandment"—"that you love one another"—which is not, in fact, new at all (John 13:34), and that expression is probably used because of the idea that the commandment has been reiterated by the mediation of the new covenant, although that term is never used (cf. 1 John 2:7–8). Whereas in Jeremiah there appeared to be continuity of content but newness of recipient, in this case there is continuity of content but newness of occasion. The gift of the spirit, which will make possible a depth of knowledge not available until after Jesus' death, also plays a prominent role in John (14:15–17, 25–26; 16:13–15). This reminds us, of course, of Peter's use of Joel's prophecy in order to explain the events of Pentecost as phenomena of the last days, with special emphasis on the wholesale outpouring of the spirit (Acts 2). We cannot follow this lead further, but must leave the subject of the gifts of the spirit with a mere reminder of their prevalence throughout the NT.

These texts have all referred to the present experiences of Christians who lived just after the death of Jesus. The prophecies of Jeremiah and Ezekiel that God would one day create a new humanity *had been fulfilled*, as far as they were concerned. But this does not remove the subject entirely from eschatology and place it in the realm of soteriology and ethics. Paul tells the Thessalonians they have no need for anyone to write to them, for they have been taught by God to love one another, affirming the fulfillment of Jer. 31:34, but he himself *is* writing to them and goes on to give them instruction and admonition (1 Thess. 4:9–12). A radical, internal change making full obedience possible *has* occurred, he tells the Romans. "We know that our old self was crucified with him so that the sinful body might be destroyed, and we might no longer be enslaved to sin" (Rom. 6:6). But then he adds a theoretically unnecessary admonition: "Let not sin therefore reign in your mortal bodies" (6:12). Even his own knowledge of God, as an apostle, remains imperfect: "Now I know in part; then I shall understand fully, even as I have been fully understood" (1 Cor. 13:12). So there remains a place for hope in Christian anthropology, even in the midst of the experiences of dramatic changes in attitude and way of life which many Christians have interpreted as fulfillment of the old promise of a new heart and a new spirit, for no matter how radical the changes or how profound the commitment, they fall far short of the perfection of which both Testaments speak. The Christian understanding of new covenant is thus one of the clearest examples of the tensions in Christianity produced by promises that seem to have been partly fulfilled, leaving an essential place for eschatology, if the full truth of the promise is not to be abandoned.[44]

Contemporary Manifestations

Whether one sees any need for a re-creation of humanity as an essential factor in the creation of the ideal world depends, of course, on one's opinion of the natural human potential for doing good. A basic difference between Judaism and Christianity at this point has already been noted, and there are also differences between Catholic and Protestant, Arminian and Calvinist, over the extent to which human beings are able to cooperate in their own salvation. Modern secularism has gone to extremes of optimism or pessimism. Pessimistic secularism, which focuses on the futility even of good intentions and the appalling excesses of evil of which the human will is capable, has nothing on which to base an eschatology, and is left without hope.[45] Optimistic secularism has produced a humanistic philosophy that exalts our potential for good and believes the evils to which we are prone are correctable by our own efforts. It develops an eschatology of its own; an ideal future that can and must be planned and that is attainable given enough education, hard work, and good will.[46] Without entering into a discussion of the merits of these two positions, it may be noted that one form of secular humanism, Marxism, has apparently begun to find that its theories about the way to produce the ideal human society have not taken an adequate account of the pervasiveness of what religious people call sin. At any rate, some dialogues between Marxists and Christians in recent years have been entered by Marxists with the hope that Christian theory might help them deal with the inadequacy of their anthropology.[47]

In modern Judaism an interesting interpretation of Jeremiah's new covenant has appeared for which we have not seen clear evidence in the ancient literature. Joseph Klausner wrote of Jer. 31:31–34:

> It is almost possible to say with certainty that this great Messianic promise is that which brought about a fundamental change in the hearts of the exiles in Babylonia and caused a complete revolution in the life of Israel after the exiles had returned to their own land. From this deep and pure fountain Israel drew the finest of its qualities: the power of concentration on the *deep inner meaning* of the Torah; and the power of revolt against deeds that do not come from the heart. . . . So the Messianic expectation, that the LORD will make a new covenant with his people for the age to come, has become a strong faith, whose *complete* realization is always expected in the future, but whose partial realization has not ceased from the time of the Babylonian exile to the most recent period.[48]

Klausner's understanding of fulfillment *in part* is thus analogous to the teachings we have found in the NT, but with the difference that he finds post-exilic Judaism already to be a manifestation of the new covenant in that the *torah* was truly becoming internalized in the Jewish experience.

In the light of Christianity's own discovery that the NT's affirmation that the last days had come and the new covenant been instituted did not mean the complete and final realization of God's purpose as yet, but rather offered the possibility of sharing in the blessings of the initiation of the eschaton, it may be suggested modern Christians might agree with Klausner that the effects of the exile on Judaism were also a fulfillment of the prophetic promise. History shows that a change in the very nature of the religion did take place in the direction of an internalization of the *torah,* with an emphasis on the importance of having the right intention and a willingness to be obedient without regard to reward.[49] In the enthusiasm of their day, the authors of the NT found it important to contrast the new covenant instituted by Christ with Sinai (i.e., with Judaism), but they soon found that for themselves as well fulfillment was still be to awaited, as well as celebrated. If what happened in the first century A.D. was a true but partial fulfillment, then why cannot Christians affirm something similar about what happened in the sixth through fifth centuries B.C.?[50]

The New Humanity

What should people be like, in order to live a truly good life? We turn now to evidence for the OT concept of the ideal person, as expressed in its portrayal of the future that God will one day create. We shall find that Israel's hopes were based on a positive estimate of the first creation; no supermen or wonderwomen are anticipated, but only the correction of what has gone wrong with the living beings whom God always intended to live under his blessing.

The OT understands the ideal human life to have one necessary and sufficient condition: uninterrupted fellowship with God. On the human side of that fellowship, obedience is the primary requisite and joy is the primary result. Given the world-affirming character of the OT, one would not expect this joy to be of the ascetic type, requiring one to learn to do without comfort and overlook pain. Since the body is part of God's good creation, its soundness and well-being is a concern, and since death is an interruption of all that is good in this world, the length of life and what becomes of the dead cannot be overlooked.

The Old Testament Tradition of the Good Life

The conviction that all humanity is living under a curse that is projected all the way back to the first people to live on earth pervades the OT. Surely this reflects the Israelite experience of the universality of personal problems that made life short, painful, and unhappy. They did not account for these trials by saying they were part of the natural order of things, or the result of an accident of some kind, or the will of a wicked deity. They were convinced that God's intentions for them were different and laid the responsibility for their miseries on human sin. But it is God who utters the curse and enforces the penalty. This understanding of the human predicament, which eschatology expects to be overcome, makes it possible for us to trace quickly the background of the promises of a new humanity by looking at several series of curses which sum up virtually everything that could go wrong in one person's life. The result of the first sin was such a series of curses (Gen. 3:16–19). There is no community, yet, with only two people on earth, and the curses are true to their setting in focusing on the fate of individuals. The curse on woman is twofold: she will suffer pain in childbearing and she must live in subordination to her husband. There is one curse specifically directed to man: he must labor against an uncooperative nature in order to get food enough to feed himself and his family. Death is also part of the curse, but that is not restricted to men alone. The human problems that Israel projected all the way back to the beginnings of life, then, were hunger and the futility of work, the inevitability of death, and the inequality of women, with a special emphasis on the pain they experience in bearing children.

Two longer series that include both blessings and curses are addressed to Israel in Leviticus 26 and Deuteronomy 28. In the blessings, only one of the curses in Genesis 3 is said to be reversible, and that involves hunger (Lev. 26:4–5, etc.). The curses contain a long list of terrors, including hunger, disease, national defeat, a complete lack of personal security, and every kind of anguish, physical and mental.[51] Of course national destiny is an important part of these curses, but they are especially useful as background for our present concerns about the destinies of individuals because so much of their content is focused that way. The needs alluded to in such vigorous and brutal language in the curses—enough to eat, freedom from disease, and security—are so obvious and so universal that there is no need to dwell on them here,[52] but something more needs to be said about the OT understanding of the relationship between illness and sin.

Illness must have been one of the most mysterious of the daily occurrences with which the Israelites had to contend, for the natural causes of disease were completely unknown.[53] Injuries could be explained naturally without the addition of any theology, as in the case of Mephibosheth's lameness, which is simply accounted for by recalling how his nurse dropped him when he was five years old (2 Sam. 4:4). No one understood the reasons for disease, however, and since the OT refuses to accept any theory of demonic causation or arbitrary acts of God, an ethical explanation is preferred: illness is a just punishment sent by God for one's sins.[54] This remains a part of popular theology to this day, despite the demonstration of its inadequacies in the Book of Job and the rejection of it by Jesus in the case of the man born blind (John 9:1–3). But in the OT period it was probably the best that could be done. The psalms of lament which complain about sickness show how it was common to associate physical disability with the spiritual problem of separation from God, with the psalmist at times confessing that both were the result of sin. The twenty-second Psalm complains:

> I am poured out like water,
> and all my bones are out of joint;
> my heart is like wax,
> it is melted within my breast;
> my strength is dried up like a potsherd,
> and my tongue cleaves to my jaws;
> thou dost lay me in the dust of death.
> (Ps. 22:14–15)

In the midst of that physical distress God has forsaken him (v. 1), does not answer (v. 2), and seems to be far off (vv. 11, 19). There is not always an explicit confession of sin in such laments; sometimes the psalmist protests his innocence instead, but elsewhere the direct connection between sin and sickness is made.

> When I declared not my sin, my body wasted away
> through my groaning all day long.
> For day and night thy hand was heavy upon me;
> my strength was dried up as by the heat of summer.
> (Ps. 32·3–4)

> There is no soundness in my flesh
> because of thy indignation;
> there is no health in my bones
> because of my sin.
> (Ps. 38:3)

And Psalm 38 concludes, "Do not forsake me, O Lord! O my God, be not far from me." Physical health is thus almost always connected with one's relationship to God, for illness is understood either as a punishment for one's sins, sent by God, or as the result of the work of an enemy, for which one asks for help from God. It has both spiritual and ethical connotations. Köhler summed it up this way:

> Loneliness is the lot of every sick man. The thought that he is guilty; the idea that to belong to him, to be with him, is shameful and suggests guilt; the conviction that one is stricken by God because afflicted with suffering—all this must be borne in mind and its nature felt if we are to get a real picture of the health and sickness of the Hebrew.[55]

Most scholars today agree that when the psalmists speak of being delivered from Sheol or the Pit they are praising God for recovery from illness, and do not speak of what we would call resurrection from the dead.[56] Israel seems to have thought of life and death as more of a continuum than we do. Life, in its fullness, meant more than just existing; to be alive meant to be in full possession of one's vigor, talents, and reputation, so that when one's vitality was decreased by illness or old age, when one was under attack by enemies or held up to scorn, then death had begun to triumph over life. We also use expressions that reflect a similar attitude in a weakened form: "dead tired"; "deathly ill." So the psalmist who is in dire distress says not only, "For my soul is full of troubles, and my life draws near to Sheol," but also, "Thou hast put me in the depths of the Pit, in the regions dark and deep" (Ps. 88:3, 6; cf. Pss. 18:4–5; 116:3). Another, against whom ruthless men have been plotting, praises God for help saying, "For great is thy steadfast love toward me; thou hast delivered my soul from the depths of Sheol" (Ps. 86:13).

Deliverance from illness, then, and not resurrection, is believed to be the subject of such lines (Ps. 30:2–3).

The practice of medicine has been little more than a form of magic in most cultures until recent times, and that may be one of the reasons the OT has so little to say about it. A few natural procedures are noted, such as Isaiah's fig poultice (Isa. 38:21), but where human beings are involved in the healing process they are most often prophets, who are able to make direct use of the healing power of God.[57] This power even included the resuscitation of those who had apparently died. One might expect, then, that eschatology, which appeals to the power of God to make right that which human beings have failed to correct, would make subjects such as illness and death the center of attention. That is not true in the OT, however. It takes the problems of human society as its major eschatological subject, and the physical problems of individuals are mentioned far less often. My sketch of Israelite attitudes toward health and sickness does not so much account for a significant stream of thought which issued in repeated expressions of hope for the future as it provides material that will be referred to in order to explain why concerns about human disabilities do not appear more often.

As for the question of life after death, which plays so large a role in later eschatologies, it is little more than an appendix to the OT view of the last days. For a book of this kind, which seeks to provide a balanced view of the OT themes, it seems out of proportion to present the kind of full-scale study of life and death which has been done in other books, just as background for two resurrection texts.[58] The traditional background for the resurrection hope will be traced in the next section, in connection with the discussion of Isa. 26:19 and Dan. 12:4.

The Transformed Person

Although the OT has an intense interest in physical matters—land, cities, food, government, and human society in general—where the fate of the individual is concerned it seems justified to say that its primary emphasis is on the spiritual, that is on the relationship between people and their God. Knowledge of God and obedience to God are the most frequently mentioned results of the re-creation of humanity described in the preceding section. In Hebrew, knowledge connotes relationship, as noted earlier, and especially in the Book of Ezekiel the fundamental result of God's judging and redeeming work is regularly said to be, "then they will know that I am Yahweh." In Ezekiel 39 the relationship between this formula and God's redeeming and transforming work is revealed. He promises to restore their fortunes (Ezek. 39:25), and to settle them securely in their land, after which they will forget their shame (39:26–27).

> Then they shall know that I am the Lord their God because I sent them into exile among the nations, and then gathered them into their own land. I will leave none of them remaining among the nations any more; and I will not hide my face any more from them, when I pour out my Spirit upon the house of Israel, says the Lord God. (Ezek. 39:28–29)

This text concerning the gift of the spirit does not speak so explicitly of internal change as most of the others, but it is associated with terms concerning one's relationship with God: knowledge and no more alienation.[59] The Book of Joel also speaks of the knowledge of God in the last days (Joel 2:26–27; 3:16–17), but two texts from Jeremiah which we have already looked at in the preceding section are of more importance to us. In Jer. 24:7 the promise is to "give them a heart to know that I am the LORD," and the results of such knowledge are repentance and the re-establishment of the relationship denoted by the covenant formula: "They shall be my people and I will be their God." To these texts promising the establishment of a new and good relationship between God and humanity may be added Jer. 31:34, which emphasizes the relationship's universality and perfection. Obviously knowledge of God is the highest human goal, for the new covenant passage concludes, "And no longer shall each man teach his neighbor and each his brother, saying, 'Know the Lord,' for they shall all know me, from the least of them to the greatest, says the Lord."

The knowledge of which Isa. 30:19–22 speaks is not the personal awareness of God, but ethical teaching, which changes the subject somewhat, but there is an element of continuity in the uninhibited relationship of which it speaks:

> And though the Lord give you the bread of adversity and the water of affliction, yet your Teacher will not hide himself any more, but your eyes shall see your Teacher. And your ears shall hear a word behind you, saying, "This is the way, walk in it," when you turn to the right or when you turn to the left. (Isa. 30:20–21)

The language and most of the ideas in the text are different from the others we have dealt with; note especially that the rejection of idolatry is the only result of divine instruction which is mentioned. But this mysterious "teacher" is surely none other than God himself. Such a promise is made more explicitly in Isa. 54:13: "All your sons shall be taught by the LORD, and great shall be the prosperity of your sons."[60] Since "way" means "way of life," ethics, in the OT, these passages are reminiscent of Jer. 32:39–41, another of the "new heart" texts.

The other element that needs to be added to the promise of an intimate relationship with God is the assurance that in the future it will remain unbroken, as in Jer. 32:39–40: "that they may fear me for ever," and "I will make with them an everlasting covenant."[61] That assurance appears also in another passage referring to the covenant, the gift of the spirit and the internalization of the word of God, which shall not depart "from this time forth and for evermore" (Isa. 59:21).

The restoration to the kind of harmonious relationship with God which man and woman enjoyed in the Garden of Eden is thus longed for, but disobedience destroyed that relationship once, and so the other side of this promise contains the assurance that one day true obedience will be possible for human beings. This theme is almost confined to Ezekiel, so it will be alluded to in passing. In Ezek. 11:19–20 the result of the gift of one heart and a new spirit is "that they may walk in my statutes and keep my ordinances and obey them," and similar statements are made in Ezek. 36:26–27 and 37:23–24 (cf. Deut. 30:8).

If the spiritual effect of the re-creation of humanity is the knowledge of God, its emotional effect is rejoicing. This theme is especially prominent in the eschatological parts of Isaiah, but it appears elsewhere as well.

> Then shall the maidens rejoice in the dance,
> and the young men and the old shall be merry.
> I will turn their mourning into joy,
> I will comfort them, and give them gladness for sorrow.
> (Jer. 31:13)[62]

So Jeremiah describes life in the new community of God's people after the restoration. The entire chapter of Isaiah 35 resounds with singing and rejoicing as the exiles make their triumphal procession home.

In that procession will be people who had been lame—poor candidates for the long march—people who had been blind—unable to find their way—and deaf—unable to hear the good news—and dumb—unable to join the singing. But all that will have been changed and no one will be left out. This is a most dramatic promise, for physical defects were a serious problem to the Israelite mind for reasons that were discussed earlier. The association of illness with sin, which we saw to have been commonplace in the OT, is continued in the picture of Zion of the future in Isa. 33:17–24:

> Then prey and spoil in abundance will be divided;
> even the lame will take the prey.
> and no inhabitant will say, "I am sick";
> the people who dwell there will be forgiven their iniquity.
> (Isa. 33:23b–24)

The reference to the lame is probably not particularly important here, as it seems merely to be an extravagant way of saying that spoil will be available to anyone with virtually no effort (cf. 2 Sam. 5:6). The truly phenomenal promise is that there will be no illness in that city; a prospect worthy, one would think, of more than four Hebrew words. It is not developed, however, except for the succeeding line, which is very likely to be causally related, since the idea is so common in the OT. There is only one other eschatological text dealing with illness! Can it be, then, that the Israelite mind-set would deduce from each of the forgiveness and re-creation passages we have encountered that physical health would be a natural result of God's restoring activity which would not need to be mentioned explicitly? That can scarcely be stated as a firm conclusion, but is at least worth considering.

The other healing text may in fact be metaphorical rather than a reference to personal health, since Jerusalem is the subject. "Behold, I will bring to it health and healing, and I will heal them and reveal to them abundance of prosperity and security" (Jer. 33:6). Illness cannot be completely ruled out, but since it is not explicitly mentioned, the more natural interpretation seems to be to take healing as a metaphor for redemption and restoration.

We began these considerations of eschatological healing with a text that listed physical afflictions other than illness, however, and those disabilities do appear more often. Lameness is found in six passages, including Isa. 33:23, which we have just virtually dismissed. In each of the others, the lame are mentioned in connection with the Lord's gathering of the exiles for return to the promised land.

> Behold, I will bring them from the north country,
>   and gather them from the farthest parts of the earth,
> among them the blind and the lame,
>   the woman with child and her who is in travail, together;
>   a great company, they shall return here.
>
> (Jer. 31:8)

Healing of the blind and lame is not explicitly mentioned, for that is not really the point. Examples of those who might not be expected to make the journey have been chosen; clearly, then, the point is the completeness of the restoration. The power of God will make it possible for all to return, despite their condition (cf. Mic. 4:6–7; Zeph. 3:19). Only in Isaiah 35, then, is the actual healing of the lame described, but since it is in the context of the return from exile, we can see that it functions in essentially the same way, to celebrate God's ability to bring all his people home.

Not only will the lame man leap like a hart, according to Isa. 35:6, but the eyes of the blind will be opened, the ears of the deaf unstopped, and the tongue of the dumb sing for joy. In Isa. 29:18 the healing of the deaf and the blind is also promised: "In that day the deaf shall hear the words of a book, and out of their gloom and darkness the eyes of the blind shall see." Along with them the meek and the poor are mentioned. Giving of sight to the blind also appears in Isa. 42:7 and 16, and blindness and deafness are used in a different way in vv. 18–19 of the same chapter. Return from exile is certainly in the background of this chapter, but God's dealings with the afflicted are expressed in somewhat more general terms. These are all the references to the blind, lame, deaf, and dumb in eschatological texts. The conclusion seems inescapable that physical health in itself is not their principal concern. Their intent is to promise complete and unhindered participation to all in the good life of the community, no matter what their condition might be. Whether that requires full healing is not always said, except in Isa. 29:18; 35:5–6; and 42:7, but it is probably safe to assume that is implied in the other texts. What is made explicit, however, sheds light on one of the principal tragedies of the disabled—they tend to be left out of the mainstream of community life. Those who expressed those hopes for a better future in Israel understood that and affirmed their belief in a God who will not have anyone denied the opportunity to participate fully in the good life.

In one of the OT's most beautiful portraits of the new Jerusalem, Isa. 65:17–25, there appears a theme that is astonishingly rare in OT eschatology: long life.

> No more shall there be in it
> an infant that lives but a few days,
> or an old man who does not fill out his days,
> for the child shall die a hundred years old,
> and the sinner a hundred years old shall be accursed.
> (Isa. 65:20)

So reads the RSV, leaving us with the confusing picture of one-hundred-year-old sinners in the ideal city! Another understanding of the word *hote'* is possible, however. It comes from a root meaning "to miss," and although it does mean "sinner" in most of its occurrences, the context here calls for us to take it in its basic sense as "one who misses or does not reach." The NEB has read it that way, giving us a line that emphasizes the near-universality of the 100-year life span in the new city: "whoever falls short of a hundred shall be despised."[63] Eschatology has at this point accepted the traditional Israelite view of life and death: that death in itself is no great tragedy, to be puzzled over and protested, but is to be accepted as the normal conclusion of a long and fulfilled life. That acceptance was possible partly because of the belief that one's true character and vitality lived on in one's children.[64] To die at a good, old age surrounded by children and grandchildren, having lived an honorable life, now to be buried with one's ancestors in the family tomb, was the proper and fitting way to bring this sojourn on earth to an end, as ancient Israel saw it (Gen. 15:15; 35:29; Job 5:26). That traditional view was accepted by the prophet who produced Isaiah 65. The usual hope was to live seventy years, according to Ps. 90:10, and eighty was exceptional. In fact, forty was probably closer to the actual average life span, but the prophet has taken the hoped-for age of seventy and increased it to one hundred for everybody, so modest are his hopes.

The passage is all the more remarkable for two reasons: it is the only eschatological text in the OT which brings up the question of life span, and it was probably written at a time when serious questions had already begun to be raised about the adequacy of the traditional Israelite views of death. Death at an early age, or without children, or by violence, or under circumstances when one could not be properly buried had always been a problem, and by the latter part of the sixth century all too many had died under such circumstances.[65] The Babylonian conquest had shattered the solidarity of the community so that it had great difficulty in supporting the assurances the sense of "corporate personality" provided that death did not mean extinction. Jewish literature from the sixth century on begins to take up the subject of death as a problem. Job (chapter 14) considered whether hope for life after death might provide a solution for his dilemma, but concluded he couldn't count on it. Much later, Ecclesiastes also dismissed the possibility on the ground of lack of evidence (Eccl. 3:19–22; 6:6). These negative voices show, however, that new ideas were being considered, even though they seem not to have made much headway for generations. It probably had always been believed that God could raise the dead if he wished, for there are stories of resuscitations here and there in the OT (1 Kings 17:17–24; 2 Kings 4:19–37; 13:21), and the belief provides the background for Ezekiel's vision of the dry bones. Probably not until the second century B.C., however, did the Jews find it possible to move from that belief to the assertion that God did intend to resurrect all the dead to new life in the last days. There are some vague hints of another kind of eschatology in the stories of the "translations" of Enoch and Elijah to the presence of God (Gen. 5:21–24; 2 Kings 2:1–12), and in the psalmists' expressions of confidence that they will be "taken," in contrast to dying (Pss. 49:15; 73:24). But for most of the OT this life is enough. Little is said about the state of the dead. Sheol or the Pit is just a kind of universal grave, neither a place of reward or punishment, and everyone goes there.[66] In the many eschatological texts that we have studied so far, nothing has been said about life after death; the ideal future has been depicted as a transformation of this world and this life in order to remove all that is evil, and apparently death at a good, old age was not considered evil. This produces the strange result of making life after death—which is all some people mean by eschatology—a kind of appendix to the eschatology of the OT. It doesn't quite fit and the logic of most OT thought doesn't require it, but there are historical reasons here that transcend logic.

The breakdown of stable, traditional Jewish communities, from the time of the exile on, led to a more individualistic view of life and to the occasional raising of the question about what will happen to *me* when I die. Some examples of such questioning have just been noted, but the concern about personal destiny did not produce significant changes in the theology of Judaism until another factor was introduced by the persecution of faithful Jews under Antiochus IV Epiphanes in the middle of the second century B.C.: the question of God's justice. It occupies the minds of apocalyptic writers as one of their major concerns, and one of the main answers they gave to questions raised by injustice in this life was to affirm that there is another life, after death, when all will be made right. The death of martyrs under torture could not be dealt with adequately in terms of traditional OT eschatology; asserting that a better world was coming one day would not help those martyrs who would not participate in it, and would not right the injustice of their sufferings. The rise of individualism and the appearance of religious persecution thus called for a new eschatology that was not in full continuity with the hope that had sustained the Jews for centuries.

This long introduction to three short OT texts has been necessary both because they are unusual for the OT and because they introduce a subject of immense proportions in the subsequent literature. Twice within the so-called Isaiah apocalypse (Isaiah 24—27), the subject of death is treated in novel ways. In Isa. 25:6–8 we hear of an eschatological banquet on Mt. Zion to which all peoples are invited.[67] Removal of "the veil that is spread over all nations" probably refers to the veil of mourning, which fits with wiping away tears and removing the reproach of his people, and in the midst of these promises we are told, "He will swallow up death for ever." These words have been called an early gloss on the text, but those who so designate them agree that they are an appropriate interpretation of the original.[68] Mourning brought to an end because there is no more death! And no further comment on so stupendous a hope! There is not much more that an exegete can do with this except to agree that it is one piece of evidence for the relatively late dating of Isaiah 24—27, showing that these chapters were produced in a time when death was seen as a problem that God needed to overcome.[69]

The other text in the Isaiah apocalypse has also been called an interpolation by some scholars, and its context provides little if any help for its interpretation. The preceding verses speak of the distress and lamentation of the past. Then comes what Robert Martin-Achard calls a prayer, not an announcement of a certainty:

> Thy dead shall live, their bodies shall rise.
>   O dwellers in the dust, awake and sing for joy!
> For thy dew is a dew of light,
>   and on the land of the shades thou wilt let it fall.
>
> (Isa. 26:19)[70]

Here is a clear reference to the resurrection of the body. It is not universal resurrection, for it speaks of "thy dead," and nothing of judgment; just rejoicing at new life is mentioned. We have little help from the text for associating this hope with the mainstream of OT eschatology, except for its relationship to God's help for those in tribulation.

Finally, in the last chapter of the ultimate OT book to be written, there appears a more detailed reference to resurrection. Daniel's vision of the history of his people during the Ptolemaic and Seleucid periods (Daniel 11) has broken off suddenly with a prediction of the death of the archtyrant, whom we can identify as Antiochus Epiphanes (11:45). Then a new time of trouble, worse than ever before, is foreseen, perhaps following the pattern of Ezekiel 38—39, with a brief promise of the deliverance of "every one whose name shall be found written in the book" (Dan. 12:1). After that:

> And many of those who sleep in the dust of the earth shall awake, some to everlasting life, and some to shame and everlasting contempt.

This is clearly resurrection for the sake of justice. It may still not be a projection of universal resurrection, since it says "many," not all, for it is possible that the author considered God's justice to be made manifest in this life for most people, as the OT ordinarily affirms, and he may have anticipated resurrection only for those special cases such as the martyrs and their tormentors whose accounts still ought to be settled. "Those who are wise shall shine like the brightness of the firmament," Daniel continues, but nowhere in the OT are we given a hint of what those who first spoke of resurrection expected that new life to be like. Those speculations, as we must call them, will soon come, and in such confusing abundance that the OT's reticence to engage in them begins to seem more a virtue than a flaw.

The New Humanity in Post–Old Testament Eschatology

For two related reasons, the subject of life after death must be omitted here, contrary to my practice of providing indications of the subsequent history of OT traditions. The subject plays a small role in the OT and it is an immense and complex subject in later Judaism and Christianity. Just an outline of subsequent thought would be out of proportion to the few texts just discussed. The reader should consult the extensive literature that will serve as a guide to this much-studied subject.[71]

The *Book of Jubilees* does speak of an ideal period before death in which God will establish a community on earth very much like that which the OT promises, with an emphasis on obedience and fellowship with God (*Jub.* 1:24–25). Other books speak briefly of God abolishing sin and of universal righteousness in the days to come. For example, the *Life of Adam and Eve* says, "Heaven and earth, nights and days, and all creatures shall obey Him, and not overstep His commandment. Men shall not change their works, but they shall be changed from forsaking the law of the Lord."[72] Even in works that show the influence of apocalyptic thought, then, there occasionally appears a picture of a world filled with righteous people living in harmony with

God, without explicit reference to how such a picture is to be related to the teachings about resurrection which appear elsewhere. Eventually the rabbis distinguish two periods, the Messianic Age, a temporary period in which the world would be greatly improved but sin not completely abolished, and the World to Come, in which things would be entirely different.[73]

Jewish literature occasionally repeats the OT promises that a time will come when all will enjoy good health and freedom from infirmity. Among the gifts of the spirit which the Qumran community listed, some were physical: healing, length of days, and eternal joy in perpetual life (1QS IV.6–8). A rather full description of an earthly paradise that, among other things, explicitly removes the curses of Genesis 3 appears in *2 Apoc. Bar.* 73–74:

> And it will happen that after he has brought down everything which is in the world, and has sat down in eternal peace on the throne of the kingdom, then joy will be revealed, and rest will appear. And then health will descend in dew, and illness will vanish, and fear and tribulation and lamentation will pass away from among men, and joy will encompass the earth. And nobody will again die untimely, nor will any adversity take place suddenly. (*2 Apoc. Bar.* 73:1–3).

Women will no longer have pain in childbirth (73:7) and work will not lead to fatigue but will be marvelously productive (74:1); furthermore, Isaiah's promise of peace among the animals will be fulfilled (73:6). *Jubilees* also speaks of "blessing and healing," probably both physical and spiritual (*Jub.* 23:29–30).

Long life is also a promise that is repeated in several works without necessarily explaining how that is related to resurrection. For Jubilees it fits rather naturally, since some sort of immortality seems to be taught, instead of resurrection. Length of life is directly and causally connected with righteousness in the eschatological section of this book, and in the dark days to come, it is predicted, "a child of three weeks shall appear old like a man of one hundred years" (*Jub.* 23:25). Then the children will begin to study the law, and as they return to the path of righteousness their life span will increase, "till their days draw nigh to one thousand years . . . and there shall be no old man nor one who is [not] satisfied with his days, for all shall be (as) children and youths" (*Jub.* 23:27–28). *Jubilees* has thus improved on the OT by a factor of ten; when death does finally come, *Jubilees* is probably closer to the OT than to later Judaism in affirming a vague kind of life after death in a way that might remind us of Pss. 49:15 and 73:24 (more than an explicit teaching of an immortal soul, which is not so common in Judaism).[74]

> And their bones shall rest in the earth,
> And their spirits shall have much joy.
> (*Jub.* 23:31)

Another rather vague portrayal of a blessed future for individual believers, without specific reference to how it should be related to the rest of eschatological hopes, appears in *1 Enoch* 5:8–9 (cf. also 25:6; 58:3). There are many rabbinic texts that speak of rejoicing in the messianic kingdom, and Isa. 25:8 is cited in order to show that there will be no death in the days of Messiah,[75] but the OT ideas of an inner transformation of human beings do not seem to have been taken up by Judaism and developed beyond what the OT originally said.

Jesus made a clear distinction between his ministry and the familiar Jewish emphasis on striving toward righteousness when he said, "Those who are well have no need of a physician, but those who are sick; I came not to call the righteous, but sinners" (Mark 2:17). Illness is used metaphorically here, but the relationship between physical and spiritual healing, both in Jesus' ministry and in the subsequent teachings of the church, is emphasized again and again.[76] In each of the Synoptic Gospels this saying is preceded by the story of the healing of the paralytic, in which Jesus *compares* (but does not relate causally) sin and sickness. "Which is easier, to say to the paralytic, 'Your sins are forgiven,' or to say, 'Rise, take up your pallet and walk'?" (Mark 2:9). He then associates his power to forgive with his power to heal. When John the Baptist sent to inquire of Jesus, "Are you he who is to come, or shall we look for another?" the eschatological question of the day, Jesus identified himself by alluding to Isa. 35:5–6 and 61:1: ". . . the blind receive their sight and the lame walk, lepers are cleansed and the deaf hear, and the dead are raised up, and the poor have good news preached to them" (Matt. 11:5). These sayings explain the prominence of the healings in the Gospels; they are not just "wonders" but are signs that the day of salvation promised in the OT has begun to dawn. Furthermore, they reveal the Christian movement's selectivity with reference to the OT promises. Healing of body and soul is not the most prominent part of the eschatology that precedes the NT, as we have seen, but it is present, and the ministry of Jesus focuses on that as his commission. The church also took that to be its commission, as Adolf von Harnack has shown in "The Gospel of the Saviour and of Salvation":[77]

> Deliberately and consciously it assumed the form of "the religion of salvation or healing," or "the medicine of soul and body," and at the same time it recognized that one of its cardinal duties was to care assiduously for the sick in body.

Here we have encountered another example of the way the followers of Jesus believed themselves to be living in the time of fulfillment of OT promises concerning God's redemptive work in the last days. The healing of body and soul which they experienced was, of course, not perfect, and so the kind of tension produced by partial fulfillment which has been discussed earlier was also felt when physical infirmity and recurrent feelings of alienation from God had to be dealt with. Briefly, we may think of Paul's interpretation of illness at Corinth in connection with unworthy participation in the Lord's Supper (1 Cor. 11:27–32) and of his own thorn in the flesh (2 Cor. 12:7–10); of his discussion of the battle between the will and the flesh in Romans 7, and of his acknowledgment of the tension between attaining and continuing to strive in Phil. 3:7–16.

Harnack's comment about the self-understanding of the early church is a valuable reminder to us of the ethical imperative that is never missing from biblical eschatology. Despite the church's emphasis on inner, spiritual healing it did not miss the physical implications of its self-designation as a religion of healing: the care of the sick was a major part of its mission on earth.

Contemporary Manifestations

Uninterrupted fellowship with God is obviously a hope that will be found only among the religious, but where healing and life after death are concerned, there exist both secular and pseudo-religious types of hope. The purely secular attitude would make healing a matter for biological science alone, although the recognition of psychosomatic elements in health problems complicates that picture. The more common form of secularism would dismiss life after death altogether, but parapsychic research now seems to open the way for a non-religious consideration of the persistence of human identity. Certain healing groups, such as Christian Science, are considered by mainstream Christianity to be heretical, and many of the efforts to probe the mysteries of death, such as spiritualism and other forms of occult practices, are, from the Christian perspective, pseudo-religious at best. Their persistence is a clear indication, however, of the continuing human need for answers to questions that the OT began to deal with long ago. The inaccessibility of any experimental evidence about life after death (the so-called "life after life" phenomena deal only with dying, not with death), suggests that there may be considerable wisdom in the OT's reticence to say too much on that subject.

Another form of realized eschatology which has appeared since NT times, based on texts such as 1 John 3:9—"No one born of God commits sin; for God's nature abides in him, and he cannot sin because he is born of God"—is perfectionism, the belief that the eschatological gift of sinlessness is in fact available in this life as the "second blessing," after conversion. The most important forms of these "holiness" movements are outgrowths of the teachings of John Wesley, although they are not necessarily in agreement with his understanding of sanctification. They all represent a serious effort to realize the NT promise that God intends to create a new humanity free from the power of sin. To the more extreme forms of perfectionism I would respond that certain of our hopes must *remain* hopes, or they begin to distort our faith.[78]

CHAPTER 4

"HIGHEST OF ALL THE HILLS"

The Transformation of Nature

There is a tradition in the OT which recognizes the need for the redemption of the natural world, as well as individuals and their societies. It does not ascribe sin to any creature other than human beings, but acknowledges the presence of two kinds of evil in the non-human world. There is an element of threat to all that is stable and ordered (the "chaotic") which can be felt lurking just beyond the edges of the normally dependable world that God has created. Within the reasonably well-ordered and predictable scheme of everyday life, nature is also a problem to us. Crops fail and we go hungry. Floods and earthquakes destroy life and property. Wild animals endanger life and health. And the OT has made the bold theological move of introducing an ethical cause for what is (from the perspective of human life and health) wrong with nature. Human sin, it says, has inflicted a curse on the natural world so that it suffers because of our misdeeds, and because of our dependence on nature that curse rebounds upon us, making life in its divinely intended fullness impossible until the curse is removed. The eschatology of the OT says it is God's intention also to make things right in nature.

This chapter is divided into two parts. The first deals with changes that concern righting what is presently wrong with the natural world; the second with texts that speak of immense changes in the earth's topography and even in the heavenly bodies.

A New Ecology

One of the principal theological issues which concerns us throughout this chapter is anthropocentrism. Theology has generally taken that for granted when it has discussed the place of nature in the Bible, but in recent years the damage we have done to the world in the name of human progress has led theologians and others to challenge this human-centered view. Many have said the Bible is the source of the whole nature-threatening attitude, and they regret it, but others claim they have found an outlook within the OT which does not say the whole of creation was made for the sake of humanity and is therefore completely subject to the human will.[1] That issue will be discussed along the way, but I want to begin with it because one of the most frequent promises concerning nature has to do with fertility, and the reason for that is anthropocentric—so that people will never have to go hungry again.

The Natural World as the Setting for Human Life in the Old Testament Tradition

The Yahwistic account of beginnings in Genesis 2—3 establishes an intimate relationship between human beings and nature. It describes the world as being at first like a desert, without vegetation of any kind, and gives two reasons for its infertility: no rain and no farmers! The man that God creates very early in the story is thus not just the recipient of the good earth, but is a participant in making it what it is. God plants the garden, but puts the man into it to till it and keep it in order to make it fertile. He also shares in the creation of the animals by giving them their names.[2] But when sin is introduced into the world it affects not just the disobedient man and woman. The Yahwist thinks of an ecosystem that has an ethical component, so that just as a physical disturbance in one part of a system will affect all creatures that are ecologically related, so the consequences of sin will have their effects on the whole world of which human beings are a part. The curse that follows the sin of man and woman thus includes enmity between human beings and serpents and turns the fertile ground into a place that produces thorns and thistles, from which a precarious living can be obtained only by unremitting labor (Gen. 3:14–19). The world is now a hostile place; the OT seems to think of human sin as having introduced an "infection" that has corrupted it. The two enemies mentioned in Genesis 3, dangerous animals and infertile ground, are standard forms of threat and curse throughout the OT, and they always carry ethical overtones. In the series of curses and blessings in Leviticus 26 and Deuteronomy 28 there is a remedy for the infection—obedience.

> If you walk in my statutes and observe my commandments and do them, then I will give you your rains in their season, and the land shall yield its increase, . . . and I will remove evil beasts from the land. (Lev. 26:3–4, 6; cf. Deut. 28:4–5, 8, 11–12)

A part of the prayer for the righteous king, in Ps. 72:15–16, associates abundance of grain with his rule. Disobedience produced the opposite results (Lev. 26:19–20, 22; Deut. 28:23–24, 26). In the prophetic books a standard element of the description of disaster is the presence of wild animals (Isa. 18:6; Jer. 15:3; Ezek. 5:17; 14:21; 33:27; Hos. 2:12). The horror of the ruined city, once the center of civilization and security, is best expressed by describing it as now the home of wild creatures. The future of the great world capital, Babylon, is depicted this way in Isa. 13:21–22:

> But wild beasts will lie down there,
> and its houses will be full of howling creatures;
> there ostriches will dwell,
> and there satyrs will dance.
> Hyenas will cry in its towers,
> and jackals in the pleasant palaces;
> its time is close at hand
> and its days will not be prolonged.

Similar dire predictions may be found in Deut. 32:24; Isa. 23:13; 34:14; Jer. 50:39; and Zeph. 2:14–15. It is evident that wildlife was abundant in Palestine throughout the OT period and that unprotected people could easily find themselves in danger from predators (1 Sam. 17:37; 2 Kings 17:25–26). As for the land, their principal source of food, there were many hazards making the harvesting of a good crop uncertain.

The Israelites were meat-eaters, but their customs and traditions concerning diet reveal another aspect of their attitude toward nature. According to the Priestly account of creation in Genesis 1, all creatures were vegetarians at the beginning (Gen. 1:29–30). The Yahwistic account is not so specific, but implies the same thing in Gen. 2:9, and in neither passage is any place made for killing in God's good creation. There is evidence from elsewhere, including eschatological texts, to support the conclusion that this reflects a deep-seated attitude among Israelites concerning the taking of life. They did kill animals for food, of course, and expressed their belief in the right to do that in terms of the blessing of Noah after the flood: "Every moving thing that lives shall be food for you; and as I gave you the green plants, I give you everything. Only you shall not eat flesh with its life, that is its blood" (Gen. 9:3–4). The right to kill and eat meat has thus been given to them by God, but it is part of life in a fallen world, not of the world as God made it, and furthermore, it is not given without restrictions. Israel understood blood to be the life of the animal, and they acknowledged by the way they treated the blood that they possessed no arbitrary power over life itself.

Long before the detailed regulations for sacrifice now contained in Leviticus were put into practice, these restrictions on random killing were part of the Israelite outlook. Once when Saul proclaimed a day-long fast for his troops as they went into battle with the Philistines, their hunger at the end of the day led them to kill some of the animals taken as booty without regard for the blood (1 Sam. 14:31–35). Saul was appalled and immediately made provisions for a large stone to be used as an altar, that the animals might be killed in the proper way. Throughout the pre-exilic period it is probable that all killing of animals for food was sacrificial, performed at the local sanctuaries that could be found throughout the country, for in Deuteronomy, which proposes to restrict sacrifice to one central sanctuary, a provision is made for the non-sacrificial slaughtering of animals which seems to be unknown in other OT sources (Deut. 12:20–28).[3] It is important to observe, however, that even when killing is non-sacrificial, the blood must be treated in a special way (Deut. 12:23–24). No full explanation of these convictions about blood and life is ever offered in the OT, probably because for Israelites no explanation was needed; they all knew it. The most extensive passage dealing with the subject occurs in Lev. 17:10–14, which adds an explanation concerning the sacrificial use of the blood that is brought to the altar: "For the life of the flesh is in the blood; and I have given it for you upon the altar to make atonement for your souls; for it is the blood that makes atonement, by reason of the life" (Lev. 17:11).

This material has been assembled in order to explain the needs to which certain eschatological passages respond, needs that are not quite so transparent to us as most of the others have been. This evidence for Israel's deep-seated feelings about the taking of life will help us to understand the reasons for some of Israel's hopes concerning the natural world.

A note should be added on the anthropocentric character of Israel's attitude toward nature. There are occasional exceptions to the general assumption in the OT that the world was made for human use. At the end of the series of blessings and curses in Leviticus 26 there comes a long section dealing with the threat of exile. An unusual reason given for exile here, and never repeated elsewhere, is what we might call "the rights of the land" (Lev. 26:34–35, 43). Leviticus contains regulations for the observance of a sabbatical year in which Israelites were not to sow their fields, prune their vineyards, or reap what grew of its own accord (25:1–7). This was not explained as being for human benefit, as in modern times land has been left to lie fallow in order to build up its moisture content, but is simply said to be "a year of solemn rest for the land." The chapter tells us the sabbatical year had not been regularly observed, and the author of Leviticus 26 concludes that one reason for exile, removing people from the land, is, "Then the land shall enjoy its sabbaths as long as it lies desolate, while you are in your enemies' land; then the land shall rest and enjoy its sabbaths. As long as it lies desolate it shall have rest, the rest which it had not in your sabbaths when you dwelt upon it" (Lev. 26:34–35). The intimate relationship between humanity and nature which we first observed in the creation stories appears here also. People have certain responsibilities to the natural world, human sin can adversely affect nature, and we now see that not only may that produce negative effects on life in the normal course of things but that also Israel could even imagine God intervening on nature's behalf, in order to make things right.

The Transformation of Nature in Old Testament Eschatology

The promise of the renewal of fertility occurs frequently in the OT, but most of what needs to be said about it can be drawn from Ezekiel 36. At first the entire subject of the chapter seems to be the natural world, for the prophet addresses not individuals or nations but the mountains of Israel. As we read on, we discover that the real subject is the people of Israel after all, for the prophet has taken a highly original approach to the promise of restoration. God promises to even accounts with those who have left the land desolate, and to make things right for the land itself. As in Genesis 2, that involves having farmers till the soil, and so the promises of renewed fertility and the return of the exiles are interwoven (Ezek. 36:8–12). The rest of Ezekiel 36 contains an excellent example of the comprehensiveness of OT eschatology. Most of the themes we have been considering are present here, and they are not neatly sorted out, but are intimately interwoven. The following chart will illustrate the relationships of physical and spiritual, human and nonhuman:

Fertility and agriculture	8–9		11							29–30			34–35		
Return and occupation of land		10		12			24		28						
Cities		10										33			
No more reproach for land					13–15										
Israel's sin and basis for restoration						16–23									
Cleansing							25			29					
New heart and spirit								26–27							
Repentance											31–32				
Nations will know														36	
Population increase															37–38

The outline shows that the text is essentially a restoration passage, with the promise of renewed fertility as the recurring theme that gives it its special character. At the same time, the spiritual requirements for restoration hold a central position in the passage. Of course, the repetitions may be an indication of the reworking of an originally shorter prophecy, as most commentators have concluded, but once again we remind ourselves that it was not what Ezekiel originally said that has influenced the hopes of generations of believers, but this rather complex canonical form, no matter how it came into existence. What this passage taught post-exilic Judaism was that the re-establishment of a proper relationship between God and his people would include changes in nature, and the reason for these changes, despite the initial address to the mountains, is clearly anthropocentric. "I will summon the grain and make it abundant and lay no famine upon you" (Ezek. 36:29). The actual curse was worse than Gen. 3:17–19 had indicated; for in addition to "in toil shall you eat of it all the days of your life," there were times when there was nothing to eat.

The first example of the hope for a transformation of nature in the last days, then, is to make possible the continuation of human life without anxiety about having enough to eat. In another passage, expressive of the same hope, Amos indulges in a kind of hyperbole much loved by the rabbis in later times (9:13–14). The days are coming when the harvest will be so large that the work will not be finished before the next planting time. As in Ezekiel 36, there is no urban-rural conflict in this vision of the future; cities and gardens go together. Of the other promises of abundant fertility in the days to come,[4] only Ezekiel 34 has been chosen for further discussion here, and that is because it provides a transition to the next theme: peace in the animal world.

There is an intriguing mixture of metaphor and realistic language in Ezekiel 34, and one must be careful in determining which way to take each verse. The prophet depicts the restorative work of Yahweh in terms of the Near Eastern royal ideology, which spoke of the king as a shepherd who guided and cared for his people (Ezek. 34:11–12).[5] But 34:13 introduces realistic language: God promises to bring his sheep out from the peoples, gather them from the countries, and bring them into their own land. This is a literal description of the future of the exiles. But the restoration and accompanying judgment is described in fully metaphorical language in 34:14–22. The mixture of realism and symbol begins in earnest with 34:23. They will have a new shepherd, who is David. Now comes a "covenant of peace," which results in banishing wild beasts from the land so that they may "dwell securely in the wilderness and sleep in the woods" (34:25). The commentaries normally take these words as a literal promise of freedom from the threat of dangerous animals, but the association of nations with beasts in 34:28 shows that this may be read either literally or figuratively. Dwelling in the wilderness and sleeping in the woods sound like a continuation of the metaphor, but the promise of abundant fertility in 34:26–27 is obviously literal. The principal themes of the chapter—security from enemy nations and freedom from hunger because of God's blessing of nature—have been closely interwoven by means of the intermingling of metaphorical and realistic language.

Hosea also speaks of a covenant that involves the animals. Nature and politics are combined as they are in Ezekiel:

> And I will make for you a covenant on that day with the beasts of the field, the birds of the air, and the creeping things of the ground; and I will abolish the bow, the sword, and war from the land; and I will make you lie down in safety. (Hos. 2:18)

This covenant will reverse Hosea's use of the tradition sketched earlier, which threatened outbreaks of wild beasts as Yahweh's agents of judgment. In 2:12 he has said of Israel's vines and fig trees "the beasts of the field shall devour them," but that disharmony in nature brought about by Israel's sin will one day be healed, and the result will be this litany:

> And in that day, says the Lord,
> I will answer the heavens
> and they shall answer the earth;
> and the earth shall answer the grain, the wine, and the oil,
> and they shall answer Jezreel;
> and I will sow him for myself in the land.
> (Hos. 2:21–23a)[6]

How far does this expectation of peace in nature go? So far we have found nothing that could be called a new ecology; only a great improvement of things as they are now. However, the OT has more to say about the wild animals than the promise that they will no longer be a threat to people (Ezek. 34:25, 28; Hos. 2:18). Those passages do not speak of an ecological change, since there is no animal that lives exclusively on people. One famous text remains, however, together with a quotation of it in another place. This is Isa. 11:6–9, quoted in part in Isa. 65:25.

> The wolf shall dwell with the lamb,
> and the leopard shall lie down with the kid,
> and the calf and the lion and the fatling together,
> and a little child shall lead them.
> The cow and the bear shall feed;
> their young shall lie down together;
> and the lion shall eat straw like the ox.
> The sucking child shall play over the hole of the asp,
> and the weaned child shall put his hand on the adder's den.
> They shall not hurt or destroy in all my holy mountain;
> for the earth shall be full of the knowledge of the Lord
> as the waters cover the sea.

In Isaiah 11 this depiction of total peace in nature is connected with the coming of the righteous king (11:1–5). The connection was not an unnatural one for Israel, as the prayer for the king in Psalm 72 shows. In Isa. 65:25 the abbreviated citation forms an appropriate conclusion to a more comprehensive picture of the new world. It begins with the creation of new heavens and new earth, then moves to the new Jerusalem, in which everyone enjoys a long life span, in which houses, vineyards, fruitful work, and children are the key blessings. God will be there—"Before they call I will answer, while they are yet speaking I will hear"—and finally there will be peace in the animal world as well.

What are we to make of this? To what human need does it respond, or have we now come for the first time to mere speculative flights of fancy? Why should the digestive system of the lion be changed so that it can eat straw like an ox? What is wrong with animals being carnivorous? Is it not in fact an absolute necessity, and thus presumably part of God's good creation, for animals to prey on one another so as to keep populations in balance? Is not the whole idea wrong-headed? To the biologist and ecologist perhaps it is, and there is no good reason to take such a hope literally. Against the background of OT theology, however, one can at least understand the reasons for it.

Earlier we noted, in spite of all the killing reported in the OT, that Israelites felt a deep sense of uneasiness about the taking of life. The extreme precautions they took in the handling of blood were regular reminders to them that all life belongs to God. They were permitted to kill, in order to have meat to eat, and they were also commanded to kill, in war or in order to execute criminals, but in no case could life be taken in an arbitrary or random way without incurring a sense of having infringed on the privileges of God himself, who "kills and brings to life" (1 Sam. 2:6). This feeling seems to have reached its most extreme expression in the Isaiah passage, the key to which is 11:9a, "They shall not hurt or destroy in all my holy mountain." Problems such as what will become of the rabbit population if the coyotes all become vegetarians are of no interest to this prophet; what concerns him is violence of any kind, even in the animal world, for he cannot accept that as being a rightful part of God's good world, and so he dreams of a day when there will no longer be any need for any living thing to kill another. He does not get very far with his projected new ecology, and we know that no one could do that, but his principle may be worth thinking about again, as we shall do shortly.

Finally, one should notice the poetic reversal of the use of strange wild creatures to indicate the thoroughness of the judgment that will befall settled and civilized places in Isa. 43:20. This is an element of the prophet's description of Yahweh's transformation of the wilderness during the return of the exiles:

> The wild beasts will honor me,
> the jackals and the ostriches;
> for I give water in the wilderness,
> rivers in the desert.

They have joined the choir.

Nature in Post–Old Testament Eschatology

The OT promise of the abundant fruitfulness of the land in the days to come caught the fancy of later interpreters, and at this point we encounter a flowering of the imagination which becomes a bit hard to take seriously. The tendency already appears in one of the earlier works of the Pseudepigrapha, *1 Enoch* 10:18–19, which speaks of the planting of trees and vines, then promises that each measure of seed which is planted will yield a thousand, and each measure of olives will yield ten presses of oil. The *Sibylline Oracles* imagine new sources of food; honey will come from heaven and sweet fountains of white milk will burst forth (3:744–55; cf. 3:620–23). The latter may be a literal interpretation of the poetry of Joel, which speaks of mountains dripping sweet wine and hills flowing with milk (Joel 3:18). In *2 Apoc. Baruch* the story is improved by depicting a day when each vine will produce a thousand branches, each branch a thousand clusters, each cluster a thousand grapes, and each grape a cor of wine (about 364 liters; *2 Apoc. Bar.* 29:5). Furthermore, other miraculous sources of food are envisioned: Behemoth and Leviathan, the sea monsters, will become food for those who are left in that day (*2 Apoc. Bar.* 29:4), and the manna will once again descend from heaven (29:8).

Christian writers also developed the theme of the fertility of the land. Irenaeus quotes Papias as having told a similar marvelous story that he ascribed to Jesus. The vine is described in almost exactly the same way as in *2 Apoc. Baruch*, except for multiplying everything by ten, but in addition Papias said that a grain of wheat would produce ten thousand ears, each ear would have ten thousand grains, and every grain would yield ten pounds of flour. Furthermore, all fruit-bearing trees, seeds, and grass would produce in similar proportions, and all the animals would live peacefully with one another and be in perfect subjection to human beings.[7] Just after this, Irenaeus cites and comments briefly on Isa. 11:6–9 as additional evidence for the restoration of nature in the kingdom that is to come.

The complete absence of such predictions from the NT makes Papias' attribution of these promises to Jesus very dubious. Although the teachings of Jesus reflect the ministry of one who lived close to the land and made good use of his knowledge of agriculture, the NT as a whole strongly suggests that early Christianity was basically an urban religion. For the Christians at Corinth, meat came from the butcher shop, not from the flock (1 Cor. 10:25), and the same is likely to have been true for most other believers, since the strong interest the OT shows in the natural world is largely missing from the NT. Even the picture of the new Jerusalem in Revelation 21—22 omits the OT's interest in the food supply save for its reference to the tree of life with its twelve kinds of fruit, yielding its fruit each month (Rev. 22:2). It would seem that the most important NT allusion to this theme is one which makes the claim that Jesus is the fulfillment of eschatological hopes. Six times in the Gospels Jesus is said to have provided food miraculously for multitudes of people (Feeding the Five Thousand: Matt. 14:13–21; Mark 6:31–44; Luke 9:11–17; John 6:5–13. Feeding the Four Thousand: Matt. 15:32–38; Mark 8:1–9). These stories are clearly intended by the evangelists as messianic signs.[8] They do not quote or even allude to the texts with which we have been dealing, concerning abundance of food in the last days; instead they seem to depict Jesus as a new Moses, providing bread in the wilderness analogous to the heavenly manna. There is evidence in *2 Apoc. Baruch*, however, that by late in the first century A.D. the Jews expected the manna to appear once again in the last days.

The rabbis seem to have used their ingenuity to elaborate every detail of the OT promises of an abundant food supply in the messianic age.[9] Only a few examples will be provided here (based on Joseph Klausner's survey). Wheat will grow as tall as a palm tree and its grains will be as large as the kidneys of a big bull. When it ripens, the wind will rub the grains together, milling fine flour that will fall to the ground where what one needs can be gathered. One grape will be brought on a wagon or a ship to one's house, put into a corner, and its contents used as if it had been a large wine cask. Grain will yield every month and trees every other month, according to some rabbis; others said trees would also bear fruit every month.[10] All this is entertaining enough, but it seems to be far removed from the modest—and essential—promise of the OT that one day hunger will be abolished.

The OT theme of peace in nature is reiterated occasionally in the later literature, but one has the impression that it does not reflect any strongly felt need. The third *Sibylline Oracle* paraphrases Isa. 11:6–8 in lines 788–95, as part of its description of the new world which also includes an abundant food supply. Once again *2 Apoc. Baruch* improves on the older tradition, although in this case it only devotes two lines to the subject: "And the wild beasts will come from the wood and serve men, and the asps and dragons will come out of their holes to subject themselves to a child" (*2 Apoc. Bar.* 73:6).

The rabbis also quoted Isa. 11:6–9 in their discussions of the messianic age, but added little to it. They attributed the dangerous character of animals to the fall of Adam and predicted that they would be restored to their original state in the last days. Some said that all but the serpent would be restored, since Gen. 3:14 says, "cursed are you above all cattle, and above all wild animals." Others said that wild animals would be removed from the world, quoting Lev. 26:6: "I will remove evil beasts from the land."[11] The evidence provided by the Jewish literature suggests no deep theological concern for the redemption of nature; the theme does not seem to be developed and applied, it is just quoted and amplified.

In contrast to the Jewish literature, the NT does not quote these texts but shows some evidence for concern about redemption on a cosmic scale which is related to OT eschatology and moves beyond it. We bypass the cosmic phenomena of Revelation for the moment and look at two well-known Pauline texts. An apparent reference to the curse on nature, the result of the sin of Adam, appears in Rom. 8:19–23: "for the creation was subjected to futility, not of its own will but by the will of him who subjected it in hope" (Rom. 8:20). This appears in the context of Paul's promise that creation itself will one day "obtain the glorious liberty of the children of God" (8:21b).[12] Although it is less obvious, Col. 1:15–20 also contains a similar breadth of concern. As in the first chapter of John, the Son of God is here connected with creation itself. Whereas John moves from creation to incarnation, this passage moves to the resurrection and its implications. "For in him all the fulness of God was pleased to dwell, and through him to reconcile to himself all things, whether on earth or in heaven, making peace by the blood of his cross" (Col. 1:19–20). There is no explicit eschatology here as in Romans 8, but both these texts speak of redemption on a scale that includes the whole natural world as well as human beings.[13]

To express those grand thoughts in more specific terms of a hope for nature which would be recognized by Christians as a response to a felt need has not been easy. For the most part, Christians have viewed the natural world as the stage on which redemption history is acted out, and as a repository of resources to be used at will.[14] Recently the Christian faith has been accused of providing the theological and philosophical justification for the human destruction of the environment.[15] Although that is based on a superficial reading of history, it has reminded us of the frequent Christian failure to take nature seriously.[16] St. Francis of Assisi has been held up as the exponent of an alternative tradition in Christianity, one that honors and respects nature as being also beloved of God; there are also other voices in our past which have taken these biblical themes more seriously.[17] As we turn to the present, however, we find that the serious treatment of this aspect of eschatology has scarcely begun.

Contemporary Manifestations

Among the sparse modern literature on this subject is Antonine De Guglielmo's article on "The Fertility of the Land in the Messianic Prophecies." It includes a summary of what scholarship has done with the material benefits promised in messianic prophecies.[18] He reports three types of interpretation:

1. The material benefits are a secondary and transient element in these prophecies. A necessary expedient to confidence in the hearts of the Israelites, they no longer had any reason for existence once the pedagogic purpose was achieved.

2. They are a secondary and conditional element, depending for their fulfillment on the faithfulness of the people.
3. They are but figures of spiritual benefits.

Otto Kaiser bluntly says the modern reader "is unable to look forward, like the Old Testament, to a time in which lions eat grass, because of his knowledge of natural history. He believes that there was conflict in the animal world at the very beginning, before there were men."[19] However, Kaiser comments about Isa. 11:6–9:

> It is not sufficient to turn the entire final stanza into a metaphor for peace among the nations. But it can serve as a metaphor for the statement that in the future which God is preparing for his creation, everything will be transformed, and that there will no longer be distress and weeping in it. . . . This hope is never valid merely for the soul of the individual, or for the renewal of the individual in another form, but is always true of the world as well.[20]

This cautious statement exceeds what other commentators have been willing to affirm about the meaning of such passages.

Until environmentalists began to speak, it seemed adequate just to reaffirm these texts without interpretation, or to call them symbolic—reinterpreting them—or to call them mythological—dismissing them—or to make no comment on them whatever. Those who speak for environmental concerns, however, have been using language that sometimes carries apocalyptic overtones. Without often using theological terms, they have, for all practical purposes, been saying that human sin has brought a curse on the natural world, that human well-being and the well-being of nature are intimately and inextricably related, and that the environment needs a "redemption" of some kind which will necessitate a radical change in human attitudes and behavior.[21] Theologians have not failed to hear that new analysis of the human situation as an integral part of world ecology and have recognized the affinities, present or potential, that such a point of view may have with the biblical faith. Some beginnings have been made with reference to creation theology, but as yet almost nothing has been done with the eschatological aspect of the Bible's theology of nature.[22]

At this point it is appropriate to offer some suggestions about the ethical imperatives that lie behind the OT affirmations of hope for peace in nature, as a way of indicating the potential value of these texts for our time. The interpretation of Isa. 11:6–9 which has been offered, with its portrayal of animals living together in harmony set against the background of concern about killing of any kind which appears elsewhere in the OT, shows that the concluding verse, "They shall not hurt or destroy in all my holy mountain," identifies the human need to which this text responds. We probably cannot even imagine a totally new ecology in which no hurting or destroying will ever occur, but as we ponder the thought, many of us may realize that it is, in fact, something we need. Our acknowledgment of that need and expression of that hope must then surely influence what we do about all hurting and destroying in the present. We need, as always, to be reminded that we will not create the new world by all becoming vegetarians, for example, but the OT witness does call our serious attention to animal as well as human pain. So far, little enough has been done about the latter, and the former is scarcely ever considered.[23]

The issue of anthropocentrism, also raised in recent discussions of environmental concerns, will need to be dealt with in a thorough and responsible way in the future. The OT does for the most part subordinate all of nature to human needs, but its eschatological texts, especially, remind us that in God's sight nature also has some rights.[24] It is doubtful that the biblical witness could ever be invoked to allow concern for the pain of nature to prevail over concern for human pain, but if its vision of the future is taken seriously as the key to what God wants, then any arbitrary or irresponsible hurting or destroying of anything in this world must surely be judged as contrary to what God is doing. Christian theology has taken passages such as "fill the earth and subdue it, and have dominion . . ." (Gen. 1:28) legalistically. Thus far, it has failed to be instructed adequately by the OT hope for a right relationship between human beings and the world in which they live.

New Heavens and New Earth

Although the first three chapters of the Bible suggest that all creation has been put under human influence (Gen. 1:28; 3:17), there is evidence that Israel sensed itself to be confronted at times by another aspect of nature—"the chaotic." That appears with clarity in the story of the flood (Genesis 6—8). As recent scholarship has shown, the flood story is the classical expression of the deep-seated human uneasiness that all that is orderly and dependable may some day break down, that chaos may still be lurking around the edges as a threat not yet finally eradicated.[25] The theology of the OT would not permit such a feeling to remain untouched by its insistence on the universality of Yahweh, however, and so the flood is not depicted as any threat to his sovereignty; it is sent by him for ethical reasons. Even so, the flood has a special quality, reflecting a different aspect of human existence from any discussed heretofore, which it shares with other elements of nature that are in no way subject to human manipulation.

Here I will be concerned with the inanimate parts of creation. Certainly the sea and the wilderness, two of the realms that need to be examined as background for the promises of the transformation of heaven and earth, are richly inhabited by animal life, but the role they ordinarily play in OT tradition is that of dangerous places, threats to human life. The other type of tradition concerns natural phenomena of heaven and earth which disrupt or threaten the normal course of life; storms, earthquakes, and perhaps volcanic eruptions.

Nature Beyond the Bounds

The classic example of the threat of chaos, the uncontrolled upsurging of torrents of water, is a common theme in the OT, usually with reference to the sea itself, but it is rare in the eschatological texts.[26] A brief survey of the theme is in order here, however, since it reappears with more prominence in apocalyptic, and the OT is clearly its origin. One of Israel's most striking ways of praising the Creator God was to exalt his victory over the waters. One support for our interpretation of the flood as an expression of a deep-seated human fear is the appearance of echoes of Near Eastern mythology in connection with the sea, more prominently than any other reflections of myth in the OT. While the chaotic quality of the deep is still indicated in Genesis 1, that chapter has otherwise thoroughly demythologized creation; God brings order simply by speaking.[27] But a more accurate reflection of the emotional connotations of creation faith is to be found in the poetic material, reminiscent of myth, which speaks of God's victory over the sea, of locking it up within boundaries that it surges against, indeed which personifies the sea as a monster, Leviathan or Rahab.[28] Israel thought of the sea as a place of great danger, as the description of the sailor's plight in Ps. 107:23–29 shows, but their creation faith affirmed it to be a danger that Yahweh had overcome for them. God's promise, in the covenant made with Noah, was thus a promise concerning the preservation of an orderly and stable world, when he said, "Never again shall all flesh be cut off by the waters of a flood, and never again shall there be a flood to destroy the earth" (Gen. 9:11, 15). The theme of victory over the sea was also historified, and elements from creation theology are associated with the crossing of the Reed Sea in Isa. 50:2; 51:10; and Ps. 66:6, and with the crossing of the Jordan in Ps. 114:3, 5.[29]

That victory at the very beginning of things and the assurance of God's continuing control of the unruly waters seem to have been reaffirmed with enough confidence in Israel that the expression of hope for some final conquest of the powers of chaos scarcely appears in the OT. It is one of the clear signs of the triumph of practical monotheism in the literature that is preserved in the canon that the existence of any real threat to the rule of God other than human sin has been so thoroughly submerged. But in the apocalyptic strain of hope, the power of evil is much more strongly emphasized than is typical for the OT. As we shall see there are a few early indications of how the sea began to be *re*-mythologized.

The wilderness was very close to the settled land where the Israelites lived, and was well known to them. Once the central ridge running from the Esdraelon Valley south to the Negev is crossed, in an easterly direction, one very quickly enters a forbidding desert that leads down to the Jordan Valley and the Dead Sea. The wilderness is visible from every high point along that ridge, and Israel's delight in the fertility of Canaan and thanksgiving for the gift of that land were heightened by the near presence of that other kind of place, where life was precarious and sometimes impossible. Hence, one of the most frightening threats that could be uttered against Israel was the prospect of having their land turned into a wilderness (Isa. 6:11; Jer. 9:10–11; Hos. 2:12, etc.). And the blossoming of the wilderness which is promised in eschatological texts seems to involve something more than promises of abundant fertility for land that already supports settled populations; hence the treatment of the theme in this section.[30]

The most violent and terrifying of natural phenomena were used by Israel to provide language to describe or designate *theophany*—the personal and immediate appearance of God to his people.[31] The classic example of theophany is the Sinai experience, which involved thunder, lightning, cloud, a loud trumpet blast, smoke, fire, and earthquakes (Exod. 19:16–20). Many scholars have deduced from this that the actual experience from which the Sinai tradition developed was the eruption of a volcano, but other theophanies such as the one in Ps. 18:7–15 sound more like descriptions of a violent storm. An alternative suggestion is that no specific natural event was associated with these accounts of the coming of God in power, but that the effort to find a way to express their feelings at being confronted by the *tremendum* of the Holy One led naturally to the use of language about the most awe-inspiring manifestations of power they had ever experienced.[32] In addition to the examples just cited, Pss. 50:3; 68:7–8, 32–33; 77:16–20; and Hab. 3:3–15 may also be noted, and it will be seen that these are songs of lament or thanksgiving in which God is depicted as coming in power to save. Earthquakes and thunderstorms are well known in Palestine and there has been volcanic activity within historic times in the Transjordan and in Midian,[33] but the tendency of all theophanic language to transcend the mere description of natural phenomena may be seen in Joel 2:30–31, which combines blood with fire and columns of smoke and speaks of the moon being turned to blood. It seems best to take all of this as evocative language rather than something based on the original identity of Yahweh as a volcanic God or a storm God, and the intent of the theophanies ought to be understood as the choice of language that will come as close as possible to the reproduction of the feelings produced by the impression of the immediate presence of God. The most terrifying of all the impressions (not descriptions) of the *tremendum* side of holiness appear in two passages that speak of the virtual dissolution of the natural world, but in ways that cannot be connected with any known type of natural disaster. Jeremiah records a vision of an apparent return to chaos which does not make use of the familiar flood imagery, in Jer. 4:23–

26, and adds to it a judgment oracle (4:27–31) that depicts a virtually complete desolation of nature. It is reminiscent of a more lengthy passage in Isa. 2:12–19, which describes the day of the Lord of hosts "against all that is proud and lofty," The use of words meaning "high" to designate pride in Hebrew is taken literally here, in a text that speaks of the complete leveling of everything lofty—the cedars of Lebanon, mountains, towers, and walls—while the people who are left on that denuded earth will seek refuge beneath its surface, in caves and holes in the ground. No natural force that could produce such a result is mentioned at all; the agent of all this destruction is "the glory of his majesty, when he rises to terrify the earth" (Isa. 2:19).[34]

The original use of theophanic language to describe the awesome power of God who comes from Sinai to save his people, as in Habakkuk 3, has thus been converted by the prophets into a picture of thoroughgoing judgment that may even involve God's destruction of the world he created. These scenes are preliminary to eschatology proper, as we have been using the word, but they are taken up and used with enthusiasm by the later apocalyptic writers as a part of their depiction of the last days, and they are clearly the background for some of the OT's depictions of the ideal future.

The darkening of sun and moon, or darkness in general, appears frequently in prophetic judgment texts, reminding us again of the close association between Yahweh and light, from the creation story onward. Since the sun and moon were worshiped in virtually every culture of the ancient Near East, it was probably for polemical reasons that Genesis 1 separates the creation of light, on the first day, from that of the heavenly bodies, on the fourth day,[35] and that independent relationship between Yahweh and light is also asserted in several of the eschatological passages of the OT. Light proved to be one of the most useful symbols for God, as the NT also reveals, and this makes the threat of the removal of light by God himself an especially potent one. Light is associated with life and darkness with death (Job 18:17–19; 22:10–11); light represents good and darkness evil (Job 24:13–17); light is used to symbolize divine guidance in a variety of ways (Exod. 13:21; Ps. 119:105); it is appropriately linked with gladness, joy, and honor in Esth. 8:16; and there is abundant evidence that it could represent the presence of God himself on earth. As in the creation story, then, the sun and moon may be treated in rather arbitrary ways by Yahweh their maker, since he is the true Light. In times of judgment their light may be extinguished as a sign of the withdrawal of the light of God, and their non-essential nature in some of the depictions of the new heaven can best be understood against this background of the theological potency of light as a symbol of God.

A few words about heaven need to be added before the eschatological texts themselves are examined. In the later apocalyptic books heaven is a subject of great importance,[36] but nothing of this kind of speculation appears in the

OT. Heaven is often just the sky, so that when coupled with earth the pair refers to all the created world, the Hebrew equivalent to cosmos (as in Gen. 1:1). But it is also used theologically to denote the place where God is. The OT could assert that no place, even heaven, was sufficient to contain God, as in 1 Kings 8:27, so that he might be encountered anywhere, but just as his holiness was felt to be manifested more directly at certain times and places on earth, so heaven was more directly associated with God than earth was. The title God of Heaven became very common in the post-exilic period (Gen. 24:7; 2 Chron. 36:23; Ezra 1:2; Neh. 1:4, 5; 2:4, 20; Jonah 1:9), and in poetry he is said to sit in the heavens and look down from heaven (Pss. 2:4; 11:4; 14:2; 33:13; 53:2; Isa. 66:1; cf. Exod. 20:22). He had a "heavenly host" around him there (1 Kings 22:19; cf. Job 1), but heaven was normally no place for human beings. Indeed, the human desire to ascend into the heavens was considered to be *hybris,* the aim to make oneself a rival to God himself, according to Isa. 14:12–15.[37] The only human being who is explicitly said to have been taken up into heaven in the OT is Elijah (2 Kings 2:1, 11).

Heaven thus plays a minor role in OT eschatology compared with its prominence later on. It is really not used in its theological sense—as the place where God is—but appears only in its physical sense as a part of the cosmos, where sun, moon, and stars are to be found, and when coupled with earth, heaven forms a term denoting all creation.

The New Creation

Although the promise "I create new heavens and a new earth" first appears in the OT in Isa. 65:17; 66:22, its occurrence does not signal the appearance of an intense interest in cosmology in the OT period. A few strikingly novel pictures of heaven and earth do occur, but in no large number. When their purpose is determined it can be seen that speculation about radical changes in the natural world was subordinated to other interests. We can in fact organize the material with reference to two places—the wilderness and Zion—which already suggests the new creation's relationship to other eschatological themes.

The transformation of the wilderness was not an important expectation in its own right, but it became an appropriate accompaniment to the announcement of a triumphant return of exiles to their homeland and to the glorification of Zion. The classic example is Isaiah 35, which deals throughout with "the way home." The wilderness is virtually personified, since the event celebrated is so great that all nature must join in. It will be glad and rejoice with joy and singing (Isa. 35:1–2). Literally (or is any of it literal?) this means the desert will blossom and become covered with vegetation like Lebanon, Carmel, and Sharon. The dry land will become a place of abundant water, with streams and pools to emphasize the radical nature of the change (35:6b–7).

This sounds like another example of the promise of fertility in the last days, but it is not the same. No settlement in this suddenly fertile desert is mentioned. In the texts dealt with earlier the re-establishment of cities always goes along with the abundance of the earth's produce, but this land seems to remain empty, a pleasant corridor through which the exiles walk with the greatest of ease. The topography will be changed in order to make comfortable travel possible—"and a highway shall be there"—and the journey will be safe—"No lion shall be there, nor shall any ravenous beast come up on it; they shall not be found there, but the redeemed shall walk there" (35:8–9). As we have seen earlier, any personal, physical disabilities that might make the trip difficult will also be removed (35:5–6), so the chapter subordinates every element to a single theme, the return of exiles to Zion, and elevates that theme to such importance that creation itself is affected; nature is a factor in the return.

Similar ideas appear in 2 Isaiah (Isa. 40:3–4; 41:18–19; 42:16; 55:13). Except for the olive, the trees that are mentioned are not those that are cultivated for the production of food. Redemption brings life to places of death, even when they are not explicitly described as places for future habitation. These brief associations of nature with the transformation of people and society may also be observed elsewhere (Isa. 29:17–21). In Isa. 32:14–20 appears what may be the only anti-urban eschatology in the OT, if v. 19 is taken to mean cities in general. Some commentators think it is a vague reference to an oppressor, such as Nineveh or Babylon, in which case the text stands in no contrast with others dealing with nature.[38] The gift of the spirit has a double function that seems strange from our perspective, although the OT background that has been sketched in this chapter shows it is not strange to Israelite thinking. The outpouring of the spirit will make the wilderness a fruitful field and the fruitful field will be deemed a forest, presumably meaning the trees of its orchards will be as many as those of a forest.[39]

> Then justice will dwell in the wilderness,
>   and righteousness abide in the fruitful field.
> And the effect of righteousness will be peace,
>   and the result of righteousness, quietness and trust for ever.
> (Isa. 32:16–17)

In a straightforward way the OT depicts the wholeness of God's expected work of redemption; justice and good crops are both the work of the spirit.

A special relationship between the wilderness and Zion is described in Ezek. 47:1–12, a good transitional passage between those two foci of promises concerning terrestrial change. In a vision the prophet was conducted on a tour of a new temple in Jerusalem, noting the details of its plan and being instructed in the cult that was to be observed there (Ezek. 40—46). Near the end of that vision he saw a stream of water flowing from below the threshold of the temple, past the altar on its south side, and out the south side of the eastern gate. His guide informed him that it flowed into the Arabah (the depression where the Dead Sea is located), and he was shown that the stream got deeper as it went, becoming a large river. The water itself had supernatural qualities; along the banks of the river grew trees that were in leaf year round, bearing edible fruit every month, and their leaves had healing properties. When this water reached the Dead Sea, the salty water of that place became fresh and was filled with an abundance of fish. A stupendous change, of one of the most barren spots on the face of the earth to a virtual Eden! But this transformation of wilderness differs in many respects from those discussed previously. It is not the accompaniment of return from exile, but a part of the glorification of Zion. It is water that comes from the temple which brings the wilderness to life; Zion is the source of life for the natural world as well as for human beings. And the bringing of fruitfulness to the Dead Sea is specifically for the benefit of that human community that has Zion as its center, providing those things that are not emphasized in other wilderness passages: fruit, healing, and fish. If there is any question about the anthropocentric nature of the vision, the matter of salt answers it. The Dead Sea did have one use, after all; it was a source of salt, and the question of what the freshening of its waters would do to the supply of that important commodity was answered by the assurance that in the marshes of the sea, salt would still be found (Ezek. 47:11).

A different emphasis appears in Ezekiel 47, and it brings us back to the beginning of our study, to the centrality of Zion in God's redeeming work and the conviction that God's life-giving power will one day flow outward from that place, transforming even the desert into the place of abundant life.[40] Other, dramatic changes in the natural world will be experienced by those who live in Zion that day. In the discussion of Isa. 4:5–6 (see chap. 1 of this book) the meaning of the canopy and pavilion, associated with cloud and smoke and fire, over the whole site of Mt. Zion was considered. The appearance of theophanic language is to be noted, but now its relationships to storm and destruction are reversed. The message of the text is one of protection for Zion from the violence of nature: "It will be for a shade by day from the heat, and for a refuge and a shelter from the storm and rain" (Isa. 4:6).

Elsewhere it is the true relationship between sun and moon and the light of God which becomes manifest over Zion. The proto-apocalyptic text, Isa. 24:21–23, speaks of victory on a cosmic scale, the defeat of both the host of heaven (which in the OT is normally on God's side) and the kings of the earth. Here the enemies of God are to be found in both spiritual and earthly realms, as in later apocalyptic, and when vanquished they are committed to "prison," perhaps a prefiguration of the hell of later works. "Then the moon will be confounded, and the sun ashamed; for the Lord of hosts will reign on Mount Zion and in Jerusalem and before his elders he will manifest his glory." Why this downgrading of the sun and moon? Are they among the enemies of God? Probably not, for other texts will suggest that "he will manifest his glory" is the key to understanding this verse. "Glory" often means physical light, in the Bible, in addition to its other meaning of "honor," and it is light that is the subject of two passages that appear to be related to this one.[41]

Several promises have converged within a few verses in Isa. 30:19–26: the abolition of mourning, the presence of "the teacher," rain and abundant food; then it is said that the moon will be as bright as the sun and the sun will be seven times as bright as usual. We can be thankful that this promise has never been literally fulfilled, since it would mean the end of all life on earth, but taken alongside Isa. 24:23 it shows that sun and moon were not regularly thought of as enemies that God would have to deal with in the last days. Light is undoubtedly used in its symbolic sense here; the author surely puts to one side the increased heat that would go with it and uses it simply to represent life and goodness.

In Isaiah 60 light on Mt. Zion forms the introduction and conclusion to the chapter. As the place where God is to be found, Zion will become a source of light for the whole world (60:1–3). These introductory verses are clear enough, and they must be kept in mind lest one be led astray by the conclusion (vv. 19–20):

> Your sun shall no more go down,
> nor your moon withdraw itself;
> for the Lord will be your everlasting light,
> and your days of mourning shall be ended.
> (Isa. 60:20)

Here is a promise of perpetual light, something for which one could scarcely feel any literal need. The replacing of sun and moon by the light of God reminds one of a return to days two and three of creation, when there was light but no heavenly bodies, and another recollection is perhaps even more startling, for God's promise to Noah was, "While earth remains . . . day and night shall not cease" (Gen. 8:22). But Isaiah 60 does not appear to contemplate an end of the world in that sense. It is surely speaking of light in a purely symbolic sense, as the manifestation of the presence of God and all his benefits in Zion. Sun and moon, physical light, have nothing to do with "days of mourning" (Isa. 60:20c) or righteousness (60:21a), but the divine presence or absence does. Hence we see that changes in nature, in their own right, are of little interest to OT writers. Typically they use elements from nature to make affirmations about God. There is no indication of any literal hope for changes involving the sun and moon; they appear in these passages because they are sources of light, and light is one of the Bible's most potent symbols for God.

A fitting conclusion to this section is provided by Zechariah 14. It reintroduces several elements that had appeared in earlier texts, using Zion as the unifying factor for all of them. The chapter begins with a reminiscence of Ezekiel 38—39, the great invasion of the holy land, but with a difference. Jerusalem will fall and half its population will go into exile, hence a more exact future parallel to past history is contemplated than we find in Ezekiel. Additional references to the Gog chapters will appear in Zech. 14:12–15, which describe the aftermath of God's victory, but before that a whole series of dramatic physical changes is presented as the result of the appearance of the Lord to do battle with the nations. This late passage is not afraid of anthropomorphism; when the Lord's feet touch the Mount of Olives it will be split in two, creating a valley through it from east to west. This would appear to have the practical effect of permitting Ezekiel's marvelous stream, which reappears in Zech. 14:8, to flow straight east into the Dead Sea. The prophet also adds to Ezekiel by having the waters flow both east and west from Zion, but he does not tell us what the stream is for! The weather will be better; on that day there shall be neither cold nor frost (if the difficult text of Zech. 14:6 has been read correctly), and Isaiah 60 is apparently cited in the promise of continuous day—but no clue is given here as to why that should be desired. The promise of Isa. 2:2, that the mountain of the house of the Lord will be the highest of the mountains, is taken literally and explained by predicting that all Palestine will be leveled off into a plain, leaving Jerusalem as the only city on a mountain (Zech. 14:10–11). Finally the eschatological pilgrimage of the nations to Zion appears combined with the emphasis on the holiness of Jerusalem, which also concludes the Books of Ezekiel and Joel. The real subject of the chapter, then, is Zion and not nature, for the prophet just seems to have collected a whole group of traditions which glorify that place, with some tendency to choose the more sensational of them, and to combine them rather haphazardly without having much to say about the meaning of the changes in the natural world. They simply reflect the power of God and the supernatural character of Jerusalem.[42]

A note also must be added concerning the sea, which appears only briefly in OT eschatology. In Isa. 27:1, the defeat of Leviathan, which is usually celebrated as belonging to God's work at creation, is projected to the future with the introductory formula "In that day." This is another of the indications of the relationship between Isaiah 24—27 and later apocalyptic. In Daniel 7 the apocalyptic use of the sea as the chaotic source of evil forces appears with clarity. "Behold, the four winds of heaven were stirring up the great sea. And four great beasts came up out of the sea, different from one another" (Dan. 7:2–3). The old threat, kept under control so well by most of the literature of the OT, reappears in apocalyptic, no doubt just because water itself is so effective a symbol of the formless and uncontrollable in nature.

Nature *in itself* thus may be said not to be a subject of great importance in the OT. When the outlook is not anthropocentric, concerned about human needs, it is theocentric, using nature as symbolic of the power and presence of God. This does not mean, however, that nature can be omitted from a serious consideration of the present or the future, for the OT does not imagine the redemption of humanity apart from a correspondingly redeemed world.

The New Heaven and New Earth in Post–Old Testament Eschatology

The mind of the apocalyptic writer ranged over the entire cosmos, exploring the hidden parts of the earth (*1 Enoch* 28—36), including the lost Garden of Eden itself, viewing the dark valleys where the wicked are punished (*1 Enoch* 53—54), and traversing the various levels of heaven. The few OT references to universal changes in the last day thus became a natural part of the efforts of apocalyptic to provide a comprehensive understanding of all history and of the entire cosmos, including realms both physical and spiritual.[43] Some of these books have concluded that before the new heaven and earth can appear, the old must be destroyed (although this is not a unanimous opinion). Fire is the favorite agent of destruction, although others are also mentioned.[44] The promise of a new creation was thus taken seriously in apocalyptic literature, but not, it would appear, because of any special interest in the natural world in its own right. References to the renewal of heaven and earth tend to be brief and without elaboration of details, as may be seen in the typical examples in *Jub.* 1:29; *1 Enoch* 45:4–5; 91:16–17; and *2 Apoc. Bar.* 32:6 (cf. 2 Pet. 3:12–13).

The symbolic value of light is used extensively in the visions reported in these books (e.g., *T. Levi* 18; *2 Enoch* 22:1), and some of the OT promises are repeated, as in *1 Enoch* 58:1–6; 91:16; and *2 Enoch* 65:9–11. *Jubilees* is somewhat creative in its combination of three elements; the renewal of heaven and earth, the establishment of the sanctuary of the Lord in Jerusalem, and the renewal of "all the luminaries . . . for healing and for peace and for blessing for all the elect of Israel" (*Jub.* 1:29).

Light becomes a very important symbol in the NT as well. When Jesus is said to be the light of the world that is surely at least in part a claim of fulfillment of the OT's promises concerning the last days, although light is of course not always used in an eschatological sense.[45] The Book of Revelation reaffirms the promises in Isaiah that God will be immediately present in the new Jerusalem by speaking again of perpetual light (Rev. 21:23–25; 22:5). Here, as in the OT, the real concern is not the sun and moon, but the presence of God.

Victory over the sea as an eschatological event appears in a striking way in the Gospels, in the stories of Jesus walking on the water (Mark 6:45–52 and par.) and stilling the storm (Mark 4:37–41 and par.). The key to understanding these unusual narratives is surely the OT material concerning the sea as a threat that God controls, and the disciples' astonished question, "Who then is this, that even wind and sea obey him?" (Mark 4:41) surely calls for an answer in eschatological terms. The special quality that the OT ascribes to the sea also makes it possible to understand what would otherwise be a very puzzling reference to cosmic change in Rev. 21:1: "Then I saw a new heaven and a new earth; for the first heaven and the first earth had passed away, and the sea was no more." In the symbolic language of apocalyptic, the sea serves no other function than to represent the threat of chaos, which will one day be completely and finally eliminated.

Except for Revelation, which reiterates Ezekiel's picture of the river flowing out of the temple, but without any of its details except for the trees along its banks (22:1–2), neither Jewish nor Christian literature of this period shows much interest in the occasional OT references to a transformation of the earth's topography and climate. The subject of the redemption of the cosmos has continued to exist as a minor theme in Christianity, however, as G. W. Williams has shown in his article on Christian attitudes toward nature.[46]

Contemporary Manifestations

All those aspects of nature which the OT considered to be somehow out of bounds to humanity have now become a part of our domain. We have irrigated the desert and people now live comfortably in the American Southwest, the Australian Outback, and the Israeli Negev. We have not yet made our habitation in the sea, but we know its depths and are learning to harvest its resources. We have ascended into the sky and have found not heaven, but outer space. Surely these aspects of OT tradition have already experienced their transformation, at human hands! Yet the Sahel region of the Sahara is devouring what was once living space for animals and people, and it is not completely clear that there will always be water enough to support those large populations in the American Southwest. The destructive power of the sea is, for all practical purposes, as far beyond human control as ever, and places where people have lived are disappearing because its encroachments cannot be stopped. Despite its magnitude, the sea also suffers because of human irresponsibility, and pollution threatens its future as a source of food for us. The sky, in its lower regions, is also a polluted place that now threatens life and health in ways the OT could not imagine. Outer space has become the newest potential site for weapons of worldwide destruction.

That relatively minor OT theme of hope for the transformation of heaven and earth, which has been considered appropriately insignificant by generations of believers, now begins to appear, because of technology's ability to increase the effectiveness of the curse human beings afflict on nature, to be a vital part of the apocalypse unfolding in our time. It is no longer adequate to ignore that part of Israel's concern about the future, or to label it "mythological," that is, unbelievable, because it is a subject about which something must be said and done.

Modern fiction shows that the human need which lay behind Israel's traditions concerning sea and flood, wilderness and theophany, has not been transcended by our conquests of sea, desert, and space; indeed, the anxiety that chaos may break loose despite what we do to keep nature under control may be as strong now as it has ever been.[47] It is thus at two levels that these almost untouched parts of our tradition can be helpful. At the ethical level, as we decide what to do on a global scale with sea, land, and sky, the concept of a humanly wrought curse on nature warns us of the immense power we have to do harm. And the hope for a divine re-creation corresponds to questions about whether human efforts to remake the world are likely to succeed. If understood properly, such hopes ought not to discourage one from trying—leaving *everything* in God's hands—but ought to produce a heavier sense of responsibility for trying to do the right thing—with respect to the future as well as the present—with the tremendous forces that we are able to use on the earth. At the emotional, or spiritual, level, the threat of chaos on a personal or a cosmic scale which seems to lie below the surface of many lives and which may cause society itself to react in panic at times is addressed by the OT's assurance that in fact there is a God who is in charge and who does intend to bring order and peace to the world. We cannot conceive of a re-creation of the heavens and the earth, but that does not mean it is therefore unimportant to say that there is a God who can and will do even that for the sake of peace and order, if need be.

CONCLUSION

Old Testament Eschatology and Contemporary Hope for the Future

What can the hopes of a small group of people who lived in the Middle East two to three thousand years ago have to say to an age in which it is possible to develop a career as a futurist? The answer in brief is this: futurists have already discovered that the essence of the problem is human nature and that what people hope for is the decisive element in their planning. What the OT says about human nature has not been rendered obsolete by technology, and the hopes of people in the Western world have been profoundly influenced by the eschatology of the Bible. But the original teachings of the Old and New Testaments have been mingled with a great variety of philosophies over the centuries and frequently have been distorted to the point where their new forms are scarcely compatible with their sources. For that reason it is necessary for each generation of believers to make its own evaluation of its sources in order to determine how it may best be faithful to them.[1] Despite the widespread secularization of our world, there are still a great many people who sincerely want to know what legitimate hopes for this troubled world can be found in the Bible. Furthermore, when secular futurists show themselves unafraid to deal with the non-material aspects of their subjects—selfishness and greed, for example—that surely presents a challenge to those who believe they have access to some unique insights into the "spiritual" side to make those insights known. One reason for writing this book was to show that the eschatology of the OT speaks with a peculiar directness to the concerns of people of the late twentieth century. The conclusions now offered will lead to suggestions concerning the potential value of what has been learned about the hopes of ancient Israel for the present.

Characteristics of Old Testament Eschatology

This study has revealed certain characteristics typical of Israel's hopes. They show how the OT's expectations and longings are distinct from those to be found in other religions and cultures. Thereby they offer a challenge for alternative forms of hope—Christian and otherwise—and insight into the nature of the eschatologies of the Western world.

1. Old Testament eschatology is a worldly hope. The OT does not scorn, ignore, or abandon the kind of life which human beings experience in this world in favor of speculation concerning some other, better place or form of existence, to be hoped for after death or achieved before death through meditation and spiritual exercises. This sets the OT in sharp contrast to Gnosticism, to the otherworldly emphases that often have appeared in Christianity, and to the concepts of salvation taught by Hinduism and Buddhism. Whether it is better and truer than those other forms of hope, or is just irredeemably "unspiritual," remains, of course, a matter for faith to decide. But this quality of the OT hope surely ought to commend its outlook to an age that is equally worldly in its concerns.

2. Old Testament eschatology understands the future to be completely in the hands of God. Having just spoken of contemporary "worldliness," which might be equated with secularism, this point must be made in order to remind ourselves that there are other ways to be worldly. The basis for hope in the OT is not faith in human progress, but the assurance of a coming divine intervention that will introduce a new thing that people have failed and will fail to accomplish. We have seen throughout that the hope of Israel was not an expression of faith in the essential goodness of humanity. Instead, it grew out of the conviction that human failure has so corrupted life on this earth that only a radical transformation initiated by God alone could make things right. This point of view thus stands in sharp contrast to modern humanism and to all "self-help" projections of the future.

It does not, however, call for a completely passive drift into the divinely wrought paradise. The OT puts a strong emphasis on human participation in one way or another. Repentance, for example, is seen as essential, at some point in the process. The emphasis on obedience in the OT portraits of the ideal future shows that at no time does the OT conceive of human beings without responsibility. They participate actively in the new world, but they cannot produce it; that will be God's work.

3. Old Testament eschatology emphasizes human society more than personal salvation. This stands in contrast to a strong emphasis in Christian teaching and to modern individualism as well. We have noticed that concern for the fate of the individual after death, which has tended to dominate Christian eschatology, is almost completely missing from the OT. This has often been observed to be one of the defects of the old, Israelite religion. In light of the human needs that arose in the post-exilic period and continue to be felt to this day, it certainly has to be called an inadequacy. But there is an

awareness today of problems created by individualism which may lead to a welcoming of the insights of the OT into the inadequacy of purely personal solutions to life's problems. The OT may be short on introspection at times, but at least this avoids the kind of anxiety over the individual's relationship with God and one's fate after death which has marked some forms of Christianity. Certainly the OT does not ignore the redemption of individuals, but it puts its strongest emphasis on the truth that full human life is life in community. Already some who are seeking to respond theologically to the futurists' identification of our root problem as selfishness have appealed to this biblical outlook. It would seem that it has still more to offer to those who are striving to find incentives to move people toward action that will improve our life together on a global scale.[2]

4. Old Testament eschatology is a comprehensive hope. The OT neither focuses on an improved social structure inhabited by the same kind of people who created the mess we are now in; nor does it promise that personal salvation will somehow make social problems go away; neither does it imagine that a healthy human society can exist without a wholesome interaction with the natural world. I have already made brief comments on the potential ethical values of OT eschatology, and I wish to expand that subject now.

An Eschatological Ethic

Until recently, theological scholarship has tended to see eschatology as irrelevant for ethics if not actually working contrary to the concern for making human life better in this world. It seemed to divert one's attention to heaven and the after-life and thus to be a very narrowly confined area of Christian thought. Carl Braaten, who has called eschatology "the key to Christian ethics," has also had to admit that most contemporary ethicists completely ignore the subject,[3] but there may be some signs of change. What theology is learning from the futurists concerning the intimate relationship between hope and action is likely to make a significant effect, and historical studies are also beginning to reveal that in practice eschatology often has had a powerful ethical component. Some examples of the ways eschatology has modified the behavior of believers may be helpful.

The type that probably comes to mind most frequently, the so-called millennarian approach, puts eschatology to use in two principal ways. A major emphasis is evangelism. Since the date-setting tendency is characteristic of these groups, the warning that the end is near is used regularly in their efforts to convert unbelievers before it is too late, and in admonitions to those within the fellowship to be sure they are right with the Lord. This latter aspect of preparation for the end also may lead to the organization of communities based on clear and strict ethical principles, although the influence of those communities on the rest of the world is often not strong, since they tend to be sectarian. Among hundreds of possible examples of such groups, only a few will be mentioned here. The Qumran community existed for several hundred years on the shores of the Dead Sea as a strictly disciplined group that withdrew from the world in order to prepare itself for the coming of the end. In America the Shakers devised a remarkable combination of worldly and heavenly millennialism: they attempted to create on earth a community and a life style that transformed earth into heaven, while in the ecstasy that accompanied their worship they enjoyed the mystical experience of the new Jerusalem. As usual in such communities, their eschatology produced a comprehensive and highly disciplined ethic for their life with one another.[4] Another striking example of the effort to create the new Jerusalem on earth, with the extensive social planning that must accompany such a dream, may be found in the history of Joseph Smith's city-building enterprise for the Mormons at Nauvoo, Illinois.[5]

Such groups as the Shakers and Mormons show how a certain kind of eschatological conviction can produce a new community that organizes and regulates its entire world in accordance with those beliefs. Others that also fit the millennarian type, such as the Jehovah's Witnesses, have eschatologies that to the outsider seem quite similar. Their activity usually does not produce far-reaching social effects however, because these groups devote much effort to evangelism and their members are distinguishable from the rest of the community only by certain special characteristics of their ethic.

This ethical ambiguity of eschatology also is illustrated by the different effects of apocalyptic movements in European Christianity. Norman Cohn's book *The Pursuit of the Millenium* selected a series of examples to show that in Christianity the effects of apocalyptic literature have been anything but quietistic—an attribute regularly ascribed to Jewish and early Christian apocalyptic.[6] His intent was to show how often revolutionary movements used millennarian literature to stir up the fervor of the downtrodden with visions of a new day about to break in with all the violence that apocalyptic imagery suggests. But a later study by Bernard McGinn showed that the establishment was also wont to produce millennarian works, for it discovered the possibility of producing support for the status quo by showing that it was already in fact in line with the divinely ordained future.[7]

If the future determines the present, as the futurists and some contemporary theologians insist, then what effects on the behavior of believers can be expected from a hope for the future which is based on the biblical promises? Furthermore, how can eschatology be used by leaders who understand its potency so as to produce good effects? The following suggestions are not original and are offered by a biblical scholar, not a professional ethicist, so they should be read accordingly. They are offered because a prolonged consideration of the OT texts has convinced me that they are valid conclusions and a necessary result of biblical exegesis and theology.

Two aspects of the ethical implications of eschatology may be identified and designated as the *object* and the *impetus*. By *object* is meant *what* eschatology says human beings can and should be doing in the world, and by *impetus* is meant *why* eschatology impels us to want to do something about the present world. The object has been a topic for continual debate; this is what has made eschatology ethically dubious for many theologians. Is it possible to define some legitimate eschatologically motivated object for ethical action, that is, one that takes the eschaton to be truly future and completely the work of God, yet sees implications in this for human behavior in the present? At this point we recall Braaten's definition of eschatological ethics: "it is the truly future eschatological kingdom of God—which has achieved a present impact in the person of Jesus and wherever the word of his presence exercises its creative power,"[8] and then add to it something drawn from the understandings offered in this book. Anything that is truly future is inaccessible to any human being except as hope, but since the Bible's central concern in speaking of the future is not time but evil, a limited participation in the eschaton as the end of evil is possible now, since God's redemptive work is already in process. It is not yet the end, of time or of evil, but in faith we believe that we do participate in events and experience conditions that already possess something of the quality of the eschaton.

This approach may help to support the affirmations of some recent writers that the objects of eschatological ethics are to provide signs of the proleptic presence of God's future.[9] As Braaten says, they are annunciation and anticipation. We do not expect, then, to create the kingdom of God—within our Christian community as the Shakers did or in society at large as the Social Gospel did—but we believe it is possible for us to do some things that are indeed in correspondence with our understanding of what God is working toward. They will be witnesses to the truth of the future hope, reminders to believers, and perhaps also to others of what God is doing. What we do in an effort to make our behavior correspond with the way we believe the world will be one day thus serves a dual purpose. On the one hand, we do some good things for other people. Where there is injustice, poverty, and illness, we do what we can to make things better for those people. Of course, eschatology is not the only incentive for such behavior; it is only one of several. But it makes a special contribution when we fail, as we regularly do. We never quite succeed in making things completely right, and sometimes we are complete failures. When that happens, in addition to the assurance of forgiveness there stands another assurance, that the future does not depend ultimately on us but on God. Whether we succeed or fail, our every effort to make things right is, therefore, a witness to the world that God is at work to bring about, someday, a time without suffering and anguish for everyone. Every little victory over evil is thus a reminder that the ultimate victory is coming.

As anticipation, ethical action that is motivated by hope results in the discovery—some would say demonstration—that God's way does in fact work.[10] For example, Eph. 2:14–16 says that Christ has broken down the dividing walls of hostility among us. In reality, not even Christians, let alone humanity as a whole, can yet live together in peace, so harmony remains a part of our hope for the future. In the meantime, however, we do believe and must take it as our solemn charge to demonstrate that some real steps toward harmonious living have been taken in this world precisely because those who follow Christ believe that this is what God is doing in and through him. Interesting examples of taking the eschaton seriously enough to try to live that way in the present are provided in the previously cited article by George Williams, which tells of medieval saints who retired to the wilderness to live in harmony, not only with their followers but even with the wild beasts.[11] In every case, of course, these anticipations are imperfect, but faith accepts them as real signs that the Bible's portrayal of God's future may already be glimpsed from time to time in the church and in the impact of Christians on the world.

So much we may expect to be able to do: to announce or remind and anticipate the final work of God. But why should it be important to do so? Are there not more important objects for action and more powerful motivating forces than the expectation of a future that God and not we will create? Consider, then, two kinds of *impetus* to action which eschatology produces: *obligation* and *attraction*. Earlier we said that the way the Bible finds to talk to us about God's future is to select from past and present the language and ideas which can be used to depict that future to which we actually have no real access. Such a choice of language thus amounts to an affirmation about which elements of the present life are the best, are the closet to ideal—and so eschatology is an affirmation about the present as well as the future. Hence when Zechariah said, "Old men and old women shall again sit in the streets of Jerusalem, each with staff in hand for very age. And the streets of the city shall be full of boys and girls playing in the streets" (8:4–5); when Isaiah said, "They shall not labor in vain, or bear children for calamity" (65:23); when Micah said, "Nation shall not lift up sword against nation, neither shall they learn war any more" (4:3), these are not only announcements of how it will be one day; they are also pronouncements of how it ought to be today.

How then does one live today, one who seriously affirms such hopes for God's future? Would one even consider doing anything that is contrary to, or at cross-purposes with, or even neutral with respect to, what one's eschatology affirms to be the ultimate purpose of God? Surely only hypocrisy or a definition of eschatology which the Bible will scarcely permit will allow that. For the biblical hope does not imply that in the meantime, before the last days arrive, God is neutral, just waiting for the time to come when he will intervene to make things right. God assures us that he is at work now and that what he is doing now is fully consistent with what will happen in that day. This is the obligation created by eschatology: to do our best to avoid doing anything contrary to what God is doing, and to be directed in our actions by our understanding of the direction of God's work.[12]

The *attraction* of eschatology is its most potent aspect, that which makes it ethically most dangerous or most helpful. It is a vision, a dream, and the power of dreams far surpasses any sense of obligation. It is sometimes merely a daydream about which we feel no need to do anything, but it need not be that. It is often the kind of dream which pulls us toward it, about which we cannot remain idle.[13] Hope for the future is one of the strongest motivating forces to which we are subject, and since demagogues know that, some of them become highly skilled in using it. All the more reason for those who are committed to the biblical faith to recognize hope's power and learn to use it for good. In our day, the best teacher of the effectiveness of eschatology to move people to take action for righting injustices was, I believe, Martin Luther King, Jr. "I have a dream" was no pie-in-the-sky by-and-by, but was a call to action here and now based on a vision of an ideal future. King was surely enough of a realist, with experience enough of the power of evil in this world, to know that it was not likely the Civil Rights Movement would ever bring that dream to pass in its fullness. But as a Christian he had an eschatology that kept him from despair, a dream that moved people to follow him and to do something new about conditions that those same people, without the dream, had endured for a long time. That his best-known speech is the one containing the line "I have a dream" is surely to be explained primarily not so much by its occasion as because it is a speech with an eschatology, because it does what eschatology at its best can do: create within us an ache for the world to be made right—when we see how wrong it is, against what God intends for us and is at work to create for us. And that ache impels us to do anything we can, to try every possible way to make this world, here and now, just a little more like that dream. The ethical power of eschatology, then, is to be found in the fact that it does not scold us for our failures, it does not warn us what will happen if we don't do better, it does not play on our guilty consciences or pity by dwelling on human misery—rather, it holds up a dream and tells us not to be afraid to go where it leads.

The City of God

It leads, of all places, to a city. For some of us that is by no means a natural conclusion, but this is where the village-born (like this author) and the city-afflicted need to learn something from the Bible. God's redemptive work, according to the OT, does not take his people back to the Garden of Eden or to the wilderness, but to Jerusalem. Neither a mythical paradise nor nature untouched by human works is an adequate symbol of God's intention. Instead, God affirms the full complexity of human society as that which is best for us, for the city represents civilization, human culture at its best, and also, in this age, at its worst.

Despite the shifts in orientation of NT theology, the concept of the city of the future still proved useful to the early church (Heb. 11:10, 16; Revelation 21—22). Another image dominates NT eschatology, however, and because of its prominence, especially in the teachings of Jesus, it has come to be equated with eschatology in Christian thought: the kingdom of God. It is not a prominent term in the OT (Pss. 103:19; 145:11–13), even though the affirmation that Yahweh is king, over Israel and over the world, is an important theme. In OT eschatology the future reign of God is certainly affirmed, but we have observed the emphasis on God's presence in and reign from Jerusalem. Surely it is fair to say, then, that for the OT the concept city of God plays a role analogous to that of kingdom of God in the NT. We have traced the continuing importance of the specific place, Jerusalem, in chapter 1. Now we need to consider the broader concept of city of God as an eschatological term. It immediately conveys the OT's emphasis on the redemption of society, but as described it does not leave out nature, for we are always introduced to a kind of garden city. The OT does not idealize the village life of its day, let alone the nomadic existence in the wilderness, for it knows better than most of us that these are existences at the bare subsistence level, while in the city, and only there, could be found wealth, the arts, and the stimulus of association with a variety of people. Despite the corruptions of city life, the abuses of power, and the inequities between rich and poor, the potential for good in that human structure is translated in the OT into a picture of the divine intention.

It must be remembered that Palestinian cities were far different from the modern metropolis: from our perspective they were small towns. The largest city in Canaan when the Israelites occupied the land was Hazor, in northern Galilee, with an area of 175 acres and an estimated population of 40,000. Jerusalem in the time of David and Solomon occupied perhaps 20 acres and in the time of Christ covered 97 acres, with a population of approximately 30,000. It grew rapidly during the first century A.D. and by the beginning of the war with Rome in A.D. 66 may have had a population of about 80,000. But the size of the average Israelite city in the OT period was about 5 to 10 acres, and using an estimate of 240 people per acre the average population would have been 1,000 to 3,000 people.[14] These figures are offered both to warn the reader not to expect the peculiar problems that beset the modern city because of its immensity even to be addressed, let alone solved, by the OT, but also to point to an element of continuity with contemporary urban life. Sociologists have observed that most city dwellers do not experience the megalopolis as an environment, but that their real environment is the neighborhood. "Psychologically, neither the slum dwellers nor the suburbanites reside in a place so large as Chicago. They have no image of the city as a human whole."[15] They suggest that there is a maximum effective size for a human community and that cities in practice are actually collections of such neighborhoods. Arnold Toynbee's forecast of the city of the future, which he called Ecumenopolis, took account of this reality and suggested that the clusters of relatively small communities which would have to make up the world-city would necessarily be kept within the dimensions of the standard-size city of the past, such as Ur in the third millennium B.C.[16] Now, it happens that the population of Ur is estimated to have been between 30,000 and 50,000, about the size of Hazor in OT times and Jerusalem in the time of Christ, which leads to this conclusion: it is fair to take all that the OT says about the city as a commentary on human community at its maximum potential.

Few of us live in kingdoms today. Those who have a king or queen may find that the term kingdom of God requires little explanation, but for Americans and others whose very reason for being goes back to anti-kingship movements, there is a real culture gap that needs to be bridged by extensive explanations of what the NT term really ought to mean to us. Since Jesus used it, however, it is not likely to be superseded by any other. Let me suggest that if in the future the OT's contribution to Christian eschatology comes to be used as extensively as this conclusion proposes it might be, then the concept of the city of the future, the city of God, might prove to be an extremely valuable supplement to the traditional kingdom of God. Few of us live in kingdoms, but most of us live in an urban culture, including those on farms, ranches, and communes. We know from daily experience what the city is, and we hear frequent projections of what the humanly devised city of the future might be like. Therefore, the promise of a coming city of God ought to speak very directly to us as a way of focusing vaguely felt hopes, directing them toward the One who alone can fulfill them, and identifying quite concretely what we can be doing about them in the meantime.

NOTES

Introduction—A New Approach to Eschatology in the Old Testament

1. R. H. Charles, *Eschatology: The Doctrine of a Future Life in Israel,* 2d ed. (New York: Schocken Books, 1963 [1913]); J. Klausner, *The Messianic Idea in Israel* (New York: Macmillian Co., 1955).

2. Compare the definitions offered by E. Jenni, "Eschatology,"*IDB* 2:126–33; J. Lindblom, *Prophecy in Ancient Israel* (Philadelphia: Fortress Press, 1962), 360; G. von Rad, *Old Testament Theology* (New York: Harper & Row, 1965), 2:118; T. M. Raitt, *A Theology of Exile: Judgment/Deliverance in Jeremiah and Ezekiel* (Philadelphia: Fortress Press, 1977), 212–22; S. Mowinckel, *He That Cometh* (Nashville: Abingdon Press, 1954), 153–54 (cf. 149); J. M. van der Ploeg, "Eschatology in the Old Testament,"*OTS* 17 (1972): 93.

3. The term "Day of Yahweh" has not been found to be a very useful way to approach OT eschatology. If it was already a term denoting a popularly held expectation of a radically different future before the time of Amos (a debated point), it still remains a term to which we can add no content from the pre-prophetic literature, except for the word which Amos negates: light (Amos 5:18). For recent discussion, see J. A. Everson, "The Days of Yahweh" *JBL* 93 (1974): 329–37; J. Gray, "The Day of Yahweh in Cultic Experience and Eschatological Prospect" *SEA* 39 (1974): 5–37; Y. Hoffmann, "The Day of the Lord as a Concept and a Term in the Prophetic Literature" *ZAW* 93 (1981): 37–50; M. Weiss, "The Origin of the 'Day of the Lord' Reconsidered" *HUCA* 37 (1966): 29–60.

It seems most appropriate to call the messages of judgment in the prophets "pre-eschatological," and to restrict the use of the word "eschatology" to those promises that the days are coming when God will make everything right. See the careful discussion in Raitt, *Theology of Exile,* 106–27, 212–22.

4. H. Seebas, " 'ahᵃrit," *TDOT* 1 (1974): 207–12; S. J. DeVries, *Yesterday, Today and Tomorrow* (Grand Rapids: Wm. B. Eerdmans, 1975), 57–136.

1. Zion—The Center of Old Testament Eschatology

1. J. C. Todd, *Politics and Religion in Ancient Israel* (New York: Macmillan Co., 1904), 1.

2. G. Fohrer, "Zion-Jerusalem in the OT," *TDNT* 7 (1971): 293–319.

3. Presented positively by H.-J. Kraus, *Worship in Israel* (Richmond: John Knox Press, 1966), 201–3; G. von Rad, *Old Testament Theology* (New York: Harper & Row, 1965), 2:155–69; criticized by R. E. Clements, *Isaiah and the Deliverance of Jerusalem*, JSOTSup 13 (Sheffield: JSOT Press, 1980), 72–89. Cf. J. J. M. Roberts, "The Davidic Origin of the Zion Tradition," *JBL* 92 (1973): 329–44.

4. J. J. M. Roberts, "Zion in the Theology of the Davidic-Solomonic Empire," in *Studies in the Period of David and Solomon*, ed. T. Ishida (Winona Lake, Ind.: Eisenbrauns, 1982), 93–108.

5. R. J. Clifford, *The Cosmic Mountain in Canaan and the Old Testament* (Cambridge: Harvard Univ. Press, 1972), 131–60; F. M. McCurley, *Ancient Myths and Biblical Faith: Scriptural Transformations* (Philadelphia: Fortress Press, 1983), 125–63.

6. Clifford, *Cosmic Mountain*, 100–103, 158–60.

7. H. Wildberger, "Die Völkerwallfahrt zum Zion, Jes. II 1–5," *VT* 7 (1957): 62–81.

8. M. Noth, "Jerusalem and the Israelite Tradition," in *The Laws in the Pentateuch and Other Essays* (Philadelphia: Fortress Press, 1967), 132–44.

9. J. H. Hayes, "The Tradition of Zion's Inviolability," *JBL* 82 (1963): 419–26; Clements, *Deliverance of Jerusalem*, 52–89; H. Wildberger, *Jesaja*, BKAT 10 (Neukirchen-Vluyn: Neukirchener Verlag, 1965), 80, 88–90; O. Kaiser, *Isaiah 1—12: A Commentary*, OTL (Philadelphia: Westminster Press, 1972), 24–30; A. S. Kapelrud, "Eschatology in the Book of Micah," *VT* 11 (1961): 392–405.

10. T. M. Raitt, *A Theology of Exile: Judgment/Deliverance in Jeremiah and Ezekiel* (Philadelphia: Fortress Press, 1977), 106–27.

11. Isa. 1:24–26; 2:2–4; 4:2–6; 11:6–9; 18:7; 24:21–23; 25:6–8; 26:1; 27:13; 28:16; 29:8; 30:19–26; 30:29; 31:4–5; 32:14–20; 33:5–6; 33:17–24; 34:8; 35:10; 37:30–32.

12. Jer. 3:14; 30:18–22; 31:6; 31:10–14; 31:23.

13. Jer. 3:15–18; 27:22; 29:10–14; 31:38–40; 32:36–41, 44; 33:4–9, 10–11, 12–13, 14–16; 50:4–5.

14. Ezek. 16:59–63; 17:22–24; 20:40–44; 34:20–30; 37:24–28; 40:2; 43:12; 45:6–8; 47:1–12; 48:35.

15. Isa. 40:2, 9; 41:27; 44:24–28; 45:13; 46:13; 48:2; 49:14–26; 51:1–3, 9–11, 12–16; 52:1–10; 54:1–17.

16. Isa. 56:3–8; 57:11–13; 59:20; 60:10–14; 61:1–11; 62:1–12; 65:17–25; 66:1, 6, 10–14, 18–21.

17. Zech. 1:14–17; 2:1–12; 3:2; 8:1–23; 9:9–10; 12:1–9; 13:1; 14:1–21.

18. R. deVaux, "Jerusalem and the Prophets," in *Interpreting the Prophetic Tradition*, ed. H. M. Orlinsky (Cincinnati: Hebrew Union College, 1969), 295–96. In Isaiah 60—62 the whole history of salvation is summed up in what is said of Jerusalem.

19. Clifford, *Cosmic Mountain*; R. L. Cohn, *The Shape of Sacred Space*, AARSR 23 (Chico, Calif.: Scholars Press, 1981), 25–42.

20. The Samaritans have always claimed that their sacred mountain, Mt. Gerizim, is the highest point on earth even though its altitude above sea level is less than that of Mt. Ebal, across the valley. M. Gaster, *The Samaritans: Their History, Doctrine and Literature* (London: H. Milford, 1925), 38, 238; J. Macdonald, *The Theology of the Samaritans* (Philadelphia: Westminster Press, 1964), 333.

21. Wildberger, *Jesaja*, 1314, without any doubts; O. Kaiser, *Isaiah 13–39*, OTL (Philadelphia: Westminster Press, 1974), 347, after discussion. Cf. R. E. Clements, *Isaiah 1–39*, NCBC (Grand Rapids: Wm. B. Eerdmans, 1980), 269.

22. Kaiser, *Isaiah 13–39*, 348–49.

23. Clements, *Isaiah 1–39*, 270. Verse 23a is most likely a gloss. Wildberger's ascription of vv. 21ab and 23ab to a fragment of an oracle originally in judgment of Egypt does not provide an adequate explanation for its appearance here (*Jesaja*, 1320–21).

24. H. Gunkel, "Jesaja 33, eine prophetische Liturgie," *ZAW* 42 (1924): 177–208; B. Childs, *Isaiah and the Assyrian Crisis*, SBT 2/3 (London: SCM Press, 1967), 112—17.

25. Esp. A. S. Kapelrud, *The Message of the Prophet Zephaniah* (Oslo: Universitetsforlaget, 1975), 70, 91–94.

26. Ibid. 38–40.

27. Studies of *shub sh^{e}but* ("to restore the fortunes"): E. Baumann, "*Shub shebut.* Eine exegetische Untersuchung," *ZAW* 47 (1929): 17–44; E. L. Dietrich, *Shub Shebut. Die Endzeitliche Widerherstellung bei den Propheten*, BZAW 40 (Giessen: A Töpelmann, 1925); E. Preuschen, "Die Bedeutung von *šûbh š^{e}bûth* im Alten Testament," *ZAW* 15 (1895): 1–74.

28. R. E. Clements, *God and Temple* (Oxford: Basil Blackwell & Mott, 1965); Y. M.-J. Congar, *The Mystery of the Temple* (Westminster, Md.: Newman Press, 1962); M. Schmidt, *Prophet und Tempel. Eine Studie zum Problem der Gottesnähe im Alten Testament* (Zurich: Evangelischer Verlag, 1948); S. Terrien, *The Elusive Presence: Toward a New Biblical Theology* (New York: Harper & Row, 1978).

29. M. Eliade, *The Sacred and the Profane* (New York: Harper & Brothers, 1961), 20–65).

30. See also Isa. 4:5; 18:7; 24:21–23; 33:21–22; 60:19; Ezek. 34:30; 37:27–28; Joel 3:17, 21; Mic. 4:7; Zech. 2:5, 10–11; 8:3.

31. A. Causse, "Le mythe de la nouvelle Jérusalem du Deutéro-Esaie à la IIIe Sibylle," *RHPR* 18 (1938); 397. The same statement is made about the temple by R. J. McKelvey, *The New Temple: The Church in the New Testament* (London: Oxford Univ. Press, 1969), 22.

32. Y. Yadin, *The Temple Scroll* (Jerusalem: Israel Exploration Society, 1983) 1:183.

33. The Qumran community also seems to have made realized eschatology of the OT promises concerning Zion. 4QpIsa^a interprets Isa. 54:11–12 in terms of the community and its leadership.

34. L. Ginzberg, *The Legends of the Jews* (Philadelphia: Jewish Publication Society, 1909–38), 3:180.

35. Ibid., 1:9.

36. Ibid., 3:446–48.

37. A. J. Wensinck, *The Ideas of the Western Semites concerning the Navel of the Earth* (Amsterdam: J. Muller, 1916), 22. It was also said that the tree from which Adam ate was used to make the cross on which Christ was crucified.

38. D. C. Munro, ed., *Translations and Reprints from the Original Sources of European History* (Philadelphia: Department of History of the University of Pennsylvania, 1897), 1/2:7–8. Some medieval maps located Jerusalem at the center of the world.

39. Justin *Dialogue with Trypho* 119.5; Tertullian *Against Marcion* III.24.3–4.

40. J. B. Payne, *Encyclopedia of Biblical Prophecy* (New York: Harper & Row, 1973), 286, offers a literal interpretation.

41. Hermas *Similitudes* 1:1, 2, 9; *Epistle to Diognetus* 5:9; Augustine *City of God* 17.20; 18.47.

42. Origen *Homily on Jeremiah* 11:1ff.; Augustine *City of God* 8.24; 16.2; Eusebius *Ecclesiastical History* X.4.7.

43. O. von Simson, *The Gothic Cathedral* (New York: Pantheon, 1956), 10–11.

44. Eusebius *Ecclesiastical History* X.4.69–70.

45. The term "Zionism" was first used by Nathan Birnbaum in the 1890s in his journal *Selbst-Emanzipation*.

2. Peace in Zion—The Transformation of Human Society

1. M. Noth, *A History of Pentateuchal Traditions* (Englewood Cliffs, N.J.: Prentice-Hall, 1972), 55–56, 81; G. von Rad, "The Promised Land and Yahweh's Land in the Hexateuch," in *The Problem of the Hexateuch and Other Essays* (New York: McGraw-Hill, 1966), 82–83; W. Brueggemann, *The Land* (Philadelphia: Fortress Press, 1977), 3–27.

2. An approach to the question is made in D. E. Gowan, "Losing the Promised Land—The Old Testament Considers the Inconceivable," in *From Faith to Faith: Essays in Honor of Donald G. Miller*, ed. D. Y. Hadidian, PTMS 31 (Pittsburgh: Pickwick Press, 1979), 247–68.

3. D. E. Gowan, "The Beginnings of Exile-Theology and the Root *glh*," *ZAW* 87 (1975): 204–8; also, idem, "Losing the Promised Land," 256–63.

4. J. T. Willis, "A Reapplied Prophetic Hope Oracle," VTSup 26 (1974), 66–76, dealing with Mic. 7:7–20.

5. T. M. Raitt, *Theology of Exile: Judgment/Deliverance in Jeremiah and Ezekiel* (Philadelphia: Fortress Press, 1977), 106–27. For opposition to the claim, see R. P. Carroll, *From Chaos to Covenant: Prophecy in The Book of Jeremiah* (New York: Crossroad, 1981), 199–200.

6. The MT has "cause to dwell" rather than "return." Note that Hosea combines theology (Egypt as the land of oppression) with present-day reality, since it is Assyria that is the real threat.

7. B. W. Anderson, "Exodus Typology in Second Isaiah," in *Israel's Prophetic Heritage: Essays in Honor of James Muilenberg*, ed. B. W. Anderson and W. Harrelson (New York: Harper & Row, 1962), 177–95; D. Baltzer, *Ezechiel und Deuterojesaja*, BZAW 121 (Berlin: Walter de Gruyter, 1971), 12–26; W. Zimmerli, "Le Nouvel 'Exode' dans le Message des Deux Grands Prophètes de l'Exil" in *Hommage à Wilhelm Vischer* (Montpellier: Causse, Graille, Castelnau, 1960), 216–27.

8. Both interests appear in so-called 3 Isaiah (Isa. 56—66), and the former is especially prominent; note Isaiah 60 and 66:18–21.

9. Pp. 4–6 of this book.

10. Other passages that deal with return: Isa. 11:12–16; 14:1–2; 27:12–13; 35:1–10; 56:8; 57:14–21; 61:1–4; Jer. 12:14–15; 23:3; 32:37, 41; 46:27; Ezek. 11:17; 28:25–26; 34:11–13; 36:8, 24, 28; 38:12; Hos. 1:10–11; 14:7; Joel 3:7, 20; Amos 9:14–15; Obadiah 17, 20–21; Mic. 2:12; 4:6–10; 7:11–15; Zeph. 3:20; Zech. 2:6–9; 10:6–12; and Deut. 30:3–5.

11. M. Knibb, "The Exile in the Literature of the Intertestamental Period," *HeyJ* 17 (1976); 253–72; D. E. Gowan, "The Exile in Jewish Apocalyptic," in *Scripture in History and Theology: Essays in Honor of J. Coert Rylaarsdam*, ed. A. L. Merrill & T. W. Overholt, PTMS 17 (Pittsburgh: Pickwick Press, 1977), 205–23.

12. M. Buber, *On Zion: The History of an Idea* (New York: Schocken Books, 1973 [1952]) (= *Israel and Palestine—The History of an Idea*); W. D. Davies, *The Territorial Dimension of Judaism* (Berkeley and Los Angeles: Univ. of California Press, 1982), 91–110; J. Klausner, *The Messianic Idea in Israel* (New York: Macmillan Co., 1955) chap. 8: "The Ingathering of the Exiles and the Reception of Proselytes," 470–82.

13. W. D. Davies, *The Gospel and the Land. Early Christianity and Jewish Territorial Doctrine* (Berkeley and Los Angeles: Univ. of California Press, 1974); Brueggemann, *The Land*, 167–83; R. C. Oudersluys, "Israel: the Land and the Scriptures" *Reformed Review* 33 (1979): 3–15; C. Thoma, "The Link between People, Land and Religion in Old and New Testaments," *SIDIC* 8:2 (1975): 4–14; W. Wirth, "Die Bedeutung der biblischen Landverheissung für die Christen," in *Jüdisches Volk—gelobtes Land*, ed. W. P. Eckert et al. (Munich: Chr. Kaiser, 1970), 312–21.

14. Tertullian *De Resurrectione Carnis* 30. Eusebius says Ezek. 37:15ff. was fulfilled in the unity of the church under Constantine: *Eccl. Hist.* X.3.2.

15. Augustine *City of God* book 17, chap. 23; book 18, chaps, 45, 46.

16. M. Vogel, "The Link between People, Land and Religion in Modern Jewish Thought," *SIDIC* 8:2 (1975): 15–32.

17. E. g., the International Jewish Labor Bund, founded originally as the General Jewish Workers Union in Lithuania, Poland, and Russia; *Encyclopedia Judaica* 2:1497–1507. Simon Dubnow called for culturally autonomous national communities in the diaspora; L. J. Silberstein, "Exile and Alienhood: Yehezkel Kaufmann on the Jewish Nation," in *Texts and Responses: Studies Presented to Nahum N. Glatzer*, ed. M. A. Fishbane and P. R. Flohr (Leiden: E. J. Brill, 1975), 239–56. See also the evidence in Davies, *Territorial Dimension*, 53–115.

18. Pinsker, Weizmann, and Herzl in their early work; Buber, *On Zion*, 123–42. Y. Kaufmann did not think it possible to establish a Jewish homeland in Palestine: Silberstein, "Exile and Alienhood," 250–56.

19. J. Bloch, "Der unwiderrufliche Rückzug auf Zion," in Eckert, *Jüdisches Volk—gelobtes Land*, 62–81.

20. U. Avnery, *Israel Without Zionists: a Plea for Peace in the Middle East* (New York: Macmillan Co., 1968).

21. In addition to the works cited in n. 13, see J. J. Stamm, *Der Staat Israel und die Landverheissungen der Bibel* (Zurich: Gotthelf-Verlag, 1957); F. W. Marquardt, *Die Bedeutung der biblischen Landverheissung für die Christen*, *TEH* 116 (Munich: Chr. Kaiser, 1964); D. M. Beegle, *Prophecy and Prediction* (Ann Arbor: Pryor Pettengill, 1978), chap. 15: "Modern Israel: Past and Future," 192–206.

22. A. G. Hebert, *The Throne of David* (London: Faber & Faber, 1941), 80.

23. J. H. Cone, *The Spirituals and the Blues* (New York: Seabury Press, 1972).

24. A. B. Davidson, *Old Testament Prophecy* (Edinburgh: T. & T. Clark, 1904), 468–500.

25. Ibid., 498–500.

26. Oudersluys, "Land and Scriptures," 10–14.

27. Wirth, "Bedeutung der biblischen Landverheissung," 314–17.

28. J. Becker, *Messianic Expectation in the Old Testament* (Philadelphia: Fortress Press, 1980); D. E. Gowan, *Bridge Between the Testaments*, PTMS 14 (Pittsburgh: Pickwick Press, 1976), 491–502. For a more traditional approach: J. Coppens, *Le messianisme royal, ses origines, son développement, son accomplissement* (Paris: Éditions du Cerf, 1968).

29. G. Cook, "The Israelite King as Son of God," *ZAW* 72 (1961): 202–25; A. Bentzen, *King and Messiah* (London: Lutterworth Press, 1955), 16–20; S. Mowinckel, *He That Cometh* (Nashville: Abingdon Press, 1954), 21–95; T. N. D. Mettinger, *King and Messiah* (Lund: C. W. K. Gleerup, 1976), 254–93.

30. O. Kaiser, *Isaiah 1—12: A Commentary*, OTL (Philadelphia: Westminster Press, 1972), 125–30; H. Wildberger, *Jesaja*, BKAT 10 (Neukirchen-Vluyn: Neukirchener Verlag, 1965), 376–89; Mowinckel, *He That Cometh*, 102–10.

31. Mowinckel, *He That Cometh*, 178–79; Wildberger, *Jesaja*, 446–55.

32. Bentzen, *King and Messiah,* 17–18.

33. D. R. Jones has suggested it might allude to David's triumphant and grieving entry into Jerusalem after the defeat of Absalom (2 Samuel 19); *Haggai, Zechariah and Malachi,* Torch Bible Commentaries (London: SCM Press, 1962), 130–33.

34. Perhaps the most famous of all, Isa. 7:14, has also been omitted, because careful exegesis of the text indicates that it is not in fact a messianic prophecy. See G. B. Gray, *A Critical and Exegetical Commentary on the Book of Isaiah,* ICC (Edinburgh: T. & T. Clark, 1912), 122–36; Mowinckel, *He That Cometh,* 110–19; and the recent commentaries. For contrary opinions, see E. J. Young, "The Immanuel Prophecy of Isaiah 7:14–16," *WTJ* 15 (1952/53): 87–124, and 16 (1953/54): 23–50; E. E. Hindson, *Isaiah's Immanuel: A Sign of His Times or the Sign of the Ages?* (Grand Rapids: Baker Book House, 1980).

35. H. Ringgren, *The Messiah in the Old Testament,* SBT 18 (London: SCM Press, 1956).

36. H. H. Rowley, "The Suffering Servant and the Davidic Messiah," *OTS* 8 (1950): 100–136.

37. Ibid.; O. S. Rankin, "The Messianic Office in the Literature of Judaism and the New Testament," *ZAW* 63 (1951): 259–70; G. Vermes, *Jesus the Jew* (New York: Macmillan Co., 1973), 129–91.

38. W. S. Lasor, "The Messianic Idea in Qumran," in *Studies and Essays in Honor of Abraham A. Neuman,* ed. M. Ben-Horin et al. (Leiden: E. J. Brill, 1962), 343–64; M. de Jonge, "The Use of the Word 'Anointed' in the Time of Jesus," NovT 8 (1966): 132–48.

39. Note the popular pressure for him to make the true messianic claim, i.e., become a king, in John 6:15, and the reappearance of such expectations among the apostles even after the resurrection, in Acts 1:6. O. Cullmann, *Christology of the New Testament* (Philadelphia: Westminster Press, 1959), 117–33.

40. Micah 5:2 and Zech. 9:9 are used in straightforward ways in Matt. 2:6 and 20:4–5, but some examples of the other kinds of uses are Ps. 110:1 as predicting the ascension in Acts 2:34; Ps. 2:1–2 with reference to the plots against Jesus in Acts 4:25–26; Isa. 11:1, 10 as foreshadowing the mission to the Gentiles in Rom. 15:12; and Pss. 2:7, 45:7–8 as indications of the deity of Christ in Heb. 1:5, 8–9.

41. Klausner, *Messianic Idea,* 519–31; E. Rivkin, "Meaning of Messiah in Jewish Thought," *USQR* 26 (1971): 383–406; S. H. Levey, *The Messiah: An Aramaic Interpretation* (Cincinnati: Hebrew Union College, 1974), xviii–xx; L. Landman, *Messianism in the Talmudic Era* (New York: Ktav, 1979), xi–xxxiv; J. Neusner, *Messiah in Context, Israel's History and Destiny in Formative Judaism* (Fortress Press, 1984).

42. J. Moltmann, *Theology of Hope* (New York: Harper & Row, 1967), 15–36; J. Macquarrie, "Eschatology and Time," in *The Future of Hope,* by J. Moltmann et al. (New York: Herder & Herder, 1970), 110–25.

43. A contrary opinion is expressed by J. L. McKenzie, *A Theology of the Old Testament* (Garden City, N.Y.: Doubleday & Co., 1974), 296.

44. H. L. Ellison, *The Mystery of Israel; an Exposition of Romans 9—11* (Grand Rapids: Wm. B. Eerdmans, 1966); J. Munck, *Christ and Israel; an Interpretation of Romans 9—11* (Philadelphia: Fortress Press, 1967); C. Plag, *Israels Wege zum Heil; eine Untersuchung zu Römer 9 bis 11* (Stuttgart: Calwer Verlag, 1969).

45. V. Lanternatori, "Messianism. Its Origin and Morphology," *HR* 2 (1962): 52–72.

46. The subject of the nations in their own right has seldom been discussed in OT theologies. Some of the relevant texts have been taken up regularly in connection

with certain theological topics, such as the problem of war, or the missionary message of the OT.

47. P. D. Miller, *The Divine Warrior in Early Israel,* HSM 5 (Cambridge: Harvard Univ. Press, 1973).

48. Cf. Joshua 10—11 with Judges 1, other passages in Judges, and 1 Samuel.

49. G. von Rad, *Der Heilige Krieg im alten Israel,* ATANT 20 (Zurich: Zwingli-Verlag, 1951); R. Smend, *Yahweh War and Tribal Confederation* (Nashville: Abingdon Press, 1970); G. H. Jones, " 'Holy War' or 'Yahweh War'?" *VT* 25 (1975): 642–58.

50. H. Gross, *Weltherrschaft als religiöse Idee im Alten Testament,* BBB 6 (Bonn: Peter Hanstein, 1953), 45–52; W. H. Schmidt, *Königtum Gottes in Ugarit und Israel,* BZAW 80 (Berlin: Walter de Gruyter, 1961), 73.

51. S. Mowinckel, *Psalmenstudien* (Oslo, 1922), 2:71. The two ideas are combined in Ps. 9:5–8.

52. J. A. Soggin, "Der prophetische Gedanke über den heiligen Krieg, als Gericht gegen Israel," *VT* 10 (1960): 79–83.

53. For a reading of the Books of Kings in this way see J. Ellul, *The Politics of God and the Politics of Man* (Grand Rapids: Wm. B. Eerdmans, 1972), 15–22, etc.

54. The covenant with Noah (Gen. 9:1–19) and the meeting between Abraham and Melchizedek (Gen. 14:18–24) provided a basis for accepting a direct relationship between Yahweh and Gentiles.

55. K. Koch, *The Growth of the Biblical Tradition* (New York: Charles Scribner's Sons, 1969), 148–58.

56. J. R. Bartlett, "The Brotherhood of Edom," *JSOT* 4 (1977): 2–27.

57. For two views of the question in Ruth see L. P. Smith, "Ruth," *IB,* 2:831; E. F. Campbell, Jr., *Ruth,* Anchor Bible (Garden City, N.Y.: Doubleday & Co., 1975), 80.

58. Unleavened bread, Exod. 12:19; Passover, if circumcised, Exod. 12:45, 48–49; Num. 9:14; Sabbath, Exod. 20:10; Deut. 5:14; Yom Kippur, Lev. 16:29; sabbatical year, Lev. 25:6; Feasts of Weeks and Booths, Deut. 16:11, 14; sacrifice, Lev. 17:8–13; Num. 15:14–16.

59. J. Milgrom, "Religious Conversion and the Revolt Model for the Formation of Israel," *JBL* 101 (1982): 169–76.

60. F. M. Derwacter, *Preparing the Way for Paul. The Proselyte Movement in Later Judaism* (New York: Macmillan Co., 1930); M. Greenberg, "Mankind, Israel and the Nations in Hebraic Heritage," in *No Man is Alien. Essays on the Unity of Mankind in honour of W. A. Visser 't Hooft,* ed. J. R. Nelson (Leiden: E. J. Brill, 1971), 15–40.

61. Another form of warlike restoration appears in Joel 3 and Zeph. 3:8–20. H.-M. Lutz, *Jahwe, Jerusalem und die Völker,* WMANT 27 (Neukirchen-Vluyn: Neukirchener Verlag, 1968), 51–97.

62. B. Erling, "Ezekiel 38—39 and the Origins of Jewish Apocalyptic," in *Ex Orbe Religionum: Studia Geo Widengren,* SHR, suppl. to Numen 21 (Leiden: E. J. Brill, 1972), 104–14.

63. D. S. Russell, *The Method and Message of Jewish Apocalyptic* (Philadelphia: Westminster Press, 1964), 224–29.

64. W. Zimmerli, "The Word of Divine Self-Manifestation," in his *I Am Yahweh* (Atlanta: John Knox Press, 1982), 99–110.

65. Isaiah 14:13. A. Lauha, *Zaphon. Der Norden und die Nordvölker im Alten Testament,* AASF 49:2 (Helsinki, 1943); B. S. Childs, "The Enemy from the North and the Chaos Tradition," *JBL* 78 (1959): 187–98.

66. M. C. Astour, "Ezekiel's Prophecy of Gog and the Cuthean Legend of Naram-Sin," *JBL* 95 (1976); 567–79.

67. Detailed studies of these texts appear in D. E. Gowan,*When Man Becomes God*, PTMS 6 (Pittsburgh: Pickwick Press, 1975), 45–116.

68. W. Vogels, "Restauration de l'Égypte et universalisme in Ez 29, 13–16," *Biblica* 53 (1972): 473–94.

69. G. H. Jones, "Abraham and Cyrus: Type and Anti-type?"*VT* 22 (1972): 304–19; K. Koch, "Die Stellung des Kyros im Geschichtsbild Deuterojesajas und ihre überlieferungsgeschichtliche Verankerung," *ZAW* 84 (1972): 352–56.

70. Isa. 45:14; 49:22–26; in "3 Isaiah": 60:5–16; 61:5–6. For explanations, see N. K. Gottwald, *All the Kingdoms of the Earth* (New York: Harper & Row, 1964), 330–46; E. J. Hamlin, *God and the World of Nations* (Association of Theological Schools in South East Asia, 1972).

71. C. Westermann, *Isaiah 40—66*, OTL (Philadelphia: Westminster Press, 1969), 425; see also R. Martin-Achard, *A Light to the Nations* (Edinburgh: Oliver & Boyd, 1962); H. H. Rowley, *The Missionary Message of the Old Testament* (London: Carey Press, 1945).

72. The passage has not received the scholarly attention it deserves. In addition to the commentaries, see A. Feuillet, "Un sommet religieux de l'Égypte" *RSR* 39 (1951): 65–87; I. Wilson, "In That Day," *Int* 21 (1967): 66–86.

73. Daniel 7:19–25; 8:9–14; 9:26–7; 11:21–5. Cf. 1 Macc. 1:10–64; 1 Macc. 5:11–20.

74. *Tg. Ps.-J. Exod.* 40:11; *Num.* 11:26; 24:17; *Tg. Neb. 1 Sam.* 2:10; *Tg. Ket. Cant.* 8:4. See Levey, *The Messiah: An Aramaic Interpretation*, 15, 17, 23, 34, 130.

75. A convenient summary of the apocalyptic views may be found in Russell, *Method and Message*, 298–303.

76. Greenberg, "Mankind, Israel and the Nations"; cf. Matt 23:15: "You traverse sea and land to make a single proselyte."

77. R. H. Charles comments on the universalism of the *Testaments of the Twelve Patriarchs* in *Apocrypha and Pseudepigrapha of the Old Testament* (Oxford: Clarendon Press, 1913) 2:294. *Sibylline Oracles* 3:741–95 speaks of a kind of United Nations in the last days.

78. Greenberg, "Mankind, Israel and the Nations"; J. Jeremias, *Jesus' Promise to the Nations*, SBT 24 (London: SCM Press, 1958), 41; C. G. Montefiore and H. Loewe, *A Rabbinic Anthology* (New York: Schocken Books, 1970), 556–79.

79. Jeremias, *Jesus' Promise*; D. Bosch, *Die Heidenmission in der Zukunftsschau Jesu*, ATANT 36 (Zurich: Zwingli Verlag, 1959).

80. C. L. Albenese, *America: Religions and Religion* (Belmont, Calif.: Wadsworth Press, 1981), 247–342.

3. The People of Zion—The Transformation of the Human Person

1. P. Ricoeur, *The Symbolism of Evil* (Boston: Beacon Press, 1967); M. Douglas, *Purity and Danger* (London: Routledge & Kegan Paul, 1966).

2. Exod. 34:6–7; cf. Exod. 20:5–6; Deut. 5:9–10; 7:9–10; 2 Chron. 30:9; Neh. 9:17, 31; Joel 2:13; Jonah 4:2; Pss. 86:15; 103:8; 145:8, etc. G. E. Wright, "The Divine Name and the Divine Nature," *Perspective* 12 (1971): 177–85.

3. J. Milgrom, *Cult and Conscience*, SJLA 18 (Leiden: E. J. Brill, 1976).

4. For detailed studies see W. Eichrodt, *Theology of the Old Testament* (Philadelphia: Westminster Press, 1967), 2:380–495; J. J. Stamm, *Erlösen und Vergeben im Alten Testament* (Bern: A. Franke, 1940).

5. Cf. Amos 4:6; Hos. 5:4; 7:10; 11:5; Isa. 6:10, 13; 9:13; Jer. 3:1; 5:3; 15:7;

23:14; T. M. Raitt, *Theology of Exile: Judgment/Deliverance in Jeremiah and Ezekiel* (Philadelphia: Fortress Press, 1977), 40–44, 47–49.

6. Self-loathing is associated with the experience of exile rather than restoration in Ezek. 6:8–10.

7. H. J. Wicks, *The Doctrine of God in the Jewish Apocryphal and Apocalyptic Literature* (London: Hunter & Longhurst, 1915), 264–346; G. F. Moore, *Judaism in the First Centuries of the Christian Era* (New York: Schocken Books, 1971 [1927]), 1:497–545.

8. M. Knibb, "The Exile in the Literature of the Intertestamental Period," *HeyJ* 17 (1976): 253–72; D. E. Gowan, "The Exile in Jewish Apocalyptic," in *Scripture in History and Theology: Essays in Honor of J. Coert Rylaarsdam*, ed. A. L. Merrill and T. W. Overholt, PTMS 17 (Pittsburgh: Pickwick Press, 1977), 205–23.

9. Wicks, *Doctrine of God*, 340–41.

10. C. G. Montefiore and H. Loewe, *A Rabbinic Anthology* (New York: Schocken Books, 1970), 315–32; Moore, *Judaism in the First Centuries*, 1.507–19.

11. *Pesiqta Rabbati* 184b–185a (quoting Mal. 3:7); Montefiore and Loewe, *Rabbinic Anthology*, 321.

12. *Tanna de Be Eliyyahu*, 29; cited from Montefiore and Loewe, *Rabbinic Anthology*, 599.

13. Cf. John the Baptist's identification of Jesus as the "Lamb of God who takes away the sins of the world." M. Barth, *Was Christ's Death a Sacrifice?* SJT Occasional Papers 9 (Edinburgh: Oliver & Boyd, 1961).

14. W. Quanbeck, "Forgiveness," *IDB* 2:314–19.

15. T. S. Eliot, "Choruses from 'The Rock'," in *Collected Poems 1909–1935* (New York: Harcourt, Brace & Co., 1936), 197.

16. Quanbeck, "Forgiveness," 315–17.

17. H. W. Wolff, *Anthropology of the Old Testament* (Philadelphia: Fortress Press, 1974), 40.

18. Wolff, *Anthropology of the Old Testament*, 32–39; D. Lys, *Rûach. Le Souffle dans l'Ancien Testament* (Paris: Presses Universitaires de France, 1962); A. Johnson, *The Vitality of the Individual in the Thought of Ancient Israel* (Cardiff: Univ. of Wales, 1949), 23–37, 83–87.

19. L. Köhler, *Old Testament Theology* (Philadelphia: Westminster Press, 1957), 113–14; Wolff, *Anthropology of the Old Testament*, 38.

20. K. Baltzer, *The Covenant Formulary in Old Testament, Jewish and Early Christian Writings* (Philadelphia: Fortress Press, 1971); P. Buis, *La notion d'alliance dans l'Ancien Testament*, LD 88 (Paris: Éditions du Cerf, 1976); D. R. Hillers, *Covenant: The History of a Biblical Idea* (Baltimore: Johns Hopkins Univ. Press, 1969); D. J. McCarthy, *Old Testament Covenant, a Survey of Current Opinions* (Richmond: John Knox Press, 1972); and *Treaty and Covenant*, AnBib 21 (Rome: Pontifical Biblical Institute, 1963); G. Mendenhall, "Law and Covenant in Israel and the Ancient Near East," *BA* 17 (1954): 26–46, 49–76.

21. Mendenhall, "Law and Covenant"; McCarthy, *Treaty and Covenant*.

22. D. N. Freedman, "Divine Commitment and Human Obligation: The Covenant Theme," *Int* 18 (1964): 419–31.

23. D. R. Hillers, *Treaty-Curses and the Old Testament Prophets*, BibOr 16 (Rome: Pontifical Biblical Institute, 1964).

24. R. E. Clements, *Prophecy and Covenant*, SBT 43 (London: SCM Press, 1965), 11–44; J. Lindblom, *Prophecy in Ancient Israel* (Philadelphia: Fortress Press, 1962), 311–15; G. von Rad, *Old Testament Theology* (New York: Harper & Row, 1965), 2:178–80, 269–72; Raitt, *Theology of Exile*, 59–81.

25. S. R. Driver, *A Critical and Exegetical Commentary on the Book of Deuteronomy*, ICC (Edinburgh: T. & T. Clark, 1895), 125.

26. W. L. Moran, "The Ancient Near Eastern Background of the Love of God in Deuteronomy," *CBQ* 25 (1963): 77–87.

27. W. Zimmerli, *Erkenntnis Gottes nach dem Buche Ezechiel*, ATANT 27 (Zurich: Zwingli-Verlag, 1954).

28. For discussions of the related texts, see P. Buis, "La Nouvelle Alliance," *VT* 18 (1968): 1–15; O. Garcia de la Fuente, "El cumplimiento de la ley en la nueva alianza segun los profetas," *EstBib* 28 (1969): 293–311.

29. Isaiah 44:5 may be another way of speaking of the "one heart and one way" to be given to Israel, but many commentators think that instead it refers to gentile proselytes, and if so it would project a totally new work of the spirit, which has been confined to Israel in our other texts. C. Westermann, *Isaiah 40—66, OTL* (Philadelphia: Westminster Press, 1969), 136–38.

30. H. W. Wolff, *Joel and Amos*, Hermeneia (Philadelphia: Fortress Press, 1977), 67.

31. Ibid., 58–59.

32. Another passage concerning the pouring out of the spirit, Isa. 32:15–20, will be discussed in the chapter on nature, since its immediate effects are fertility of the land. It also brings righteousness and peace, but nothing is said about its effects on individuals.

33. S. Böhmer, *Heimkehr und neuer Bund*, GThA 5 (Göttingen: Vandenhoeck & Ruprecht, 1976), 11–20.

34. G. Gerleman, "Die sperrende Grenze. Die Wurzel *'lm* im Hebräischen," *ZAW* 91 (1979): 338–49.

35. Other occurrences: Isa. 55:3; 61:8; Jer. 32:40; 50:5; Ezek. 37:26. In Isa 54:10 it is said, "But my steadfast love shall not depart from you, and my covenant of peace shall not be removed."

36. G. F. Moore, *Judaism in the First Centuries*, 1:266.

37. Cf. *T. Dan* 6:6; *T. Jud.* 24:3; 4 Ezra 6:26. P. Volz, *Die Eschatologie der jüdischen Gemeinde im neutestamentlichen Zeitalter* (Hildesheim: Georg Olms, 1966 [1934], 392–93.

38. Other similar ideas may be found in *Midr. Rab. Cant.* I.2,4; II.13,4; *Yalq. Shim'oni* on Jer. 31:33; and *Pesiq. R.* 12:21.

39. Moore, *Judaism in the First Centuries*, 1:n. 43.

40. Ibid., 1:272.

41. A. Dupont-Sommer, *The Essene Writings from Qumran* (Magnolia, Mass.: Peter Smith, 1961), 126.

42. R. Bultmann, *Theology of the New Testament* (New York: Charles Scribner's Sons, 1951), 1:190–352; W. G. Kummel, *The Theology of the New Testament* (Nashville: Abingdon Press, 1973), 185–244.

43. T. J. Deidun, *New Covenant Morality in Paul*, AnBib 89 (Rome: Biblical Institute Press, 1981), 19–20, 33–34.

44. Consider Bultmann's effort to redefine eschatology so as to eliminate the future element: R. Bultmann, "New Testament and Mythology," in *Kerygma and Myth*, ed. H. W. Bartsch (New York: Harper & Row, 1961), 5, 38–44; idem, *Theology of the New Testament*, 1:4–11.

45. A striking example in fiction of such an outlook is the picture of the future in G. Orwell's *1984* (New York: Harcourt Brace Jovanovich, 1949).

46. E.g., from the Humanist Manifesto of 1933: "The goal of humanism is a free

and universal society in which people voluntarily and intelligently cooperate for the common good."

47. J. M. Lochman, *Encountering Marx* (Philadelphia: Fortress Press, 1977), 32–34, 71–75.

48. J. Klausner, *The Messianic Idea in Israel* (New York: Macmillan Co., 1955), 98–99; cf. S. Sandmel, *The Hebrew Scriptures* (New York: Alfred A. Knopf, 1963), 147.

49. D. E. Gowan, *Bridge Between the Testaments* PTMS 14 (Pittsburgh: Pickwick Press, 1976), 15–19, 49–54, 413–42.

50. D. E. Gowan, *Reclaiming the Old Testament for the Christian Pulpit* (Atlanta: John Knox Press, 1980), 134–38.

51. Hillers, *Treaty-Curses.*

52. Cf. the assumptions about what constitutes the good life in Job's "negative confession": Job 31.

53. A. Lods, "Les idées des Israélites sur la maladie, ses causes et ses remédes," BZAW 41 (Giessen: Alfred Töpelmann, 1925), 181–93; L. Köhler, *Hebrew Man* (Nashville: Abingdon Press, 1956), 32–51; J. Hempel, *Heilung als Symbol und Wirklichkeit im biblischen Schrifttum* (Göttingen: Vandenhoeck & Ruprecht, 1965); R. K. Harrison, "Disease," *IDB* 1:847–54; "Healing, Health," *IDB* 2:541–48; K. Seybold and U. B. Mueller, *Sickness and Healing* (Nashville: Abingdon Press, 1981), 15–96.

54. For the theory of demonic causation, see T. H. Gaster, "Demon, Demonology," *IDB* 1:817–24; Harrison, "Disease," *IDB* 1:853–54; S. Mowinckel, *The Psalms in Israel's Worship* (Oxford: Basil Blackwell & Mott, 1962), 2:1–8.

55. Köhler, *Hebrew Man,* 51.

56. C. Barth, *Die Errettung vom Tode in den individuellen Klage und Dankliedern des Alten Testaments* (Zollikom: Evangelischer Verlag, 1947); B. Vawter, "Intimations of Immortality and the Old Testament," *JBL* 91 (1972): 158–71. Contrary opinion by M. Dahood, *Psalms 101—150,* Anchor Bible (Garden City, N.Y.: Doubleday & Co., 1970), xli–lii.

57. Ahijah and Jeroboam's son, 1 Kings 14:1–13; Elijah and the widow's son, 1 Kings 17:17–24; Elisha and the Shunammite's son, 2 Kings 4:29–37; Elisha and Naaman, 2 Kings 5:1–14.

58. The best study, among many, is by R. Martin-Achard, *From Death to Life* (Edinburgh: Oliver & Boyd, 1960).

59. Also in Ezek. 20:41–44; 28:25–26; 34:22–30.

60. Much was made of this promise in later Jewish eschatology, but it is interesting to note that if one accepts Westermann's emendation from "sons" to (Zion's) "builders," the kind of promise we have been looking for virtually evaporates (*Isaiah 40–66,* 276–78). Jesus' saying "But you are not to be called rabbi, for you have one teacher, and you are all brethren" (Matt. 23:8) may be a reference to these texts.

61. Assuming "everlasting" is the correct way to understand *'olam;* the context strongly suggests it.

62. Isa. 25:9; 35:1–10; 51:3, 11; 52:8; 56:7; 65:18–19; Jer. 33:9–11; Joel 2:21, 23; Zeph. 3:14; Zech. 2:10; 8:19; 9:9, among others.

63. Today's English Version of the Bible brings in some OT theology from elsewhere, but is probably on the right track in its paraphrase: "to die before that would be considered a sign that I had punished them."

64. H. W. Robinson, "The Hebrew Conception of Corporate Personality," BZAW 66 (Berlin: Alfred Töpelmann, 1936), 49–62.

65. A. Lods, "Note sur deux croyances hebräiques relatives à la mort et à ce qui la suit: Le sort des incirconcis dans l'au delà et la victoire sur Leviatan," in *Comptes rendues de l'Acadḗmie des Inscriptions et Belles-Lettres de Paris* (1943), 271–97; O. Eissfeldt,

"Schwerterslagene bei Hesekiel," in *Studies in Old Testament Prophecy*, ed. H. H. Rowley (Edinburgh: T. & T. Clark, 1950), 73–81.

66. Martin-Achard, *From Death to Life*, 36–46; J. Pedersen, *Israel* (Copenhagen: Branner og Korch, 1926), 1—2:461–70; A. Heidel, *The Gilgamesh Epic and Old Testament Parallels* (Chicago: Univ. of Chicago Press, 1949), 137–223.

67. H. Wildberger, "Das Freudenmahl auf dem Zion," *TZ* 33 (1977): 373–83.

68. Martin-Achard, *From Death to Life*, 128; O. Kaiser, *Isaiah 13—39*, OTL (Philadelphia: Westminster Press, 1974), 201. Klausner, *Messianic Idea*, 201, considers it to be dated too early to be a literal reference to the problem of death, so calls it a metaphor for the end of war.

69. W. R. Millar, *Isaiah 24—27 and the Origin of Apocalyptic*, HSM 11 (Chico, Calif.: Scholars Press, 1976); R. J. Coggins, "The Problem of Isaiah 24—27," *ExpTim* 90 (1978/79): 328–33.

70. This is the RSV's emended text, reading "their bodies" for the Heb. "my body," in order to agree with the plural verb. Martin-Achard (*From Death to Life*, 130) reads the last line in a more natural way: "And the earth shall bring forth the Rephaim," i.e., the shades of the dead.

71. A sampling of recent books: C. F. Evans, *Resurrection and the New Testament*, SBT 2:12 (London: SCM Press, 1970); G. W. E. Nickelsburg, *Resurrection, Immortality and Eternal Life in Intertestamental Judaism*, HTS 26 (Cambridge: Harvard Univ. Press, 1972); G. Stemberger, *Der Leib der Auferstehung: Studien zur Anthropologie und Eschatologie des palästinischen Judentums in neutestamentlichen Zeitalter*, AnBib 56 (Rome: Biblical Institute Press, 1972); H. C. C. Cavallin, *Life After Death. Paul's Argument for the Resurrection of the Dead in 1 Cor. 15.* part 1: *An Enquiry into the Jewish background*, ConBNT 7:1 (Lund: C. W. K. Gleerup, 1974); P. Lapide, *Auferstehung. Ein jüdisches Glaubenerlebnis* (Stüttgart: Calwer Verlag, 1977); U. Fischer, *Eschatologie und Jenseitserwartung in hellenistischen Diasporajüdentum*, BZNW 44 (Berlin: Walter de Gruyter, 1978).

72. *Life of Adam and Eve* 29:8; *1 Enoch* 10:22; 58:4; 69:29; 92:5; *Jub.* 4:26; 50:5; *Pss. Sol.* 17:36; *T. Levi* 18:9.

73. Klausner, *Messianic Idea*, 516.

74. For a careful study of the varying points of view in intertestamental Judaism, see Cavallin, *Life After Death*.

75. H. L. Strack and P. Billerbeck, *Kommentar zum Neuen Testament aus Talmud und Midrasch* (Munich: C. H. Beck, 1956 [1928]), 4/2:943–44, 965–66.

76. Seybold and Mueller, *Sickness and Healing*, 114–94.

77. A. von Harnack, *The Expansion of Christianity in the First Three Centuries* (New York: G. P. Putnam's Sons, 1904), vol I, book 2, chap. 2, 131–32.

78. A brief, fair account of perfectionism may be found in S. Neill, *Christian Holiness* (New York: Harper & Brothers, 1960), 25–43.

4. "Highest of All the Hills"—The Transformation of Nature

1. F. Elder, *Crisis in Eden: A Religious Study of Man and Environment* (Nashville: Abingdon Press, 1970).

2. G. von Rad, *Genesis*, OTL (Philadelphia: Westminster Press, 1961), 82–83.

3. S. R. Driver, *A Critical and Exegetical Commentary on Deuteronomy*, ICC (Edinburgh: T. & T. Clark, 1895), 145–46.

4. Isa. 4:2; 7:22?; 30:23–25; 32:15–16; Jer. 31:12; Hos. 2:21–22; Joel 2:19, 22, 23–26; 3:18; Zech. 8:12; 9:17; 10:1.

5. W. Eichrodt, *Ezekiel*, OTL (Philadelphia: Westminster Press, 1970), 469–72;

L. Dürr, *Ursprung und Ausbau der israelitisch-jüdischen Heilandserwartung* (Berlin: Schwetschke, 1925), 116–24.

6. Jezreel should probably be translated here "God sows," rather than being taken as a reference to the valley that bears that name. J. L. Mays, *Hosea*, Old Testament Library (Philadelphia: Westminster Press, 1969), 52–53.

7. Irenaeus *Against Heresies*, V.33.3.

8. A. Richardson, *The Miracle Stories of the Gospels* (London: SCM Press, 1941), 94–99.

9. H. L. Strack and P. Billerbeck, *Kommentar zum Neuen Testament als Talmud und Midrasch* (Munich: C. H. Beck, 1956 [1928]), 4/2:888–90, 948–58.

10. J. Klausner, *The Messianic Idea in Israel* (New York: Macmillan Co., 1955), 507–10.

11. Strack-Billerbeck, *Kommentar zum Neuen Testament*, 4/2:945, 964–65; Klausner, *Messianic Idea*, 511.

12. W. Sanday and A. C. Headlam, *A Critical and Exegetical Commentary on the Epistle to the Romans*, ICC (New York: Charles Scribner's Sons, 1896), 207, 210–12.

13. J. G. Gibbs, "Pauline Cosmic Christology and Ecological Crisis," *JBL* 90 (1971): 466–79.

14. Evidence for a more positive treatment of nature in the Greek fathers of the first four centuries has been gathered by D. S. Wallace-Hadrill, *The Greek Patristic View of Nature* (New York: Barnes & Noble, 1968).

15. L. White, Jr., "The Historic Roots of Our Ecologic Crisis," *Science* 155 (10 March, 1967): 1203–7; reprinted many times since.

16. There have been many responses to White's article. See, e.g., those in *Ecology and Religion in History*, ed. D. and E. Spring (New York: Harper & Row, 1974).

17. G. W. Williams, "Christian Attitudes Toward Nature,"*Christian Scholar's Review* 2 (1971/2): 3–35, 112–26.

18. A. De Guglielmo, "The Fertility of the Land in the Messianic Prophecies," *CBQ* 19 (1957): 306–11; citing A. Meli, "I beni temporali nelle profezie messianische,"*Biblica* 16 (1935): 307–29.

19. O. Kaiser, *Isaiah 1—12*, OTL (Philadelphia: Westminster Press, 1972), 161.

20. Ibid., 161–62; cf. O. Kaiser, *Isaiah 13—39*, OTL (Philadelphia: Westminster Press, 1974), 303; H. Wildberger, *Jesaja*, BKAT 10 (Neukirchen-Vluyn; Neukirchener Verlag, 1965), 456–57, 460. A conservative, J. B. Payne, just cites the passages without saying anything about what they should mean for the faith of the modern Christian. He does insist that Isa. 11:9 restricts the ecological changes to Jerusalem: *The Theology of the Older Testament* (Grand Rapids: Zondervan, 1962), 493–94.

21. G. Wald, "Decision and Destiny; the Future of Life on Earth," *Zygon* 5 (1970): 159–71; and the articles in *The Dying Generations*, ed. T. R. Harney and R. Disch (New York: Dell Books, 1971).

22. K. Froehlich, "Ecology of Creation," *TToday* 27 (1970): 263–76; H. Barnette, *The Church and the Ecological Crisis* (Grand Rapids: Wm. B. Eerdmans, 1972), 63–64, 75–78; articles in *Western Man and Environmental Ethics*, ed. I. G. Barbour (Reading, Mass.: Addison-Wesley, 1973); J. Moltmann, *The Future of Creation* (Philadelphia: Fortress Press, 1979), 115–30: "Creation as an Open System"; H. Schwarz, "The Eschatological Dimension of Ecology," *Zygon* 9 (1974): 323–38; G. Kaufman, "A Problem for Theology: The Concept of Nature," *HTR* 65 (1972): 337–66; O. H. Steck, *World and Environment* (Nashville: Abingdon Press, 1980).

23. J. B. Cobb, Jr., "The Population Explosion and the Rights of the Subhuman World," *IDOC* 9 (12 Sept. 1970): 40–62.

24. D. T. Asselin, "The Notion of Dominion in Genesis 1—3," *CBQ* 16 (1954): 277–94; J. Limburg, "What Does It Mean to Have Dominion over the Earth?" *Dialog* 10 (1971): 221–23; W. Houston, " 'And let them have dominion . . .' Biblical Views of Man in Relation to the Environmental Crisis," *Studia Biblica 1978. 1. Papers on Old Testament and Related Themes*, JSOTSup 11 (1979), 161–84.

25. Von Rad, *Genesis*, 128.

26. P. Reymond, *L'Eau, sa Vie, et sa Signification dans L'Ancien Testament*, VTSup 6 (Leiden: E. J. Brill, 1958).

27. Von Rad, *Genesis*, 51–52.

28. Job 7:12; 9:8; 26:12; 38:8; Pss. 33:7; 46:2–3; 74:13–14; 89:9–10; 93:3–4; Prov. 8:29. G. R. Driver, "Mythical Monsters in the Old Testament," in *Studi Orientalistici in onore di Giorgio Levi della Vida*, "Its Pubblicazioni" 52 (Roma: Rome Universita, Scuola orientali, Studi orientali, 1956), 234–49; M. K. Wakeman, *God's Battle with the Monster. A Study in Biblical Imagery* (Leiden: E. J. Brill, 1973), 56–105. On chaos as a biblical theme see S. Niditch, *Chaos to Cosmos: Studies in Biblical Patterns of Creation* (Chico, Calif.: Scholars Press, 1985).

29. Cf. the projection of this same power over the Nile into the future in Isa. 11:15.

30. S. Talmon, "Wilderness," IDBSup, 946–49; G. H. Williams, *Wilderness and Paradise in Christian Thought* (New York: Harper & Row, 1962), 3–27.

31. J. Jeremias, *Theophanie. Die Geschichte einer Alttestamentliche Gattung*, WMANT 10 (Neukirchen-Vluyn: Neukirchener Verlag, 1965).

32. J. H. Eaton, "The Origin and Meaning of Habakkuk iii," *ZAW* 76 (1964): 144–71. For *tremendum*, see R. Otto, *The Idea of the Holy* (Oxford: Clarendon, 1923), 12–24; Penguin edition, 26–38. For the effects of natural phenomena on the Israelites, see D. Baly, *The Geography of the Bible* (New York: Harper & Row, 1957), 76–82.

33. Baly, *Geography of the Bible*, 22–24.

34. D. E. Gowan, *When Man Becomes God*, PTMS 6 (Pittsburgh: Pickwick Press, 1975), 38–43.

35. Von Rad, *Genesis*, 55–56.

36. P. Volz, *Die Eschatologie der Jüdischen Gemeinde im Neutestamentlichen Zeitalter* (Hildesheim: Georg Olms, 1966 [1934]), 418, 420–21. Cf. two brief articles in *Heaven*, ed. B. van Iersel and E. Schillebeeckx (New York: Seabury Press, 1979): J. Nelis, "God and Heaven in the Old Testament," 22–33; A. Cody, "The New Testament," 34–42.

37. Gowan, *When Man Becomes God*, 45–67.

38. Wildberger, *Jesaja*, 1275.

39. Ibid., 1278.

40. The difficult text, Isa. 33:21, may be an alternate and fragmentary form of a similar tradition of the stream from Zion, which also appears in the old cultic tradition, as in Ps. 46:4. R. E. Clements, *Isaiah 1—39*, New Century Bible (Grand Rapids: Wm. B. Eerdmans, 1980), 270.

41. S. Aalen, "'or," *TDOT* 2 (1975): 238–42.

42. B. Otzen, *Studien über Deuterosacharja*, Acta Theologica Danica 6 (Copenhagen: Munksgaard, 1964); H.-M. Lutz, *Jahwe, Jerusalem und die Völker*, WMANT 27 (Neukirchen-Vluyn: Neukirchener Verlag, 1968).

43. D. S. Russell, *The Method and Message of Jewish Apocalyptic* (Philadelphia: Westminster Press, 1964), 280–84.

44. *Sib. Or.* 3:542–43, 690–91; 4:176–80; *Adam and Eve* 49:3; *2 Apoc Bar.* 70:8; *Pss. Sol.* 15:6–7; cf. 2 Thess. 1:5–8; 2 Pet. 3:7.

45. H. Conzelmann, "phos," *TDNT* 9 (1974): 316–58. John 1:4, 9; 3:19; 8:12; 11:9–10; 1 John 1:5.

46. Williams, "Christian Attitudes Toward Nature," 122–24.

47. Consider the genre of novel based essentially on the theme of Noah and the flood, i.e., some natural disaster wipes out almost the whole population of the world, leaving a small group to start all over again. E.g., G. R. Stewart, *Earth Abides* (New York: Houghton Mifflin, 1949); P. Frank, *Alas, Babylon* (New York: Lippincott, 1959); F. Clement, *The Birth of an Island* (New York: Simon & Schuster, 1975); L. Niven and J. Pournelle, *Lucifer's Hammer* (New York: Fawcett, 1977).

Conclusion—Old Testament Eschatology and Contemporary Hope for the Future

1. J. Moltmann, *Theology of Hope* (New York: Harper & Row, 1967); H. Schwarz, *On the Way to the Future* (Minneapolis: Augsburg Pub. House, 1979); M. L. Stackhouse, *Ethics and the Urban Ethos* (Boston: Beacon Press, 1972), 90–107.

2. T. Peters, *Futures—Human and Divine* (Atlanta: John Knox Press, 1978), 11–13, 26.

3. C. E. Braaten, *Eschatology and Ethics* (Minneapolis: Augsburg Pub. House, 1974), 105–22.

4. D. Hayden, *Seven American Utopias* (Cambridge: M.I.T. Press, 1976), 67–68.

5. Ibid., 110.

6. N. Cohn, *The Pursuit of the Millennium*, rev. and expanded ed. (New York: Oxford Univ. Press, 1970).

7. B. McGinn, *Visions of the End: Apocalyptic Tradition in the Middle Ages* (New York: Columbia Univ. Press, 1979), 28–36.

8. Braaten, *Eschatology and Ethics*, 117.

9. Schwarz, *On the Way*, 242–56; Braaten, *Eschatology and Ethics*, 110.

10. F. Schaeffer, *Pollution and the Death of Man: The Christian View of Ecology* (London: Hodder & Stoughton, 1970), 65–93.

11. G. W. Williams, "Christian Attitudes Toward Nature,"*Christian Scholar's Review* 2 (1971/72): 31–33.

12. Cf. Peters, *Futures—Human and Divine*, 23–27, who does not express it as obligation.

13. Braaten, *Eschatology and Ethics*, 23.

14. F. Frick, *The City in Ancient Israel*, SBLDS 36 (Missoula, Mont.: Scholars Press, 1977), 79.

15. D. W. Shriver and K. A. Ostrom, *Is There Hope for the City?* (Philadelphia: Westminster Press, 1977), 21.

16. A. Toynbee, *Cities on the Move* (New York: Oxford Univ. Press, 1970), 246.

APPENDIX
The Problem of Time: What Can We Say About the Future?

If, to put it very simply, the future is that which has not *happened* yet, how can it be possible to know anything about it? Isn't the whole enterprise called eschatology a futile effort to get at something which is in fact completely inaccessible? Can it be anything more than speculation, or wishful thinking, or just projections of possible developments from present circumstances? We have no control over time; we remember the past but cannot change it, and we have very imperfect success in controlling even the immediate future. What validity, then, can language about the future be expected to have? We shall consider three general questions before turning to the Old Testament specifically: time as an existential problem to which every religion responds, the difficulty of finding adequate language to speak about time, and the question of prediction—whether it is possible to *know* anything about the future.

Time as an Existential Problem

As far as we can tell, all sentient beings are capable of responding to matter, but only human beings have a sense of time to which they respond. Other creatures may possibly have some consciousness of *change*, which seems to be the fundamental experience producing a consciousness of time, but human beings think about change, plan change, recall change, regret change, fear change, and find ways of measuring intervals between changes. We remember that things have not always been the same as they are now, and so we develop a sense of "past," in distinction from "present." As we accumulate a series of such memories we become persuaded, to a greater or lesser extent, that what is present may change again, and so we conceive of a "future," which will in some respects be different from past or present. A fair number of the changes that we remember, between past and present, have been unfortunate; we regret them, but we have found no effective way of undoing the past. Past then has a quality which distinguishes it from present, as we conceive them; we can make decisions and take actions which affect our present state, but there is nothing we can do to affect the past. Some of the changes which produce a future for us, that is, a situation different from the present, are thus the apparent results of our own decisions and actions. We can affect the future, but once again memory creates a problem for us, for we remember that previous changes have occurred which we did not plan and apparently did not cause, and we assume that similar regrettable (or felicitous) changes might occur again. We can partly affect the future, but cannot entirely control it; neither can we know the precise results of any action nor what factors extraneous to us may also produce changes. Whereas our inability to affect the past produces regret, our inability to control or even perceive accurately the future produces anxiety.

This aspect of the human time-sense is so basic to human nature that it is addressed by each of the world's religions, with varying answers being offered. Historians of religion have shown how the terror of time has been overcome by the affirmation that time is illusion, or by the assurance that there is something truly unchanging to which one has regular access in myth and ritual. In such studies the uniqueness of the Old Testament's acceptance of the reality and indeed of the revelatory character of change (i.e. of history) is always acknowledged.[1] Here I shall deal with only one aspect of that large subject, namely the ways in which the Old Testament speaks of the future with a response to that powerful sense of insecurity which the awareness of time produces in human beings. It takes time with the utmost seriousness, neither denying its reality nor affirming that human beings may aspire to some superior reality which transcends it. God is known only in the midst of temporal events—things which pass away and thus are preserved only in memory. This is likely to have created extreme feelings of uncertainty about the future, which the Israelite cult responded to with assurances of God's presence and God's permanence, in ways not unknown to other religions (cf. Pss. 46, 90, 91, etc.).

But the most distinctive feature of the Old Testament's "time-determined" outlook is its eschatology. It takes change with the utmost seriousness in that it is not afraid to affirm a time to come which will be radically different from the present. The fears which such an assertion is bound to raise are met in two ways: by a selective use of traditions from the past and by an appeal to faith in the God who is already known from his interventions in human existence in time.

The problem created by our awareness of time, then, is met head on by the Old Testament's teachings concerning the future, which declare that there is a divine intent which is somehow also time-bound. It is not yet fully experienced in human life or anywhere in creation, but the acts of God which are experienced in history have a discernable direction. Eschatology then affirms that the future, which is not completely under human control, is in fact completely determinable by God, and it expresses the hope that the direction of his past and present actions will, in good time, achieve the goal toward which God's work in time is pointing.

Language About Time

A very able Old Testament scholar, in what must be considered one of his lesser works, began a discussion of time in the Old Testament with the unabashed affirmation that there are three kinds of time: circular, horizontal, and vertical. This hasty and unexamined conversion of time into space provides a good introduction to the problem of language about time, for it illustrates the difficulty of the subject, which has been called the most intractable problem of philosophy.[2] I shall not enter into the complexities of the philosophers' discussions but it will be helpful to reflect on the linguistic choices human beings make as they talk about time, and especially about the future, so as to avoid previous blunders.

Is time linear or circular? The debate over the question continues on all fronts, but surely the common sense answer is that it is neither. Lines and circles are spatial, and we talk that way about time not because we are dunces but precisely because of time's peculiar difficulties. There is no way that we can really get at it; it is not experienced by any of the primary senses; our "measurements" of it might—given a certain amount of perverseness—be called only creations of the mind, without any essential relationship to the sensed world. St. Augustine's words remain the classic statement of the problem:

> What, then, is time? If no one asks me, I know what it is.
> If I wish to explain it to him who asks me, I do not know.[3]

If we can partly free ourselves of the spatial terminology which is regularly used in theological discussions of time, it may be an advantage to us. After all, surely no one *experiences* time as a line or a circle! Those are concepts which have been imposed on human experience as it has been intellectualized.[4] And the supposed helpfulness of those concepts, as they have been used to attempt to explain the difference between Greek and Hebrew thought, or between the ancient and the modern mind, has been shown by careful study to be dubious indeed.[5] It has been shown that *both* Greeks and Hebrews show evidence of acknowledging repetitive events, that is, essentially the same thing recurring periodically (sun, moon, seasons, and the corresponding holy times celebrated in the cult) and also in identifying significant events which were unprecedented and brought lasting change.[6] Furthermore, the Old Testament shows evidence of focusing on "times," moments which are identified by the event or the quality of event which occurs in that time, and also shows the ability to conceive of time as a continuum, the way the modern historian does, by which events may be related to one another along an abstract scale.[7]

In Hebrew, as in English, there is an interchangeable vocabulary for time and space. The past is *behind* us, we say, and we face the future. We *go back* into the past and move forward into the future. Some events are *near* to us in time and others are distant. This apparently inevitable tendency to turn to language about space has produced a curious difficulty for some when they have learned the Hebrew words for past and future, which are also used both for space and time. The word *qedem* may mean "in front of" or "before," but as a temporal term it refers to the past. In the same way, *'ahar* may mean "behind" or "after," but from it the word for future is formed (*'aḥarit*). Speakers of English have thus been tempted to conclude that for Israel the past was in front of them and the future behind them, and to picture them as backing into the future! But this is a mistaken conversion from time to space. For Hebrew speakers, the past is not "in front of" them; it is what happened *before* the present situation, and the future is not "behind"; it is what happens after this.

These observations may alert the reader to the trickiness of our time vocabulary, suggest some of the reasons for it, and, it is hoped, produce some caution in drawing theological conclusions from time language. Now a brief consideration of the Old Testament vocabulary of the future is in order.

The concept of "eternity" in the sense of timelessness does not appear at all in the Old Testament. Numerous extended studies of *'olam*, the term often translated "forever," have all agreed in concluding that it never suggests the end of time or timelessness. It means an extremely long time or a time far away from the present—either toward the past or the future. Contrary to what our expectations might be, then, the word *'olam* does not point us toward a significant body of passages which fit our definition of eschatology.[8]

Another word which one might expect to appear as a technical eschatological term is "end" (*qeṣ*), but in fact it is used that way only in the book of Daniel (8:17, 19; 9:26; 11:35, 40; 12:4, 9, 13). Israel did not in fact develop a technical vocabulary to designate its affirmations of hope concerning the ultimate triumph of right. The word *'aḥarit*, which has also been investigated with this question in mind, means generally "that which comes after," and may be used of various kinds of futures: those which are normal developments out of the present (Prov. 23:17–18), and in a few cases those which involve radical, eschatological change (Isa. 2:2 = Mic. 4:1; Hos. 3:5; Ezek. 38:16; Dan. 2:28; 10:14).[9] The temporal term which occurs most often in introductions to eschatological passages is the word "day" (*yom*), which has been called the "elemental Hebrew word for time.[10] This is what we may expect to find:

In/on that day
In those days
After many days
In the latter days
Behold, the days are coming (or, Days are coming)
Behold, a day of the Lord is coming
For the day of the Lord is near

The vagueness of the language must be noted. The most common expression, "on that day," is used to refer to events in the past as well as the future.[11] And only "the day of the Lord is near" (Isa. 13:6; Ezek. 7:7; 30:3; Joel 1:15; 2:1; 3:14; Obad. 15; Zeph. 1:7, 14) offers even a suggestion that a limited period of time that could be calculated or even estimated is in mind. The only things remotely approaching date-setting in the Old Testament (aside from those assurances of imminence) are the cryptic time-references in Dan. 7:25; 9:24–27 and 12:11–12, plus specific intervals which are predicted for the Judean exile in Jer. 25:11; 29:10 (70 years, cf. 27:7), and exiles of other peoples in Isa. 23:17 (Tyre) and Ezek. 29:13 (Egypt).

We may draw a few, limited conclusions at this point. These time words are significant in several ways. The hope of Israel was clearly focused on an expected change to occur in history. There is no other-worldly dimension to be found in the Old Testament hope, nor is there anything that might be interpreted as "realized eschatology," in the way that some New Testament texts have been read. There is no expectation of an end of time; it is assumed that history will continue, but it will be transformed, rid of all evil. That change is expected to come at some unpredictable moment in the future, with no further definition except for occasions when prophetic enthusiasm concludes that the time is near. Since "that day" is never said to involve the end of time and since it is doubtful that there can be any sense of time apart from change we may assume that the Old Testament expects history in a significant sense to continue, with meaningful changes, developments and movement (cf. Isa. 65: 17–25; Zechariah 8). Time is not the problem for the Old Testament; the problem is evil.

Because the emphasis throughout Old Testament eschatology is on the transformation of present reality in order to be done with evil "forever," its use of the word "new" (*ḥadash*) may be of greater help to our understanding of its central concern than the relatively small number of occurrences of the word might at first suggest. For instance, note how something new, some radical change in what presently exists, is expected to be accomplished by God, within time, in that day:

> Behold the days are coming, says the Lord, when I will make a new covenant with the house of Israel and the house of Judah, not like the covenant which I made with their fathers . . . (Jer. 31:31–32a)

> A new heart I will give you, and a new spirit I will put within you; and I will take out of your flesh the heart of stone and give you a heart of flesh. (Ezek. 36:26)

> From this time forth I make you hear new things, hidden things which you have not known. (Isa. 48:6b)

> For behold, I create new heavens and a new earth; and the former things shall not be remembered or come into mind. (Isa. 65:17)

How Does the Old Testament Speak of the Future?

If the future is to a great extent, virtually by definition, unknown, how can people talk about it at all? Obviously, only by projecting from the known—past and present—to the unknown, by assuming a significant continuity between present and future. For the immediate future we assume that we and others will still be alive, that we shall still enjoy the benefits of a stable society, that the "laws" of nature can be depended on, and so forth. But when the distant future is projected the question of discontinuity becomes more important. Furthermore, we have insisted that eschatology, by definition, involves a radical discontinuity. How different can things be and still be conceivable to us? What would we do for language to describe a future utterly different from anything we have ever experienced? In the extravagant symbolism of some apocalyptic literature we encounter such a struggle with the limits of language, but not so much in the Old Testament. It speaks of a future which involves radical change, but which is still comprehensible—up to a point.

The Old Testament concept of the ideal future is based, without apology, on the best of human experiences in the past and present. Its use of the word "new" does not denote something completely different, utterly unparalleled, but refers to the transformation of the best that Israel has known in order to purge it of all that has gone wrong with it. The redemption of Israel is described as a new exodus in Ezekiel and Second Isaiah, since exodus is the archetypal redemptive event. Israel's greatest king, David, becomes the model for a promise of government as it should be. Israel's history with Yahweh becomes the pattern for projecting the histories of other nations. There will even be a new covenant, according to Jeremiah, but that will not be something completely unlike the Sinai covenant.

Certainly there are passages which speak of things that had never happened in Israel's memory. Daniel promises resurrection, and that had never happened; other texts speak of cosmic and ecological changes. But the Old Testament does record some resuscitations from apparent death, and its theophanic language had always drawn from the most awe-inspiring of natural events imagery which moved beyond ordinary experience, so even the most extreme eschatological statements can be shown to have grown out of Israelite tradition. They stand in some continuity with what people knew and believed, hence they could be understood.

One might draw from this the negative conclusion that eschatology is no more than the projection of human hopes—wishful thinking. One might expect a new exodus without any special insight or revelation from heaven. I take the position that the divine impetus cannot be ruled out, that the Old Testament message concerning the future is more than wishful thinking, but must assert that the Old Testament does not convey *knowledge* about the future, for that is not possible for human beings to attain. It conveys *hope*. As prediction, then, it is fallible, but as a message of hope, it speaks with divine authority. The preceding chapters have considered how Israel's hopes clashed with realities which seemed to label them "wishful thinking," how they were modified by reality, how those who acted on their hopes found that reality could also be modified, and how certain convictions about the purpose of God survived every challenge: physical, intellectual, and emotional. The language of the Old Testament has been examined as human language, not as heavenly oracles, and it was considered to be the expression of human hopes, not the transmission of a divinely written "future history." But hope was not taken to be a purely human subject, an aspect, perhaps of our fallibility. One of the threads running through this book was the contrast between the uncertainty of knowledge about the future, because it really is inaccessible to us, and the certainty of hope, because it is grounded in a God whom we already know, to whom the future belongs.

Notes

1. G. F. Brandon, *History, Time and Deity* (New York: Barnes & Noble, 1965), 5, 107–47; M. Eliade, *The Sacred and the Profane* (New York: Harper & Row, Torchbooks, 1961), 68–113; *Cosmos and History: The Myth of the Eternal Return* (New York: Harper & Row Torchbooks, 1959), 49–92, 139–62.

2. R. H. Gale, "Preface" and "What Then Is Time?," in *The Philosophy of Time*, ed. R. H. Gale (Garden City, N.Y.: Doubleday & Co., 1967), vii–viii, 1–8.

3. Augustine, *Confessions and Enchiridion*, ET by A. C. Cutler, Library of Christian Classics 7 (Philadelphia: Westminster Press, 1955), XI.14.17 (p. 254). Charles Lamb had his own version of it: "Nothing puzzles me more than time and space; yet nothing troubles me less, as I never think about them." *The Harper Book of Quotations*, ed. Robert I. Fitzhenry (New York: HarperCollins Publishers, 1993), 39.

4. Eliade, *Cosmos and History*, 86–90, 112–30.

5. Contrasting J. Barr, *Biblical Words for Time*, SBT 33 (London: SCM Press, 1962); A. Momigliano, "Time in Ancient Historiography," in *History and the Concept of Time*, History and Theory 6 (Middletown, Conn.: Wesleyan University, 1966), 1–23; and C. G. Starr, "Historical and Philosophical Time," in *History and the Concept of Time*, 24–35; with T. Boman, *Hebrew Thought Compared with Greek* (Philadelphia: Westminster

Press, 1956), 129–54; J. Marsh, *The Fullness of Time* (New York: Harper & Brothers, 1952); N. H. Snaith, "Time in the Old Testament," in *Promise and Fulfillment*, ed. F. F. Bruce (Edinburgh: T. & T. Clark, 1963), 175–86; and G. von Rad, "Les idèes sur le temps et l'histoire en Israel et l'eschatologie des Prophetes," in *Maqqel Shaqed: Hommage à W. Vischer* (Montpellier: Causse Graille Castelna, 1960), 198–209.

6. Momigliano, "Time in Ancient Historiography," 8–18.

7. Momigliano, "Time in Ancient Historiography," 6; against von Rad, "Les idèes sur le temps," 198–200. Note, for example, Exod. 12:41; 2 Kings 15:1–2, or the three days in Gen. 22:3–4, in which nothing happens.

8. E. Jenni, "Des Word *ʿolam* im Alten Testament," *ZAW* 64 (1952): 197–248 and *ZAW* 65 (1953): 1–35; Robinson, *Inspiration and Revelation*, 113–20; cf. G. Gerleman, "Die sperrende Grenze. Die Wurzel *ʿlm* im Hebraischen," *ZAW* 91 (1979): 338–49.

9. H. Seebas, "*ʾaḥarit*", *TDOT* 1 (1974): 207–12.

10. S. J. DeVries, Yesterday, *Today and Tomorrow* (Grand Rapids: Wm. B. Eerdmans, 1975), 337.

11. Ibid., 57–136.

INDEX OF PASSAGES

OLD TESTAMENT

Jeremiah

Apocrypha

Pseudepigrapha

New Testament

RABBINIC LITERATURE